SPSS
Advanced Models™ 10.0

For more information about SPSS® software products, please visit our WWW site at *http://www.spss.com* or contact

Marketing Department
SPSS Inc.
233 South Wacker Drive, 11th Floor
Chicago, IL 60606-6307
Tel: (312) 651-3000
Fax: (312) 651-3668

Preface

SPSS® 10.0 is a powerful software package for microcomputer data management and analysis. The Advanced Models option is an add-on enhancement that provides additional statistical analysis techniques. The procedures in Advanced Models must be used with the SPSS 10.0 Base and are completely integrated into that system.

The Advanced Models option includes procedures for:

- GLM—General linear models, which can accommodate analysis of variance (ANOVA), regression, and analysis of covariance (ANCOVA), in both univariate and multivariate models. Repeated measures and doubly repeated measures models are also available.

- Variance components.

- Model selection loglinear analysis (hierarchical).

- General loglinear analysis.

- Logit loglinear analysis.

- Ordinal regression analysis.

- Survival analysis, including life tables, Kaplan-Meier survival analysis, and Cox regression.

Installation

To install Advanced Models, follow the instructions for adding and removing features in the installation instructions supplied with the SPSS Base. (To start, double-click on the SPSS Setup icon.)

Compatibility

The SPSS system is designed to operate on many computer systems. See the materials that came with your system for specific information on minimum and recommended requirements.

Serial Numbers

Your serial number is your identification number with SPSS Inc. You will need this serial number when you call SPSS Inc. for information regarding support, payment, or an upgraded system. The serial number was provided with your Base system. Before using the system, please copy this number to the registration card.

Registration Card

Don't put it off: *fill out and send us your registration card.* Until we receive your registration card, you have an unregistered system. Even if you have previously sent a card to us, please fill out and return the card enclosed in your Advanced Models package. Registering your system entitles you to:

- Technical support services
- New product announcements and upgrade announcements

Customer Service

If you have any questions concerning your shipment or account, contact your local office, listed on page vi. Please have your serial number ready for identification when calling.

Training Seminars

SPSS Inc. provides both public and onsite training seminars for SPSS. All seminars feature hands-on workshops. SPSS seminars will be offered in major U.S. and European cities on a regular basis. For more information on these seminars, call your local office, listed on page vi.

Technical Support

The services of SPSS Technical Support are available to registered customers. Customers may call Technical Support for assistance in using SPSS products or for installation help for one of the supported hardware environments. To reach Technical Support, see the SPSS home page on the World Wide Web at *http://www.spss.com*, or call your local office, listed on page vi. Be prepared to identify yourself, your organization, and the serial number of your system.

Additional Publications

Additional copies of SPSS product manuals may be purchased from Prentice Hall, the exclusive distributor of SPSS publications. To order, fill out and mail the Publications order form included with your system or call toll-free. If you represent a bookstore or have an account with Prentice Hall, call 1-800-223-1360. If you are not an account customer, call 1-800-374-1200. In Canada, call 1-800-567-3800. Outside of North America, contact your local Prentice Hall office.

Except for academic course adoptions, manuals can also be purchased from SPSS Inc. Contact your local SPSS office, listed on page vi.

Tell Us Your Thoughts

Your comments are important. Please send us a letter and let us know about your experiences with SPSS products. We especially like to hear about new and interesting applications using the SPSS system. Write to SPSS Inc. Marketing Department, Attn: Director of Product Planning, 233 South Wacker Drive, 11th Floor, Chicago, IL 60606-6307.

About This Manual

This manual documents the graphical user interface. Illustrations of dialog boxes are taken from SPSS for Windows. Dialog boxes in other operating systems are similar. In addition, this manual provides examples of statistical procedures and advice on interpreting the output. Complete command syntax for all of the commands included in the Advanced Models option are contained in the *SPSS Syntax Reference Guide*. The Advanced Models command syntax is also available online with the CD-ROM version of SPSS.

Contacting SPSS

If you would like to be on our mailing list, contact one of our offices, listed on page vi, or visit our WWW site at *http://www.spss.com*. We will send you a copy of our newsletter and let you know about SPSS Inc. activities in your area.

SPSS Inc.
Chicago, Illinois, U.S.A.
Tel: 1.312.651.3000
www.spss.com/corpinfo
Customer Service:
1.800.521.1337
Sales:
1.800.543.2185
sales@spss.com
Training:
1.800.543.6607
Technical Support:
1.312.651.3410
support@spss.com

SPSS Federal Systems
Tel: 1.703.527.6777
www.spss.com

SPSS Argentina srl
Tel: +5411.4814.5030
www.spss.com

SPSS Asia Pacific Pte. Ltd.
Tel: +65.245.9110
www.spss.com

SPSS Australasia Pty. Ltd.
Tel: +61.2.9954.5660
www.spss.com

SPSS Belgium
Tel: +32.162.389.82
www.spss.com

SPSS Benelux BV
Tel: +31.183.651777
www.spss.com

SPSS Brasil Ltda
Tel: +55.11.5505.3644
www.spss.com

SPSS Czech Republic
Tel: +420.2.24813839
www.spss.cz

SPSS Danmark A/S
Tel: +45.45.46.02.00
www.spss.com

SPSS Finland Oy
Tel: +358.9.524.801
www.spss.com

SPSS France SARL
Tel: +01.55.35.27.00 x03
www.spss.com

SPSS Germany
Tel: +49.89.4890740
www.spss.com

SPSS Hellas SA
Tel: +30.1.72.51.925/72.51.950
www.spss.com

SPSS Hispanoportuguesa S.L.
Tel: +34.91.447.37.00
www.spss.com

SPSS Hong Kong Ltd.
Tel: +852.2.811.9662
www.spss.com

SPSS India
Tel: +91.80.225.0260
www.spss.com

SPSS Ireland
Tel: +353.1.496.9007
www.spss.com

SPSS Israel Ltd.
Tel: +972.9.9526700
www.spss.com

SPSS Italia srl
Tel: +39.51.252573
www.spss.it

SPSS Japan Inc.
Tel: +81.3.5466.5511
www.spss.com

SPSS Kenya Limited
Tel: +254.2.577.262/3
www.spss.com

SPSS Korea KIC Co., Ltd.
Tel: +82.2.3446.7651
www.spss.co.kr

SPSS Latin America
Tel: +1.312.651.3539
www.spss.com

SPSS Malaysia Sdn Bhd
Tel: +60.3.7873.6477
www.spss.com

SPSS Mexico SA de CV
Tel: +52.5.682.87.68
www.spss.com

SPSS Norway
Tel: +47.22.40.20.60
www.spss.com

SPSS Polska
Tel: +48.12.6369680
www.spss.pl

SPSS Russia
Tel: +7.095.125.0069
www.spss.com

SPSS Schweiz AG
Tel: +41.1.266.90.30
www.spss.com

SPSS Sweden AB
Tel: +46.8.506.105.68
www.spss.com

SPSS BI (Singapore) Pte. Ltd.
Tel: +65.324.5150
www.spss.com

SPSS South Africa
Tel: +27.11.807.3189
www.spss.com

SPSS Taiwan Corp.
Taipei, Republic of China
Tel: +886.2.25771100
www.sinter.com.tw/spss/

SPSS (Thailand) Co., Ltd.
Tel: +66.2.260.7070, +66.2.260.7080
www.spss.com

SPSS UK Ltd.
Tel: +44.1483.719200
www.spss.com

Contents

3 Variance Components Analysis 33

4 Model Selection Loglinear Analysis 41

5 General Loglinear Analysis 47

6 Logit Loglinear Analysis 55

7 Ordinal Regression 63

8 Life Tables 71

15 Model Selection Loglinear Analysis Examples

16 General Loglinear Analysis Examples

17   *Multinomial Logit Models Examples*   *205*

18   *Ordinal Regression*   *241*

19 Life Tables Examples

Appendix
Categorical Variable Coding Schemes   *313*

Bibliography   *321*

Index   *325*

GLM Multivariate Analysis

The GLM Multivariate procedure provides regression analysis and analysis of variance for multiple dependent variables by one or more factor variables or covariates. The factor variables divide the population into groups. Using this general linear model procedure, you can test null hypotheses about the effects of factor variables on the means of various groupings of a joint distribution of dependent variables. You can investigate interactions between factors as well as the effects of individual factors. In addition, the effects of covariates and covariate interactions with factors can be included. For regression analysis, the independent (predictor) variables are specified as covariates.

Both balanced and unbalanced models can be tested. A design is balanced if each cell in the model contains the same number of cases. In a multivariate model, the sums of squares due to the effects in the model and error sums of squares are in matrix form rather than the scalar form found in univariate analysis. These matrices are called SSCP (sums-of-squares and cross-products) matrices. If more than one dependent variable is specified, the multivariate analysis of variance using Pillai's trace, Wilks' lambda, Hotelling's trace, and Roy's largest root criterion with approximate F statistic are provided as well as the univariate analysis of variance for each dependent variable. In addition to testing hypotheses, GLM Multivariate produces estimates of parameters.

Commonly used *a priori* contrasts are available to perform hypothesis testing. Additionally, after an overall F test has shown significance, you can use post hoc tests to evaluate differences among specific means. Estimated marginal means give estimates of predicted mean values for the cells in the model, and profile plots (interaction plots) of these means allow you to visualize some of the relationships easily. The post hoc multiple comparison tests are performed for each dependent variable separately.

Residuals, predicted values, Cook's distance, and leverage values can be saved as new variables in your data file for checking assumptions. Also available are a residual SSCP matrix, which is a square matrix of sums of squares and cross-products of residuals, a residual covariance matrix, which is the residual SSCP matrix divided by the degrees of freedom of the residuals, and the residual correlation matrix, which is the standardized form of the residual covariance matrix.

WLS Weight allows you to specify a variable used to give observations different weights for a weighted least-squares (WLS) analysis, perhaps to compensate for different precision of measurement.

Example. A manufacturer of plastics measures three properties of plastic film: tear resistance, gloss, and opacity. Two rates of extrusion and two different amounts of additive are tried, and the three properties are measured under each combination of extrusion rate and additive amount. The manufacturer finds that the extrusion rate and the amount of additive individually produce significant results but that the interaction of the two factors is not significant.

Methods. Type I, Type II, Type III, and Type IV sums of squares can be used to evaluate different hypotheses. Type III is the default.

Statistics. Post hoc range tests and multiple comparisons: least significant difference, Bonferroni, Sidak, Scheffé, Ryan-Einot-Gabriel-Welsch multiple F, Ryan-Einot-Gabriel-Welsch multiple range, Student-Newman-Keuls, Tukey's honestly significant difference, Tukey's-b, Duncan, Hochberg's GT2, Gabriel, Waller Duncan t test, Dunnett (one-sided and two-sided), Tamhane's T2, Dunnett's T3, Games-Howell, and Dunnett's C. Descriptive statistics: observed means, standard deviations, and counts for all of the dependent variables in all cells; the Levene test for homogeneity of variance; Box's M test of the homogeneity of the covariance matrices of the dependent variables; and Bartlett's test of sphericity.

Plots. Spread-versus-level, residual, and profile (interaction).

Data. The dependent variables should be quantitative. Factors are categorical and can have numeric values or string values of up to eight characters. Covariates are quantitative variables that are related to the dependent variable.

Assumptions. For dependent variables, the data are a random sample of vectors from a multivariate normal population; in the population, the variance-covariance matrices for all cells are the same. Analysis of variance is robust to departures from normality, although the data should be symmetric. To check assumptions, you can use homogeneity of variances tests (including Box's M) and spread-versus-level plots. You can also examine residuals and residual plots.

Related procedures. Use the Explore procedure to examine the data before doing an analysis of variance. For a single dependent variable, use GLM Univariate. If you measured the same dependent variables on several occasions for each subject, use GLM Repeated Measures.

To Obtain a GLM Multivariate Analysis of Variance

▶ From the menus choose:

Analyze
  General Linear Model
    Multivariate...

Figure 1-1
Multivariate dialog box

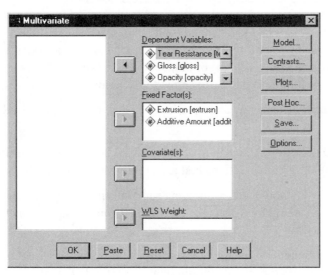

▶ Select at least two dependent variables.

Optionally, you can specify Fixed Factor(s), Covariate(s), and WLS Weight.

GLM Multivariate Model

Figure 1-2
Multivariate Model dialog box

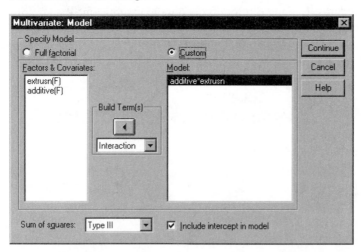

Specify Model. A full factorial model contains all factor main effects, all covariate main effects, and all factor-by-factor interactions. It does not contain covariate interactions. Select Custom to specify only a subset of interactions or to specify factor-by-covariate interactions. You must indicate all of the terms to be included in the model.

Factors and Covariates. The factors and covariates are listed with (F) for fixed factor and (C) for covariate.

Model. The model depends on the nature of your data. After selecting Custom, you can select the main effects and interactions that are of interest in your analysis.

Sum of squares. The method of calculating the sums of squares. For balanced or unbalanced models with no missing cells, the Type III sum-of-squares method is the most commonly used type.

Include intercept in model. The intercept is usually included in the model. If you can assume that the data pass through the origin, you can exclude the intercept.

Build Terms

For the selected factors and covariates:

Interaction. Creates the highest-level interaction term of all selected variables. This is the default.

Main effects. Creates a main-effects term for each variable selected.

All 2-way. Creates all possible two-way interactions of the selected variables.

All 3-way. Creates all possible three-way interactions of the selected variables.

All 4-way. Creates all possible four-way interactions of the selected variables.

All 5-way. Creates all possible five-way interactions of the selected variables.

Sums of Squares

For the model, you can choose a type of sum of squares. Type III is the most commonly used and is the default.

Type I. This method is also known as the hierarchical decomposition of the sum-of-squares method. Each term is adjusted only for the term that precedes it in the model. The Type I sum-of-squares method is commonly used for:

- A balanced ANOVA model in which any main effects are specified before any first-order interaction effects, any first-order interaction effects are specified before any second-order interaction effects, and so on.
- A polynomial regression model in which any lower-order terms are specified before any higher-order terms.
- A purely nested model in which the first-specified effect is nested within the second-specified effect, the second-specified effect is nested within the third, and so on. (This form of nesting can be specified only by using syntax.)

Type II. This method calculates the sums of squares of an effect in the model adjusted for all other "appropriate" effects. An appropriate effect is one that corresponds to all effects that do not contain the effect being examined. The Type II sum-of-squares method is commonly used for:

- A balanced ANOVA model.
- Any model that has main factor effects only.

- Any regression model.
- A purely nested design. (This form of nesting can be specified by using syntax.)

Type III. This method, the default, calculates the sums of squares of an effect in the design as the sums of squares adjusted for any other effects that do not contain it and orthogonal to any effects (if any) that contain it. The Type III sums of squares have one major advantage in that they are invariant with respect to the cell frequencies as long as the general form of estimability remains constant. Therefore, this type is often considered useful for an unbalanced model with no missing cells. In a factorial design with no missing cells, this method is equivalent to the Yates' weighted-squares-of-means technique. The Type III sum-of-squares method is commonly used for:

- Any models listed in Type I and Type II.
- Any balanced or unbalanced model with no empty cells.

Type IV. This method is designed for a situation in which there are missing cells. For any effect F in the design, if F is not contained in any other effect, then Type IV = Type III = Type II. When F is contained in other effects, Type IV distributes the contrasts being made among the parameters in F to all higher-level effects equitably. The Type IV sum-of-squares method is commonly used for:

- Any models listed in Type I and Type II.
- Any balanced model or unbalanced model with empty cells.

GLM Multivariate Contrasts

Figure 1-3
Multivariate Contrasts dialog box

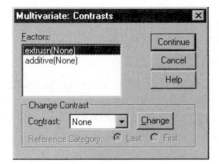

Contrasts are used to test whether the levels of an effect are significantly different from one another. You can specify a contrast for each factor in the model. Contrasts represent linear combinations of the parameters.

Hypothesis testing is based on the null hypothesis $\mathbf{LBM = 0}$, where $\mathbf{L}$ is the contrast coefficients matrix, $\mathbf{M}$ is the identity matrix, which has dimension equal to the number of dependent variables, and $\mathbf{B}$ is the parameter vector. When a contrast is specified, SPSS creates an $\mathbf{L}$ matrix such that the columns corresponding to the factor match the contrast. The remaining columns are adjusted so that the $\mathbf{L}$ matrix is estimable.

In addition to the univariate test using F statistics and the Bonferroni-type simultaneous confidence intervals based on Student's t distribution for the contrast differences across all dependent variables, the multivariate tests using Pillai's trace, Wilks' lambda, Hotelling's trace, and Roy's largest root criteria are provided.

Available contrasts are deviation, simple, difference, Helmert, repeated, and polynomial. For deviation contrasts and simple contrasts, you can choose whether the reference category is the last or first category.

Contrast Types

Deviation. Compares the mean of each level (except a reference category) to the mean of all of the levels (grand mean). The levels of the factor can be in any order.

Simple. Compares the mean of each level to the mean of a specified level. This type of contrast is useful when there is a control group. You can choose the first or last category as the reference.

Difference. Compares the mean of each level (except the first) to the mean of previous levels. (Sometimes called reverse Helmert contrasts.)

Helmert. Compares the mean of each level of the factor (except the last) to the mean of subsequent levels.

Repeated. Compares the mean of each level (except the last) to the mean of the subsequent level.

Polynomial. Compares the linear effect, quadratic effect, cubic effect, and so on. The first degree of freedom contains the linear effect across all categories; the second degree of freedom, the quadratic effect; and so on. These contrasts are often used to estimate polynomial trends.

GLM Multivariate Profile Plots

Figure 1-4
Multivariate Profile Plots dialog box

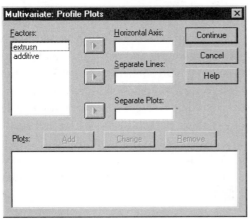

Profile plots (interaction plots) are useful for comparing marginal means in your model. Profile plots are created for each dependent variable. A profile plot is a line plot in which each point indicates the estimated marginal mean of a dependent variable (adjusted for covariates) at one level of a factor. The levels of a second factor can be used to make separate lines. Each level in a third factor can be used to create a separate plot. All fixed factors are available for plots.

A profile plot of one factor shows whether the estimated marginal means are increasing or decreasing across levels. For two or more factors, parallel lines indicate that there is no interaction between factors, which means that you can investigate the levels of only one factor. Lines that cross each other indicate an interaction.

Figure 1-5
Nonparallel plot (left) and parallel plot (right)

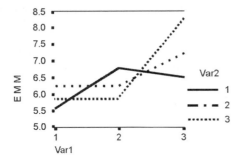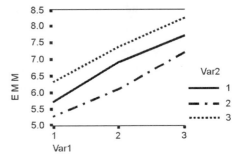

After a plot is specified by selecting factors for the horizontal axis, and optionally, factors for separate lines and separate plots, the plot must be listed in the Plots list.

GLM Multivariate Post Hoc Multiple Comparisons for Observed Means

Figure 1-6

Post Hoc Multiple Comparisons for Observed Means dialog box

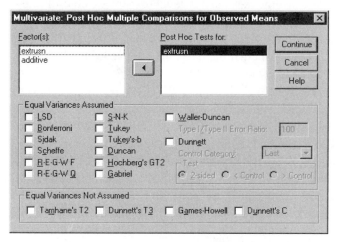

Post hoc multiple comparison tests. Once you have determined that differences exist among the means, post hoc range tests and pairwise multiple comparisons can determine which means differ. Comparisons are made on unadjusted values. These tests are used for between-subjects factors only. The post hoc multiple comparison tests are performed for each dependent variable separately.

The Bonferroni and Tukey's honestly significant difference tests are commonly used multiple comparison tests. The **Bonferroni test**, based on Student's t statistic, adjusts the observed significance level for the fact that multiple comparisons are made. **Sidak's t test** also adjusts the significance level and provides tighter bounds than the Bonferroni test. **Tukey's honestly significant difference test** uses the Studentized range statistic to make all pairwise comparisons between groups and sets the experimentwise error rate to the error rate for the collection for all pairwise comparisons. When testing a large number of pairs of means, Tukey's honestly significant difference test is more powerful than the Bonferroni test. For a small number of pairs, Bonferroni is more powerful.

Hochberg's GT2 is similar to Tukey's honestly significant difference test, but the Studentized maximum modulus is used. Usually, Tukey's test is more powerful. **Gabriel's pairwise comparisons test** also uses the Studentized maximum modulus and is generally more powerful than Hochberg's GT2 when the cell sizes are unequal. Gabriel's test may become liberal when the cell sizes vary greatly.

Dunnett's pairwise multiple comparison *t* test compares a set of treatments against a single control mean. The last category is the default control category. Alternatively, you can choose the first category. You can also choose a two-sided or one-sided test. To test that the mean at any level (except the control category) of the factor is not equal to that of the control category, use a two-sided test. To test whether the mean at any level of the factor is smaller than that of the control category, select < Control. Likewise, to test whether the mean at any level of the factor is larger than that of the control category, select > Control.

Ryan, Einot, Gabriel, and Welsch (R-E-G-W) developed two multiple step-down range tests. Multiple step-down procedures first test whether all means are equal. If all means are not equal, subsets of means are tested for equality. **R-E-G-W *F*** is based on an *F* test and **R-E-G-W *Q*** is based on the Studentized range. These tests are more powerful than Duncan's multiple range test and Student-Newman-Keuls (which are also multiple step-down procedures), but they are not recommended for unequal cell sizes.

When the variances are unequal, use **Tamhane's T2** (conservative pairwise comparisons test based on a *t* test), **Dunnett's T3** (pairwise comparison test based on the Studentized maximum modulus), **Games-Howell pairwise comparison test** (sometimes liberal), or **Dunnett's *C*** (pairwise comparison test based on the Studentized range).

Duncan's multiple range test, Student-Newman-Keuls (**S-N-K**), and **Tukey's-*b*** are range tests that rank group means and compute a range value. These tests are not used as frequently as the tests previously discussed.

The **Waller-Duncan *t* test** uses a Bayesian approach. This range test uses the harmonic mean of the sample size when the sample sizes are unequal.

The significance level of the **Scheffé test** is designed to allow all possible linear combinations of group means to be tested, not just pairwise comparisons available in this feature. The result is that the Scheffé test is often more conservative than other tests, which means that a larger difference between means is required for significance.

The least significant difference (**LSD**) pairwise multiple comparison test is equivalent to multiple individual *t* tests between all pairs of groups. The disadvantage of this test is that no attempt is made to adjust the observed significance level for multiple comparisons.

Tests displayed. Pairwise comparisons are provided for LSD, Sidak, Bonferroni, Games and Howell, Tamhane's T2 and T3, Dunnett's *C*, and Dunnett's T3. Homogeneous subsets for range tests are provided for S-N-K, Tukey's-*b*, Duncan, R-E-G-W *F*, R-E-G-W *Q*, and Waller. Tukey's honestly significant difference test, Hochberg's GT2, Gabriel's test, and Scheffé's test are both multiple comparison tests and range tests.

GLM Multivariate Save

Figure 1-7
Multivariate Save dialog box

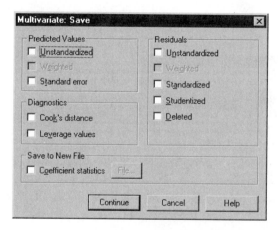

You can save values predicted by the model, residuals, and related measures as new variables in the Data Editor. Many of these variables can be used for examining assumptions about the data. To save the values for use in another SPSS session, you must save the current data file.

Predicted Values. The values that the model predicts for each case. Unstandardized predicted values and the standard errors of the predicted values are available. If a WLS variable was chosen, weighted unstandardized predicted values are available.

Diagnostics. Measures to identify cases with unusual combinations of values for the independent variables and cases that may have a large impact on the model. Available are Cook's distance and uncentered leverage values.

Residuals. An unstandardized residual is the actual value of the dependent variable minus the value predicted by the model. Standardized, Studentized, and deleted residuals are also available. If a WLS variable was chosen, weighted unstandardized residuals are available.

Save to New File. Writes an SPSS data file containing a variance-covariance matrix of the parameter estimates in the model. Also, for each dependent variable, there will be a row of parameter estimates, a row of significance values for the *t* statistics corresponding to the parameter estimates, and a row of residual degrees of freedom. For a multivariate model, there are similar rows for each dependent variable. You can use this data in other SPSS procedures.

GLM Multivariate Options

Figure 1-8
Multivariate Options dialog box

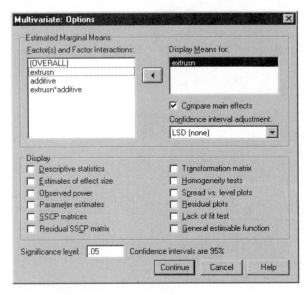

Optional statistics are available from this dialog box. Statistics are calculated using a fixed-effects model.

Estimated Marginal Means. Select the factors and interactions for which you want estimates of the population marginal means in the cells. These means are adjusted for the covariates, if any. Interactions are available only if you have specified a custom model.

- **Compare main effects.** Provides uncorrected pairwise comparisons among estimated marginal means for any main effect in the model, for both between- and within-subjects factors. This item is available only if main effects are selected under the Display Means For list.

- **Confidence interval adjustment.** Select least significant difference (LSD), Bonferroni, or Sidak adjustment to the confidence intervals and significance. This item is available only if Compare main effects is selected.

Display. Select Descriptive statistics to produce observed means, standard deviations, and counts for all of the dependent variables in all cells. Estimates of effect size gives a partial eta-squared value for each effect and each parameter estimate. The eta-squared statistic describes the proportion of total variability attributable to a factor. Select Observed power to obtain the power of the test when the alternative hypothesis is set based on the observed value. Select Parameter estimates to produce the parameter estimates, standard errors, *t* tests, confidence intervals, and the observed power for each test. You can display the hypothesis and error SSCP matrices and the Residual SSCP matrix plus Bartlett's test of sphericity of the residual covariance matrix.

Homogeneity tests produces the Levene test of the homogeneity of variance for each dependent variable across all level combinations of the between-subjects factors, for between-subjects factors only. Also, homogeneity tests include Box's *M* test of the homogeneity of the covariance matrices of the dependent variables across all level combinations of the between-subjects factors. The spread-versus-level and residual plots options are useful for checking assumptions about the data. This item is disabled if there are no factors. Select Residual plots to produce an observed-by-predicted-by-standardized residuals plot for each dependent variable. These plots are useful for investigating the assumption of equal variance. Select Lack of fit test to check if the relationship between the dependent variable and the independent variables can be adequately described by the model. General estimable function allows you to construct custom hypothesis tests based on the general estimable function. Rows in any contrast coefficient matrix are linear combinations of the general estimable function.

Significance level. You might want to adjust the significance level used in post hoc tests and the confidence level used for constructing confidence intervals. The specified value is also used to calculate the observed power for the test. When you specify a significance level, the associated level of the confidence intervals is displayed in the dialog box.

GLM Command Additional Features

These features may apply to univariate, multivariate, or repeated measures analysis. The SPSS command language also allows you to:

■ Specify nested effects in the design (using the DESIGN subcommand).

■ Specify tests of effects versus a linear combination of effects or a value (using the TEST subcommand).

■ Specify multiple contrasts (using the CONTRAST subcommand).

■ Include user-missing values (using the MISSING subcommand).

■ Specify EPS criteria (using the CRITERIA subcommand).

■ Construct a custom **L** matrix, **M** matrix, or **K** matrix (using the LMATRIX, MMATRIX, or KMATRIX subcommands).

■ For deviation or simple contrasts, specify an intermediate reference category (using the CONTRAST subcommand).

■ Specify metrics for polynomial contrasts (using the CONTRAST subcommand).

■ Specify error terms for post hoc comparisons (using the POSTHOC subcommand).

■ Compute estimated marginal means for any factor or factor interaction among the factors in the factor list (using the EMMEANS subcommand).

■ Specify names for temporary variables (using the SAVE subcommand).

■ Construct a correlation matrix data file (using the OUTFILE subcommand).

■ Construct a matrix data file that contains statistics from the between-subjects ANOVA table (using the OUTFILE subcommand).

■ Save the design matrix to a new data file (using the OUTFILE subcommand).

See the *SPSS Syntax Reference Guide* for complete syntax information.

GLM Repeated Measures

The GLM Repeated Measures procedure provides analysis of variance when the same measurement is made several times on each subject or case. If between-subjects factors are specified, they divide the population into groups. Using this general linear model procedure, you can test null hypotheses about the effects of both the between-subjects factors and the within-subjects factors. You can investigate interactions between factors as well as the effects of individual factors. In addition, the effects of constant covariates and covariate interactions with the between-subjects factors can be included.

In a doubly multivariate repeated measures design, the dependent variables represent measurements of more than one variable for the different levels of the within-subjects factors. For example, you could have measured both pulse and respiration at three different times on each subject.

The GLM Repeated Measures procedure provides both univariate and multivariate analyses for the repeated measures data. Both balanced and unbalanced models can be tested. A design is balanced if each cell in the model contains the same number of cases. In a multivariate model, the sums of squares due to the effects in the model and error sums of squares are in matrix form rather than the scalar form found in univariate analysis. These matrices are called SSCP (sums-of-squares and cross-products) matrices. In addition to testing hypotheses, GLM Repeated Measures produces estimates of parameters.

Commonly used *a priori* contrasts are available to perform hypothesis testing on between-subjects factors. Additionally, after an overall *F* test has shown significance, you can use post hoc tests to evaluate differences among specific means. Estimated marginal means give estimates of predicted mean values for the cells in the model, and profile plots (interaction plots) of these means allow you to visualize some of the relationships easily.

Residuals, predicted values, Cook's distance, and leverage values can be saved as new variables in your data file for checking assumptions. Also available are a residual SSCP matrix, which is a square matrix of sums of squares and cross-products of residuals, a residual covariance matrix, which is the residual SSCP matrix divided by the degrees of freedom of the residuals, and the residual correlation matrix, which is the standardized form of the residual covariance matrix.

WLS Weight allows you to specify a variable used to give observations different weights for a weighted least-squares (WLS) analysis, perhaps to compensate for different precision of measurement.

Example. Twelve students are assigned to a high- or low-anxiety group based on their scores on an anxiety-rating test. The anxiety rating is called a between-subjects factor because it divides the subjects into groups. The students are each given four trials on a learning task, and the number of errors for each trial is recorded. The errors for each trial are recorded in separate variables, and a within-subjects factor (trial) is defined with four levels for the four trials. The trial effect is found to be significant, while the trial-by-anxiety interaction is not significant.

Methods. Type I, Type II, Type III, and Type IV sums of squares can be used to evaluate different hypotheses. Type III is the default.

Statistics. Post hoc range tests and multiple comparisons (for between-subjects factors): least significant difference, Bonferroni, Sidak, Scheffé, Ryan-Einot-Gabriel-Welsch multiple F, Ryan-Einot-Gabriel-Welsch multiple range, Student-Newman-Keuls, Tukey's honestly significant difference, Tukey's-b, Duncan, Hochberg's GT2, Gabriel, Waller Duncan t test, Dunnett (one-sided and two-sided), Tamhane's T2, Dunnett's T3, Games-Howell, and Dunnett's C. Descriptive statistics: observed means, standard deviations, and counts for all of the dependent variables in all cells; the Levene test for homogeneity of variance; Box's M; and Mauchly's test of sphericity.

Plots. Spread-versus-level, residual, and profile (interaction).

Data. The dependent variables should be quantitative. Between-subjects factors divide the sample into discrete subgroups, such as male and female. These factors are categorical and can have numeric values or string values of up to eight characters. Within-subjects factors are defined in the Repeated Measures Define Factor(s) dialog box. Covariates are quantitative variables that are related to the dependent variable. For a repeated measures analysis, these should remain constant at each level of a within-subjects variable.

The data file should contain a set of variables for each group of measurements on the subjects. The set has one variable for each repetition of the measurement within the group. A within-subjects factor is defined for the group with the number of levels equal to the number of repetitions. For example, measurements of weight could be taken on different days. If measurements of the same property were taken on five days, the within-subjects factor could be specified as *day* with five levels.

For multiple within-subjects factors, the number of measurements for each subject is equal to the product of the number of levels of each factor. For example, if measurements were taken at three different times each day for four days, the total number of measurements is 12 for each subject. The within-subjects factors could be specified as *day(4)* and *time(3)*.

Assumptions. A repeated measures analysis can be approached in two ways, univariate and multivariate.

The univariate approach (also known as the split-plot or mixed-model approach) considers the dependent variables as responses to the levels of within-subjects factors. The measurements on a subject should be a sample from a multivariate normal distribution, and the variance-covariance matrices are the same across the cells formed by the between-subjects effects. Certain assumptions are made on the variance-covariance matrix of the dependent variables. The validity of the F statistic used in the univariate approach can be assured if the variance-covariance matrix is circular in form (Huynh and Mandeville, 1979).

To test this assumption, Mauchly's test of sphericity can be used, which performs a test of sphericity on the variance-covariance matrix of an orthonormalized transformed dependent variable. Mauchly's test is automatically displayed for a repeated measures analysis. For small sample sizes, this test is not very powerful. For large sample sizes, the test may be significant even when the impact of the departure on the results is small. If the significance of the test is large, the hypothesis of sphericity can be assumed. However, if the significance is small and the sphericity assumption appears to be violated, an adjustment to the numerator and denominator degrees of freedom can be made in order to validate the univariate F statistic. Three estimates of this adjustment, which is called **epsilon**, are available in the GLM Repeated Measures procedure. Both the numerator and denominator degrees of freedom must be multiplied by epsilon, and the significance of the F ratio must be evaluated with the new degrees of freedom.

The multivariate approach considers the measurements on a subject to be a sample from a multivariate normal distribution, and the variance-covariance matrices are the same across the cells formed by the between-subjects effects. To test whether the variance-covariance matrices across the cells are the same, Box's M test can be used.

Related procedures. Use the Explore procedure to examine the data before doing an analysis of variance. If there are *not* repeated measurements on each subject, use GLM Univariate or GLM Multivariate. If there are only two measurements for each subject (for example, pre-test and post-test), and there are no between-subjects factors, you can use the Paired-Samples T Test procedure.

GLM Repeated Measures Define Factor(s)

GLM Repeated Measures analyzes groups of related dependent variables that represent different measurements of the same attribute. This dialog box lets you define one or more within-subjects factors for use in GLM Repeated Measures. Note that the order in which you specify within-subjects factors is important. Each factor constitutes a level within the previous factor.

To use Repeated Measures, you must set up your data correctly. You must define within-subjects factors in this dialog box. Notice that these factors are not existing variables in your data but rather factors that you define here.

Example. In a weight-loss study, suppose the weights of several people are measured each week for five weeks. In the data file, each person is a subject or case. The weights for the weeks are recorded in the variables *weight1*, *weight2*, and so on. The gender of each person is recorded in another variable. The weights, measured for each subject repeatedly, can be grouped by defining a within-subjects factor. The factor could be called *week*, defined to have five levels. In the main dialog box, the variables *weight1*, ..., *weight5* are used to assign the five levels of *week*. The variable in the data file that groups males and females (*gender*) can be specified as a between-subjects factor to study the differences between males and females.

Measures. If subjects were tested on more than one measure at each time, click Measure to define the measures. For example, the pulse and respiration rate could be measured on each subject every day for a week. These measures do not exist as variables in the data file but are defined here. A model with more than one measure is sometimes called a doubly multivariate repeated measures model.

To Obtain a GLM Repeated Measures Analysis

▶ From the menus choose:

Analyze
  General Linear Model
    Repeated Measures...

Figure 2-1
Repeated Measures Define Factor(s) dialog box

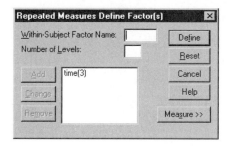

▶ Type a within-subject factor name and its number of levels.

▶ Click Add.

▶ Repeat these steps for each within-subjects factor.

To define measure factors for a doubly multivariate repeated measures design:

▶ Click Measure.

Chapter 2

Figure 2-2
Expanded Repeated Measures Define Factor(s) dialog box

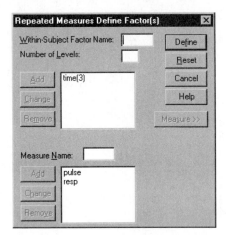

▶ Type the measure name.

▶ Click Add.

After defining all of your factors and measures:

▶ Click Define.

Figure 2-3
Repeated Measures dialog box

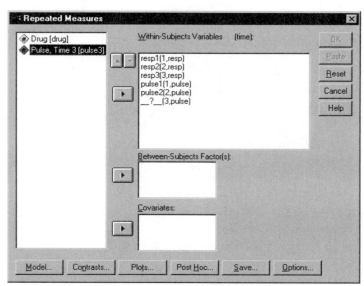

▶ Select a dependent variable that corresponds to each combination of within-subjects factors (and optionally, measures) on the list.

To change positions of the variables, use the up and down pushbuttons.

To make changes to the within-subjects factors, you can reopen the Repeated Measures Define Factor(s) dialog box without closing the main dialog box.

Optionally, you can specify between-subjects factor(s) and covariates.

GLM Repeated Measures Model

Figure 2-4
Repeated Measures Model dialog box

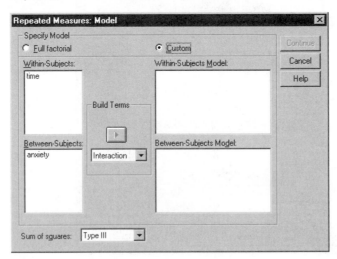

Specify Model. A full factorial model contains all factor main effects, all covariate main effects, and all factor-by-factor interactions. It does not contain covariate interactions. Select Custom to specify only a subset of interactions or to specify factor-by-covariate interactions. You must indicate all of the terms to be included in the model.

Between-Subjects. The covariates are listed with (C) for covariate.

Model. The model depends on the nature of your data. After selecting Custom, you can select the within-subjects effects and interactions and the between-subjects effects and interactions that are of interest in your analysis.

Sum of squares. The method of calculating the sums of squares for the between-subjects model. For balanced or unbalanced between-subjects models with no missing cells, the Type III sum-of-squares method is the most commonly used.

Build Terms

For the selected factors and covariates:

Interaction. Creates the highest-level interaction term of all selected variables. This is the default.

Main effects. Creates a main-effects term for each variable selected.

All 2-way. Creates all possible two-way interactions of the selected variables.

All 3-way. Creates all possible three-way interactions of the selected variables.

All 4-way. Creates all possible four-way interactions of the selected variables.

All 5-way. Creates all possible five-way interactions of the selected variables.

Sums of Squares

For the model, you can choose a type of sum of squares. Type III is the most commonly used and is the default.

Type I. This method is also known as the hierarchical decomposition of the sum-of-squares method. Each term is adjusted for only the term that precedes it in the model. The Type I sum-of-squares method is commonly used for:

- A balanced ANOVA model in which any main effects are specified before any first-order interaction effects, any first-order interaction effects are specified before any second-order interaction effects, and so on.

- A polynomial regression model in which any lower-order terms are specified before any higher-order terms.

- A purely nested model in which the first-specified effect is nested within the second-specified effect, the second-specified effect is nested within the third, and so on. (This form of nesting can be specified only by using syntax.)

Type II. This method calculates the sums of squares of an effect in the model adjusted for all other "appropriate" effects. An appropriate effect is one that corresponds to all effects that do not contain the effect being examined. The Type II sum-of-squares method is commonly used for:

- A balanced ANOVA model.

- Any model that has main factor effects only.

- Any regression model.

- A purely nested design. (This form of nesting can be specified by using syntax.)

Type III. This method, the default, calculates the sums of squares of an effect in the design as the sums of squares adjusted for any other effects that do not contain it and orthogonal to any effects (if any) that contain it. The Type III sums of squares have one major advantage in that they are invariant with respect to the cell frequencies as long as the general form of estimability remains constant. Therefore, this type is often considered useful for an unbalanced model with no missing cells. In a factorial design with no missing cells, this method is equivalent to the Yates' weighted-squares-of-means technique. The Type III sum-of-squares method is commonly used for:

■ Any models listed in Type I and Type II.

■ Any balanced or unbalanced model with no empty cells.

Type IV. This method is designed for a situation in which there are missing cells. For any effect F in the design, if F is not contained in any other effect, then Type IV = Type III = Type II. When F is contained in other effects, Type IV distributes the contrasts being made among the parameters in F to all higher-level effects equitably. The Type IV sum-of-squares method is commonly used for:

■ Any models listed in Type I and Type II.

■ Any balanced model or unbalanced model with empty cells.

GLM Repeated Measures Contrasts

Figure 2-5
Repeated Measures Contrasts dialog box

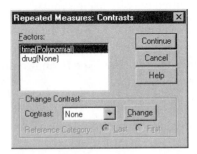

Contrasts are used to test for differences among the levels of a between-subjects factor. You can specify a contrast for each between-subjects factor in the model. Contrasts represent linear combinations of the parameters.

Hypothesis testing is based on the null hypothesis $\mathbf{LBM}=0$, where $\mathbf{L}$ is the contrast coefficients matrix, $\mathbf{B}$ is the parameter vector, and $\mathbf{M}$ is the average matrix that corresponds to the average transformation for the dependent variable. You can display this transformation matrix by selecting Transformation matrix in the Repeated Measures Options dialog box. For example, if there are four dependent variables, a within-subjects factor of four levels, and polynomial contrasts (the default) are used for within-subjects factors, the $\mathbf{M}$ matrix will be (0.5 0.5 0.5 0.5)'. When a contrast is specified, SPSS creates an $\mathbf{L}$ matrix such that the columns corresponding to the between-subjects factor match the contrast. The remaining columns are adjusted so that the $\mathbf{L}$ matrix is estimable.

Available contrasts are deviation, simple, difference, Helmert, repeated, and polynomial. For deviation contrasts and simple contrasts, you can choose whether the reference category is the last or first category.

Contrast Types

Deviation. Compares the mean of each level (except a reference category) to the mean of all of the levels (grand mean). The levels of the factor can be in any order.

Simple. Compares the mean of each level to the mean of a specified level. This type of contrast is useful when there is a control group. You can choose the first or last category as the reference.

Difference. Compares the mean of each level (except the first) to the mean of previous levels. (Sometimes called reverse Helmert contrasts.)

Helmert. Compares the mean of each level of the factor (except the last) to the mean of subsequent levels.

Repeated. Compares the mean of each level (except the last) to the mean of the subsequent level.

Polynomial. Compares the linear effect, quadratic effect, cubic effect, and so on. The first degree of freedom contains the linear effect across all categories; the second degree of freedom, the quadratic effect; and so on. These contrasts are often used to estimate polynomial trends.

GLM Repeated Measures Profile Plots

Figure 2-6
Repeated Measures Profile Plots dialog box

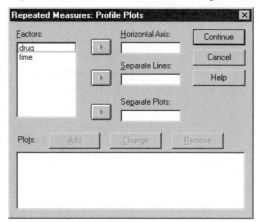

Profile plots (interaction plots) are useful for comparing marginal means in your model. A profile plot is a line plot in which each point indicates the estimated marginal mean of a dependent variable (adjusted for any covariates) at one level of a factor. The levels of a second factor can be used to make separate lines. Each level in a third factor can be used to create a separate plot. Both between-subjects factors and within-subjects factors can be used in profile plots.

A profile plot of one factor shows whether the estimated marginal means are increasing or decreasing across levels. For two or more factors, parallel lines indicate that there is no interaction between factors, which means that you can investigate the levels of only one factor. Nonparallel lines indicate an interaction.

Figure 2-7
Nonparallel plot (left) and parallel plot (right)

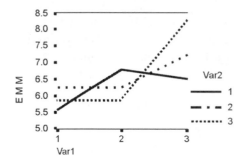 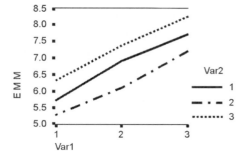

After a plot is specified by selecting factors for the horizontal axis and, optionally, factors for separate lines and separate plots, it must be added to the Plots list.

GLM Repeated Measures Post Hoc Multiple Comparisons for Observed Means

Figure 2-8
Post Hoc Multiple Comparisons for Observed Means dialog box

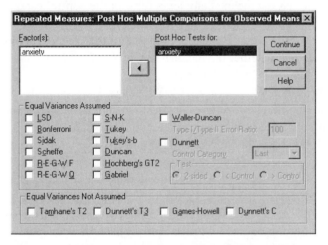

Post hoc multiple comparison tests. Once you have determined that differences exist among the means, post hoc range tests and pairwise multiple comparisons can determine which means differ. These tests are used for fixed *between-subjects* factors only. They are not available if there are no between-subjects factors. The post hoc multiple comparison tests are performed for each dependent variable separately.

The Bonferroni and Tukey's honestly significant difference tests are commonly used multiple comparison tests. The **Bonferroni test**, based on Student's *t* statistic, adjusts the observed significance level for the fact that multiple comparisons are made. **Sidak's *t* test** also adjusts the significance level and provides tighter bounds than the Bonferroni test. **Tukey's honestly significant difference test** uses the Studentized range statistic to make all pairwise comparisons between groups and sets the experimentwise error rate to the error rate for the collection for all pairwise comparisons. When testing a large number of pairs of means, Tukey's honestly significant difference test is more powerful than the Bonferroni test. For a small number of pairs, Bonferroni is more powerful.

Hochberg's GT2 is similar to Tukey's honestly significant difference test, but the Studentized maximum modulus is used. Usually, Tukey's test is more powerful. **Gabriel's pairwise comparisons test** also uses the Studentized maximum modulus and is generally more powerful than Hochberg's GT2 when the cell sizes are unequal. Gabriel's test may become liberal when the cell sizes vary greatly.

Dunnett's pairwise multiple comparison *t* test compares a set of treatments against a single control mean. The last category is the default control category. Alternatively, you can choose the first category. You can also choose a two-sided or one-sided test. To test that the mean at any level (except the control category) of the factor is not equal to that of the control category, use a two-sided test. To test whether the mean at any level of the factor is smaller than that of the control category, select < Control. Likewise, to test whether the mean at any level of the factor is larger than that of the control category, select > Control.

Ryan, Einot, Gabriel, and Welsch (R-E-G-W) developed two multiple step-down range tests. Multiple step-down procedures first test whether all means are equal. If all means are not equal, subsets of means are tested for equality. **R-E-G-W *F*** is based on an *F* test and **R-E-G-W *Q*** is based on the Studentized range. These tests are more powerful than Duncan's multiple range test and Student-Newman-Keuls (which are also multiple step-down procedures), but they are not recommended for unequal cell sizes.

When the variances are unequal, use **Tamhane's T2** (conservative pairwise comparisons test based on a *t* test), **Dunnett's T3** (pairwise comparison test based on the Studentized maximum modulus), **Games-Howell pairwise comparison test** (sometimes liberal), or **Dunnett's *C*** (pairwise comparison test based on the Studentized range).

Duncan's multiple range test, Student-Newman-Keuls (**S-N-K**), and **Tukey's-*b*** are range tests that rank group means and compute a range value. These tests are not used as frequently as the tests previously discussed.

The **Waller-Duncan *t* test** uses a Bayesian approach. This range test uses the harmonic mean of the sample size when the sample sizes are unequal.

The significance level of the **Scheffé test** is designed to allow all possible linear combinations of group means to be tested, not just pairwise comparisons available in this feature. The result is that the Scheffé test is often more conservative than other tests, which means that a larger difference between means is required for significance.

The least significant difference (**LSD**) pairwise multiple comparison test is equivalent to multiple individual *t* tests between all pairs of groups. The disadvantage of this test is that no attempt is made to adjust the observed significance level for multiple comparisons.

Tests displayed. Pairwise comparisons are provided for LSD, Sidak, Bonferroni, Games and Howell, Tamhane's T2 and T3, Dunnett's *C*, and Dunnett's T3. Homogeneous subsets for range tests are provided for S-N-K, Tukey's-*b*, Duncan, R-E-G-W *F*, R-E-G-W *Q*, and Waller. Tukey's honestly significant difference test, Hochberg's GT2, Gabriel's test, and Scheffé's test are both multiple comparison tests and range tests.

GLM Repeated Measures Save

Figure 2-9
Repeated Measures Save dialog box

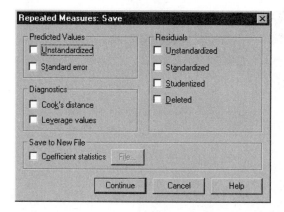

You can save values predicted by the model, residuals, and related measures as new variables in the Data Editor. Many of these variables can be used for examining assumptions about the data. To save the values for use in another SPSS session, you must save the current data file.

Predicted Values. The values that the model predicts for each case. Unstandardized predicted values and the standard errors of the predicted values are available.

Diagnostics. Measures to identify cases with unusual combinations of values for the independent variables and cases that may have a large impact on the model. Available are Cook's distance and uncentered leverage values.

Residuals. An unstandardized residual is the actual value of the dependent variable minus the value predicted by the model. Standardized, Studentized, and deleted residuals are also available.

Save to New File. Writes an SPSS data file containing a variance-covariance matrix of the parameter estimates in the model. Also, for each dependent variable, there will be a row of parameter estimates, a row of significance values for the *t* statistics corresponding to the parameter estimates, and a row of residual degrees of freedom. For a multivariate model, there are similar rows for each dependent variable. You can use this matrix file in other procedures that read an SPSS matrix file.

GLM Repeated Measures Options

Figure 2-10
Repeated Measures Options dialog box

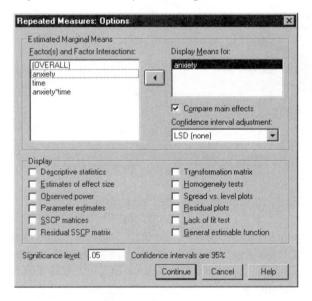

Optional statistics are available from this dialog box. Statistics are calculated using a fixed-effects model.

Estimated Marginal Means. Select the factors and interactions for which you want estimates of the population marginal means in the cells. These means are adjusted for the covariates, if any. Both within-subjects and between-subjects factors can be selected.

■ **Compare main effects.** Provides uncorrected pairwise comparisons among estimated marginal means for any main effect in the model, for both between- and within-subjects factors. This item is available only if main effects are selected under the Display Means For list.

■ **Confidence interval adjustment.** Select least significant difference (LSD), Bonferroni, or Sidak adjustment to the confidence intervals and significance. This item is available only if Compare main effects is selected.

Display. Select Descriptive statistics to produce observed means, standard deviations, and counts for all of the dependent variables in all cells. Estimates of effect size gives a partial eta-squared value for each effect and each parameter estimate. The eta-squared statistic describes the proportion of total variability attributable to a factor. Select Observed power to obtain the power of the test when the alternative hypothesis is set based on the observed value. Select Parameter estimates to produce the parameter estimates, standard errors, *t* tests, confidence intervals, and the observed power for each test. You can display the hypothesis and error SSCP matrices and the Residual SSCP matrix plus Bartlett's test of sphericity of the residual covariance matrix.

Homogeneity tests produces the Levene test of the homogeneity of variance for each dependent variable across all level combinations of the between-subjects factors, for between-subjects factors only. Also, homogeneity tests include Box's *M* test of the homogeneity of the covariance matrices of the dependent variables across all level combinations of the between-subjects factors. The spread-versus-level and residual plots options are useful for checking assumptions about the data. This item is disabled if there are no factors. Select Residual plots to produce an observed-by-predicted-by-standardized residuals plot for each dependent variable. These plots are useful for investigating the assumption of equal variance. Select Lack of fit test to check if the relationship between the dependent variable and the independent variables can be adequately described by the model. General estimable function allows you to construct custom hypothesis tests based on the general estimable function. Rows in any contrast coefficient matrix are linear combinations of the general estimable function.

Significance level. You might want to adjust the significance level used in post hoc tests and the confidence level used for constructing confidence intervals. The specified value is also used to calculate the observed power for the test. When you specify a significance level, the associated level of the confidence intervals is displayed in the dialog box.

GLM Command Additional Features

These features may apply to univariate, multivariate, or repeated measures analysis. The SPSS command language also allows you to:

- Specify nested effects in the design (using the DESIGN subcommand).

- Specify tests of effects versus a linear combination of effects or a value (using the TEST subcommand).

- Specify multiple contrasts (using the CONTRAST subcommand).

- Include user-missing values (using the MISSING subcommand).

- Specify EPS criteria (using the CRITERIA subcommand).

- Construct a custom **L** matrix, **M** matrix, or **K** matrix (using the LMATRIX, MMATRIX, and KMATRIX subcommands).

- For deviation or simple contrasts, specify an intermediate reference category (using the CONTRAST subcommand).

- Specify metrics for polynomial contrasts (using the CONTRAST subcommand).

- Specify error terms for post hoc comparisons (using the POSTHOC subcommand).

- Compute estimated marginal means for any factor or factor interaction among the factors in the factor list (using the EMMEANS subcommand).

- Specify names for temporary variables (using the SAVE subcommand).

- Construct a correlation matrix data file (using the OUTFILE subcommand).

- Construct a matrix data file that contains statistics from the between-subjects ANOVA table (using the OUTFILE subcommand).

- Save the design matrix to a new data file (using the OUTFILE subcommand).

See the *SPSS Syntax Reference Guide* for complete syntax information.

Variance Components Analysis

The Variance Components procedure, for mixed-effects models, estimates the contribution of each random effect to the variance of the dependent variable. This procedure is particularly interesting for analysis of mixed models such as split plot, univariate repeated measures, and random block designs. By calculating variance components, you can determine where to focus attention in order to reduce the variance.

Four different methods are available for estimating the variance components: minimum norm quadratic unbiased estimator (MINQUE), analysis of variance (ANOVA), maximum likelihood (ML), and restricted maximum likelihood (REML). Various specifications are available for the different methods.

Default output for all methods includes variance component estimates. If the ML method or the REML method is used, an asymptotic covariance matrix table is also displayed. Other available output includes an ANOVA table and expected mean squares for the ANOVA method, and an iteration history for the ML and REML methods. The Variance Components procedure is fully compatible with the GLM Univariate procedure.

WLS Weight allows you to specify a variable used to give observations different weights for a weighted analysis, perhaps to compensate for different precision of measurement.

Example. At an agriculture school, weight gains for pigs in six different litters are measured after one month. The litter variable is a random factor with six levels. (The six litters studied are a random sample from a large population of pig litters.) The investigator finds out that the variance in weight gain is attributable to the difference in litters much more than to the difference in pigs within a litter.

Data. The dependent variable is quantitative. Factors are categorical. They can have numeric values or string values of up to eight characters. At least one of the factors must be random. That is, the levels of the factor must be a random sample of possible levels. Covariates are quantitative variables that are related to the dependent variable.

Assumptions. All methods assume that model parameters of a random effect have zero means and finite constant variances and are mutually uncorrelated. Model parameters from different random effects are also uncorrelated.

The residual term also has a zero mean and finite constant variance. It is uncorrelated with model parameters of any random effect. Residual terms from different observations are assumed to be uncorrelated.

Based on these assumptions, observations from the same level of a random factor are correlated. This fact distinguishes a variance component model from a general linear model.

ANOVA and MINQUE do not require normality assumptions. They are both robust to moderate departures from the normality assumption.

ML and REML require the model parameter and the residual term to be normally distributed.

Related procedures. Use the Explore procedure to examine the data before doing variance components analysis. For hypothesis testing, use GLM Univariate, GLM Multivariate, and GLM Repeated Measures.

To Obtain a Variance Components Analysis

▶ From the menus choose:

Analyze
  General Linear Model
    Variance Components...

Figure 3-1
Variance Components dialog box

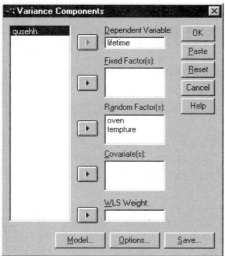

▶ Select a dependent variable.

▶ Select variables for Fixed Factor(s), Random Factor(s), and Covariate(s), as appropriate for your data. For specifying a weight variable, use WLS Weight.

Variance Components Model

Figure 3-2
Variance Components Model dialog box

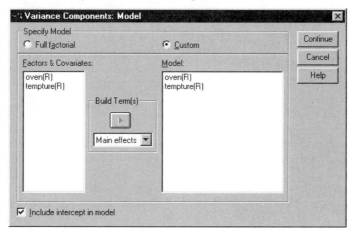

Specify Model. A full factorial model contains all factor main effects, all covariate main effects, and all factor-by-factor interactions. It does not contain covariate interactions. Select Custom to specify only a subset of interactions or to specify factor-by-covariate interactions. You must indicate all of the terms to be included in the model.

Factors and Covariates. The factors and covariates are listed with (F) for a fixed factor, (R) for a random factor, and (C) for a covariate.

Model. The model depends on the nature of your data. After selecting Custom, you can select the main effects and interactions that are of interest in your analysis. The model must contain a random factor.

Include intercept in model. Usually the intercept is included in the model. If you can assume that the data pass through the origin, you can exclude the intercept.

Build Terms

For the selected factors and covariates:

Interaction. Creates the highest-level interaction term of all selected variables. This is the default.

Main effects. Creates a main-effects term for each variable selected.

All 2-way. Creates all possible two-way interactions of the selected variables.

All 3-way. Creates all possible three-way interactions of the selected variables.

All 4-way. Creates all possible four-way interactions of the selected variables.

All 5-way. Creates all possible five-way interactions of the selected variables.

Variance Components Options

Figure 3-3
Variance Components Options dialog box

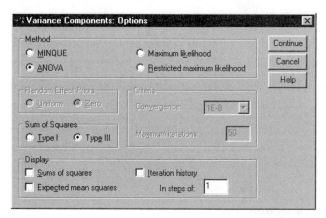

Method. You can choose one of four methods used to estimate the variance components.

- MINQUE (minimum norm quadratic unbiased estimator) produces estimates that are invariant with respect to the fixed effects. If the data are normally distributed and the estimates are correct, this method produces the least variance among all unbiased estimators. You can choose a method for random-effect prior weights.

- ANOVA (analysis of variance) computes unbiased estimates using either the Type I or Type III sums of squares for each effect. The ANOVA method sometimes produces negative variance estimates, which can indicate an incorrect model, an inappropriate estimation method, or a need for more data.

- Maximum likelihood (ML) produces estimates that would be most consistent with the data actually observed, using iterations. These estimates can be biased. This method is asymptotically normal. ML and REML estimates are invariant under translation. This method does not take into account the degrees of freedom used to estimate the fixed effects.

- Restricted maximum likelihood (REML) estimates reduce the ANOVA estimates for many (if not all) cases of balanced data. Because this method is adjusted for the fixed effects, it should have smaller standard errors than the ML method. This method takes into account the degrees of freedom used to estimate the fixed effects.

Random-Effect Priors. Uniform implies that all random effects and the residual term have an equal impact on the observations. The Zero scheme is equivalent to assuming zero random-effect variances. Available only for the MINQUE method.

Sum of Squares. Type I sums of squares are used for the hierarchical model, which is often used in variance component literature. If you choose Type III, the default in GLM, the variance estimates can be used in GLM Univariate for hypothesis testing with Type III sums of squares. Available only for the ANOVA method.

Criteria. You can specify the convergence criterion and the maximum number of iterations. Available only for the ML or REML methods.

Display. For the ANOVA method, you can choose to display sums of squares and expected mean squares. If you selected Maximum likelihood or Restricted maximum likelihood, you can display a history of the iterations.

Sums of Squares (Variance Components)

For the model, you can choose a type of sum of squares. Type III is the most commonly used and is the default.

Type I. This method is also known as the hierarchical decomposition of the sum-of-squares method. Each term is adjusted for only the term that precedes it in the model. The Type I sum-of-squares method is commonly used for:

■ A balanced ANOVA model in which any main effects are specified before any first-order interaction effects, any first-order interaction effects are specified before any second-order interaction effects, and so on.

■ A polynomial regression model in which any lower-order terms are specified before any higher-order terms.

■ A purely nested model in which the first-specified effect is nested within the second-specified effect, the second-specified effect is nested within the third, and so on. (This form of nesting can be specified only by using syntax.)

Type III. This method, the default, calculates the sums of squares of an effect in the design as the sums of squares adjusted for any other effects that do not contain it and orthogonal to any effects (if any) that contain it. The Type III sums of squares have one major advantage in that they are invariant with respect to the cell frequencies as long as the general form of estimability remains constant. Therefore, this type is often considered useful for an unbalanced model with no missing cells. In a factorial design with no missing cells, this method is equivalent to the Yates' weighted-squares-of-means technique. The Type III sum-of-squares method is commonly used for:

■ Any models listed in Type I.

■ Any balanced or unbalanced model with no empty cells.

Variance Components Save to New File

Figure 3-4
Variance Components Save to New File dialog box

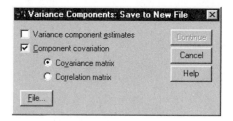

You can save some results of this procedure to a new SPSS data file.

Variance component estimates. Saves estimates of the variance components and estimate labels to a data file. These can be used in calculating more statistics or in further analysis in the GLM procedures. For example, you can use them to calculate confidence intervals or test hypotheses.

Component covariation. Saves a variance-covariance matrix or a correlation matrix to a data file. Available only if Maximum likelihood or Restricted maximum likelihood has been specified.

Save to File. Allows you to specify a filename for the file containing the variance component estimates and/or the matrix.

You can use the MATRIX command to extract the data you need from the new file and then compute confidence intervals or perform tests.

VARCOMP Command Additional Features

The SPSS command language also allows you to:

- Specify nested effects in the design (using the DESIGN subcommand).
- Include user-missing values (using the MISSING subcommand).
- Specify EPS criteria (using the CRITERIA subcommand).

See the *SPSS Syntax Reference Guide* for complete syntax information.

Model Selection Loglinear Analysis

The Model Selection Loglinear Analysis procedure analyzes multiway crosstabulations (contingency tables). It fits hierarchical loglinear models to multidimensional crosstabulations using an iterative proportional-fitting algorithm. This procedure helps you find out which categorical variables are associated. To build models, forced entry and backward elimination methods are available. For saturated models, you can request parameter estimates and tests of partial association. A saturated model adds 0.5 to all cells.

Example. In a study of user preference for one of two laundry detergents, researchers counted people in each group, combining various categories of water softness (soft, medium, or hard), previous use of one of the brands, and washing temperature (cold or hot). They found how temperature is related to water softness and also to brand preference.

Statistics. Frequencies, residuals, parameter estimates, standard errors, confidence intervals, and tests of partial association. For custom models, plots of residuals and normal probability plots.

Data. Factor variables are categorical. All variables to be analyzed must be numeric. Categorical string variables can be recoded to numeric variables before starting the model selection analysis.

Avoid specifying many variables with many levels. Such specifications can lead to a situation where many cells have small numbers of observations, and the chi-square values may not be useful.

Related procedures. The Model Selection procedure can help identify the terms needed in the model. Then you can continue to evaluate the model using General

Loglinear Analysis or Logit Loglinear Analysis. You can use Autorecode to recode string variables. If a numeric variable has empty categories, use Recode to create consecutive integer values.

To Obtain a Model Selection Loglinear Analysis

From the menus choose:

Analyze
  Loglinear
    Model Selection...

Figure 4-1
Model Selection Loglinear Analysis dialog box

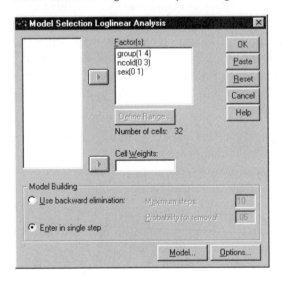

▶ Select two or more numeric categorical factors.

▶ Select one or more factor variables in the Factor(s) list, and click Define Range.

▶ Define the range of values for each factor variable.

▶ Select an option in the Model Building group.

Optionally, you can select a cell weight variable to specify structural zeros.

Loglinear Analysis Define Range

Figure 4-2
Loglinear Analysis Define Range dialog box

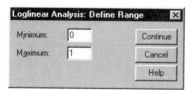

You must indicate the range of categories for each factor variable. Values for Minimum and Maximum correspond to the lowest and highest categories of the factor variable. Both values must be integers, and the minimum value must be less than the maximum value. Cases with values outside of the bounds are excluded. For example, if you specify a minimum value of 1 and a maximum value of 3, only the values 1, 2, and 3 are used. Repeat this process for each factor variable.

Loglinear Analysis Model

Figure 4-3
Loglinear Analysis Model dialog box

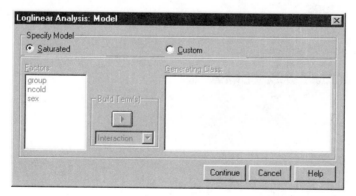

Specify Model. A saturated model contains all factor main effects and all factor-by-factor interactions. Select Custom to specify a generating class for an unsaturated model.

Generating Class. A generating class is a list of the highest-order terms in which factors appear. SPSS builds a hierarchical model containing the terms that define the generating class and all lower-order relatives. Suppose you select variables *A*, *B*, and *C* in the Factors list and then select Interaction from the Build Terms drop-down list. The resulting model will contain the specified 3-way interaction $A*B*C$, the 2-way interactions $A*B$, $A*C$, and $B*C$, and main effects for *A*, *B*, and *C*. Do not specify the lower-order relatives in the generating class.

Build Terms

For the selected factors and covariates:

Interaction. Creates the highest-level interaction term of all selected variables. This is the default.

Main effects. Creates a main-effects term for each variable selected.

All 2-way. Creates all possible two-way interactions of the selected variables.

All 3-way. Creates all possible three-way interactions of the selected variables.

All 4-way. Creates all possible four-way interactions of the selected variables.

All 5-way. Creates all possible five-way interactions of the selected variables.

Loglinear Analysis Options

Figure 4-4
Loglinear Analysis Options dialog box

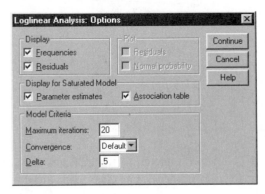

Display. You can choose Frequencies, Residuals, or both. In a saturated model, the observed and expected frequencies are equal, and the residuals are equal to 0.

Display for Saturated Model. For a saturated model, you can choose Parameter estimates. The parameter estimates may help determine which terms can be dropped from the model. An association table, which lists tests of partial association, is also available. This option is computationally expensive for tables with many factors.

Plot. For custom models, you can choose one or both types of plots, Residuals and Normal probability. These will help determine how well a model fits the data.

Model Criteria. SPSS uses an iterative proportional-fitting algorithm to obtain parameter estimates. You can override one or more of the estimation criteria by specifying Maximum iterations, Convergence, or Delta (a value added to all cell frequencies for saturated models).

HILOGLINEAR Command Additional Features

The SPSS command language also allows you to:

- Specify cell weights in matrix form (using the CWEIGHT subcommand).
- Generate analyses of several models with a single command (using the DESIGN subcommand).

See the *SPSS Syntax Reference Guide* for complete syntax information.

General Loglinear Analysis

The General Loglinear Analysis procedure analyzes the frequency counts of observations falling into each cross-classification category in a crosstabulation or a contingency table. Each cross-classification in the table constitutes a cell, and each categorical variable is called a factor. The dependent variable is the number of cases (frequency) in a cell of the crosstabulation, and the explanatory variables are factors and covariates. This procedure estimates maximum likelihood parameters of hierarchical and nonhierarchical loglinear models using the Newton-Raphson method. Either a Poisson or a multinomial distribution can be analyzed.

You can select up to 10 factors to define the cells of a table. A cell structure variable allows you to define structural zeros for incomplete tables, include an offset term in the model, fit a log-rate model, or implement the method of adjustment of marginal tables. Contrast variables allow computation of generalized log-odds ratios (GLOR).

SPSS automatically displays model information and goodness-of-fit statistics. You can also display a variety of statistics and plots or save residuals and predicted values in the working data file.

Example. Data from a report of automobile accidents in Florida are used to determine the relationship between wearing a seat belt and whether an injury was fatal or nonfatal. The odds ratio indicates significant evidence of a relationship.

Statistics. Observed and expected frequencies; raw, adjusted, and deviance residuals; design matrix; parameter estimates; odds ratio; log-odds ratio; GLOR; Wald statistic; and confidence intervals. Plots: adjusted residuals, deviance residuals, and normal probability.

Data. Factors are categorical, and cell covariates are continuous. When a covariate is in the model, SPSS applies the mean covariate value for cases in a cell to that cell.

Contrast variables are continuous. They are used to compute generalized log-odds ratios. The values of the contrast variable are the coefficients for the linear combination of the logs of the expected cell counts.

A cell structure variable assigns weights. For example, if some of the cells are structural zeros, the cell structure variable has a value of either 0 or 1. Do not use a cell structure variable to weight aggregated data. Instead, choose Weight Cases from the Data menu.

Assumptions. Two distributions are available in General Loglinear Analysis: Poisson and multinomial.

Under the Poisson distribution assumption:

- The total sample size is not fixed before the study, or the analysis is not conditional on the total sample size.
- The event of an observation being in a cell is statistically independent of the cell counts of other cells.

Under the multinomial distribution assumption:

- The total sample size is fixed, or the analysis is conditional on the total sample size.
- The cell counts are not statistically independent.

Related procedures. Use the Crosstabs procedure to examine the crosstabulations. Use the Logit Loglinear procedure when it is natural to regard one or more categorical variables as the response variables and the others as the explanatory variables.

To Obtain a General Loglinear Analysis

▶ From the menus choose:

Analyze
  Loglinear
    General...

Figure 5-1
General Loglinear Analysis dialog box

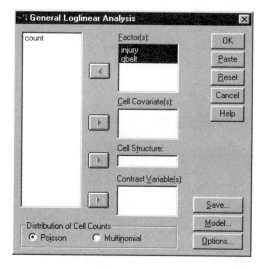

▶ In the General Loglinear Analysis dialog box, select up to 10 factor variables.

Optionally, you can:

■ Select cell covariates.

■ Select a cell structure variable to define structural zeros or include an offset term.

■ Select a contrast variable.

General Loglinear Analysis Model

Figure 5-2
General Loglinear Analysis Model dialog box

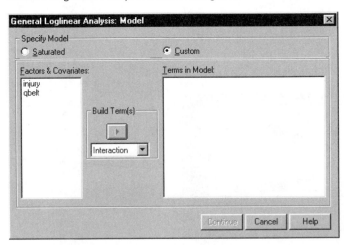

Specify Model. A saturated model contains all main effects and interactions involving factor variables. It does not contain covariate terms. Select Custom to specify only a subset of interactions or to specify factor-by-covariate interactions.

Factors and Covariates. The factors and covariates are listed, with (Cov) indicating a covariate.

Terms in Model. The model depends on the nature of your data. After selecting Custom, you can select the main effects and interactions that are of interest in your analysis. You must indicate all of the terms to be included in the model.

Build Terms

For the selected factors and covariates:

Interaction. Creates the highest-level interaction term of all selected variables. This is the default.

Main effects. Creates a main-effects term for each variable selected.

All 2-way. Creates all possible two-way interactions of the selected variables.

All 3-way. Creates all possible three-way interactions of the selected variables.

All 4-way. Creates all possible four-way interactions of the selected variables.

All 5-way. Creates all possible five-way interactions of the selected variables.

General Loglinear Analysis Options

Figure 5-3
General Loglinear Analysis Options dialog box

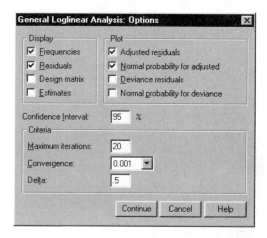

The General Loglinear Analysis procedure displays model information and goodness-of-fit statistics. In addition, you can choose one or more of the following:

Display. Several statistics are available for display—observed and expected cell frequencies; raw, adjusted, and deviance residuals; a design matrix of the model; and parameter estimates for the model.

Plot. Plots, available for custom models only, include two scatterplot matrices (adjusted residuals or deviance residuals against observed and expected cell counts). You can also display normal probability and detrended normal plots of adjusted residuals or deviance residuals.

Confidence Interval. The confidence interval for parameter estimates can be adjusted.

Criteria. The Newton-Raphson method is used to obtain maximum likelihood parameter estimates. You can enter new values for the maximum number of iterations, the convergence criterion, and delta (a constant added to all cells for initial approximations). Delta remains in the cells for saturated models.

To Specify Options

▶ From the menus choose:

Analyze
  Loglinear
    General...

▶ In the General Loglinear Analysis or Logit Loglinear Analysis dialog box, click Options.

General Loglinear Analysis Save

Figure 5-4
General Loglinear Analysis Save dialog box

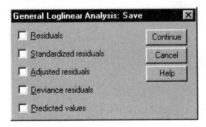

Select the values you want to save as new variables in the working data file. The suffix *n* in the new variable names increments to make a unique name for each saved variable.

The saved values refer to the aggregated data (cells in the contingency table), even if the data are recorded in individual observations in the Data Editor. If you save residuals or predicted values for unaggregated data, the saved value for a cell in the contingency table is entered in the Data Editor for each case in that cell. To make sense of the saved values, you should aggregate the data to obtain the cell counts.

Four types of residuals can be saved: raw, standardized, adjusted, and deviance. The predicted values can also be saved.

GENLOG Command Additional Features

The SPSS command language also allows you to:

- Calculate linear combinations of observed cell frequencies and expected cell frequencies, and print residuals, standardized residuals, and adjusted residuals of that combination (using the GERESID subcommand).

- Change the default threshold value for redundancy checking (using the CRITERIA subcommand).

- Display the standardized residuals (using the PRINT subcommand).

See the *SPSS Syntax Reference Guide* for complete syntax information.

Logit Loglinear Analysis

The Logit Loglinear Analysis procedure analyzes the relationship between dependent (or response) variables and independent (or explanatory) variables. The dependent variables are always categorical, while the independent variables can be categorical (factors). Other independent variables, cell covariates, can be continuous, but they are not applied on a case-by-case basis. The weighted covariate mean for a cell is applied to that cell. The logarithm of the odds of the dependent variables is expressed as a linear combination of parameters. A multinomial distribution is automatically assumed; these models are sometimes called multinomial logit models. This procedure estimates parameters of logit loglinear models using the Newton-Raphson algorithm.

You can select from 1 to 10 dependent and factor variables combined. A cell structure variable allows you to define structural zeros for incomplete tables, include an offset term in the model, fit a log-rate model, or implement the method of adjustment of marginal tables. Contrast variables allow computation of generalized log-odds ratios (GLOR). The values of the contrast variable are the coefficients for the linear combination of the logs of the expected cell counts.

SPSS automatically displays model information and goodness-of-fit statistics. You can also display a variety of statistics and plots or save residuals and predicted values in the working data file.

Example. A study in Florida included 219 alligators. How does the alligators' food type vary with their size and the four lakes in which they live? The study found that the odds of a smaller alligator preferring reptiles to fish is 0.70 times lower than for larger alligators; also, the odds of selecting primarily reptiles instead of fish were highest in lake 3.

Statistics. Observed and expected frequencies; raw, adjusted, and deviance residuals; design matrix; parameter estimates; generalized log odds ratio; Wald statistic; and confidence intervals. Plots: adjusted residuals, deviance residuals, and normal probability plots.

Data. The dependent variables are categorical. Factors are categorical. Cell covariates can be continuous, but when a covariate is in the model, SPSS applies the mean covariate value for cases in a cell to that cell. Contrast variables are continuous. They are used to compute generalized log odds ratios (GLOR). The values of the contrast variable are the coefficients for the linear combination of the logs of the expected cell counts.

A cell structure variable assigns weights. For example, if some of the cells are structural zeros, the cell structure variable has a value of either 0 or 1. Do not use a cell structure variable to weight aggregate data. Instead, use Weight Cases on the Data menu.

Assumptions. The counts within each combination of categories of explanatory variables are assumed to have a multinomial distribution. Under the multinomial distribution assumption:

- The total sample size is fixed, or the analysis is conditional on the total sample size.

- The cell counts are not statistically independent.

Related procedures. Use the Crosstabs procedure to display the contingency tables. Use the General Loglinear Analysis procedure when you want to analyze the relationship between an observed count and a set of explanatory variables.

To Obtain a Logit Loglinear Analysis

▶ From the menus choose:

Analyze
  Loglinear
    Logit...

Figure 6-1
Logit Loglinear Analysis dialog box

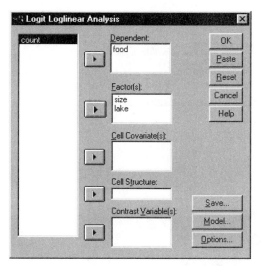

▶ In the Logit Loglinear Analysis dialog box, select one or more dependent variables.

▶ Select one or more factor variables.

The total number of dependent and factor variables must be less than or equal to 10.

Optionally, you can:

- Select cell covariates.

- Select a cell structure variable to define structural zeros or include an offset term.

- Select one or more contrast variables.

Logit Loglinear Analysis Model

Figure 6-2
Logit Loglinear Analysis Model dialog box

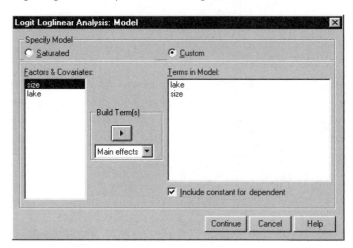

Specify Model. A saturated model contains all main effects and interactions involving factor variables. It does not contain covariate terms. Select Custom to specify only a subset of interactions or to specify factor-by-covariate interactions.

Factors and Covariates. The factors and covariates are listed, with (Cov) indicating a covariate.

Terms in Model. The model depends on the nature of your data. After selecting Custom, you can select the main effects and interactions that are of interest in your analysis. You must indicate all of the terms to be included in the model.

Terms are added to the design by taking all possible combinations of the dependent terms and matching each combination with each term in the model list. If Include constant for dependent is selected, there is also a unit term (1) added to the model list.

For example, suppose variables *D1* and *D2* are the dependent variables. A dependent terms list is created by the Logit Loglinear Analysis procedure (*D1*, *D2*, *D1*D2*). If the Terms in Model list contains *M1* and *M2* and a constant is included, the model list contains 1, *M1*, and *M2*. The resultant design includes combinations of each model term with each dependent term:

D1, D2, D1*D2
M1*D1, M1*D2, M1*D1*D2
M2*D1, M2*D2, M2*D1*D2.

Include constant for dependent. Includes a constant for the dependent variable in a custom model.

Build Terms

For the selected factors and covariates:

Interaction. Creates the highest-level interaction term of all selected variables. This is the default.

Main effects. Creates a main-effects term for each variable selected.

All 2-way. Creates all possible two-way interactions of the selected variables.

All 3-way. Creates all possible three-way interactions of the selected variables.

All 4-way. Creates all possible four-way interactions of the selected variables.

All 5-way. Creates all possible five-way interactions of the selected variables.

Logit Loglinear Analysis Options

Figure 6-3
Logit Loglinear Analysis Options dialog box

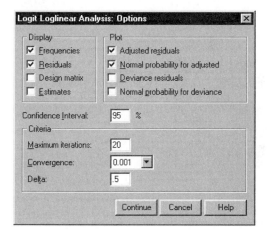

The Logit Loglinear Analysis procedure displays model information and goodness-of-fit statistics. In addition, you can choose one or more of the following options:

Display. Several statistics are available for display: observed and expected cell frequencies; raw, adjusted, and deviance residuals; a design matrix of the model; and parameter estimates for the model.

Plot. Plots available for custom models include two scatterplot matrices (adjusted residuals or deviance residuals against observed and expected cell counts). You can also display normal probability and detrended normal plots of adjusted residuals or deviance residuals.

Confidence Interval. The confidence interval for parameter estimates can be adjusted.

Criteria. The Newton-Raphson method is used to obtain maximum likelihood parameter estimates. You can enter new values for the maximum number of iterations, the convergence criterion, and delta (a constant added to all cells for initial approximations). Delta remains in the cells for saturated models.

To Specify Options

▶ From the menus choose:

Analyze
  Loglinear
    Logit...

▶ In the Logit Loglinear Analysis dialog box, click Options.

Logit Loglinear Analysis Save

Figure 6-4
Logit Loglinear Analysis Save dialog box

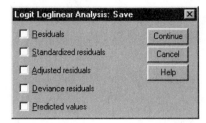

Select the values you want to save as new variables in the working data file. The suffix *n* in the new variable names increments to make a unique name for each saved variable.

The saved values refer to the aggregated data (to cells in the contingency table), even if the data are recorded in individual observations in the Data Editor. If you save residuals or predicted values for unaggregated data, the saved value for a cell in the contingency table is entered in the Data Editor for each case in that cell. To make sense of the saved values, you should aggregate the data to obtain the cell counts.

Four types of residuals can be saved: raw, standardized, adjusted, and deviance. The predicted values can also be saved.

GENLOG Command Additional Features

The SPSS command language also allows you to:

■ Calculate linear combinations of observed cell frequencies and expected cell frequencies, and print residuals, standardized residuals, and adjusted residuals of that combination (using the GERESID subcommand).

■ Change the default threshold value for redundancy checking (using the CRITERIA subcommand).

■ Display the standardized residuals (using the PRINT subcommand).

See the *SPSS Syntax Reference Guide* for complete syntax information.

Ordinal Regression

Ordinal Regression allows you to model the dependence of a polytomous ordinal response on a set of predictors, which can be factors or covariates. The design of Ordinal Regression is based on the methodology of McCullagh (1980, 1998), and the procedure is referred to as PLUM in the syntax.

Standard linear regression analysis involves minimizing the sum of squared differences between a response (dependent) variable and a weighted combination of predictor (independent) variables. The estimated coefficients reflect how changes in the predictors affect the response. The response is assumed to be numerical, in the sense that changes in the level of the response are equivalent throughout the range of the response. For example, the difference in height between a person who is 150cm tall and a person who is 140cm tall is 10cm, which has the same meaning as the difference in height between a person who is 210cm tall and a person who is 200cm tall. These relationships do not necessarily hold for ordinal variables, in which the choice and number of response categories can be quite arbitrary.

Example. Ordinal Regression could be used to study patient reaction to drug dosage. The possible reactions may be classified as "none," "mild," "moderate," or "severe." The difference between a mild and moderate reaction is difficult or impossible to quantify and is based on perception. Moreover, the difference between a mild and moderate response may be greater or less than the difference between a moderate and severe response.

Statistics and plots. Observed and expected frequencies and cumulative frequencies, Pearson residuals for frequencies and cumulative frequencies, observed and expected probabilities, observed and expected cumulative probabilities of each response category by covariate pattern, asymptotic correlation and covariance matrices of parameter estimates, Pearson's chi-square and likelihood ratio chi-square, goodness-of-fit statistics, iteration history, test of parallel lines assumption, parameter estimates, standard errors, confidence intervals, and Cox and Snell's, Nagelkerke's, and McFadden's R^2 statistics.

Data. The dependent variable is assumed to be ordinal and can be numeric or string. The ordering is determined by sorting the values of the dependent variable in ascending order. The lowest value defines the first category. Factor variables are assumed to be categorical. Covariate variables must be numeric. Note that using more than one continuous covariate can easily result in the creation of a very large cell probabilities table.

Assumptions. Only one response variable is allowed, and it must be specified. Also, for each distinct pattern of values across the independent variables, the responses are assumed to be independent multinomial variables.

Related procedures. Nominal logistic regression uses similar models for nominal dependent variables.

To Obtain an Ordinal Regression

▶ From the menus choose:

Analyze
  Regression
    Ordinal...

Figure 7-1
Ordinal Regression dialog box

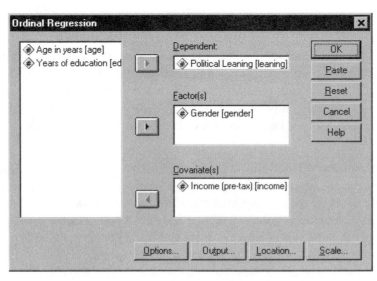

▶ Select one dependent variable.

▶ Click OK.

Ordinal Regression Options

The Options dialog box allows you to adjust parameters used in the iterative estimation algorithm, choose a level of confidence for your parameter estimates, and select a link function.

Figure 7-2
Ordinal Regression Options dialog box

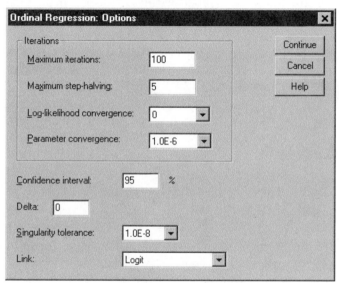

Iterations. You can customize the iterative algorithm.

■ **Maximum iterations.** Specify a non-negative integer. If 0 is specified, the procedure returns the initial estimates.

■ **Maximum step-halving.** Specify a positive integer.

■ **Log-likelihood convergence.** The algorithm stops if the absolute or relative change in the log-likelihood is less than this value. The criterion is not used if 0 is specified.

■ **Parameter convergence.** The algorithm stops if the absolute or relative change in each of the parameter estimates is less than this value. The criterion is not used if 0 is specified.

Confidence Interval. Specify a value greater than or equal to 0 and less than 100.

Delta. The value added to zero cell frequencies. Specify a non-negative value less than 1.

Singularity tolerance. Used for checking for highly dependent predictors. Select a value from the list of options.

Link. Choose between the Cauchit, complementary log-log, logit, negative log-log, and probit functions.

Ordinal Regression Output

The Output dialog box allows you to produce tables for display in the Viewer and save variables to the working file.

Figure 7-3
Ordinal Regression Output dialog box.

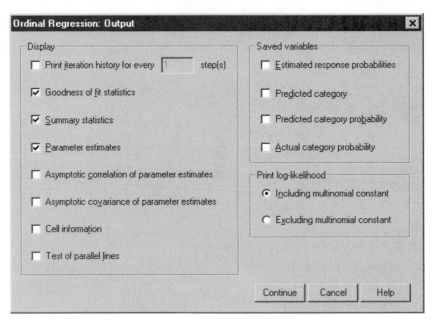

Display. Produces tables for:

- **Iteration history.** The log-likelihood and parameter estimates are printed for the print iteration frequency specified. The first and last iterations are always printed.

- **Goodness-of-fit statistics.** The Pearson and Likelihood ratio chi-square statistics. They are computed based on the classification specified on the variable list.

- **Summary statistics.** Cox and Snell's, Nagelkerke's, and McFadden's R^2 statistics.

- **Parameter estimates.** Parameter estimates, standard errors, and confidence intervals.

- **Asymptotic correlation of parameter estimates.** Matrix of parameter estimate correlations.

- **Asymptotic covariance of parameter estimates.** Matrix of parameter estimate covariances.

- **Cell information.** Observed and expected frequencies and cumulative frequencies, Pearson residuals for frequencies and cumulative frequencies, observed and expected probabilities, and observed and expected cumulative probabilities of each response category by covariate pattern. Note that for models with many covariate patterns (for example, models with continuous covariates), this option can generate a very large, unwieldy table.

- **Test of parallel lines.** Test of the hypothesis that the location parameters are equivalent across the levels of the dependent variable. This is available only for the location-only model.

Saved variables. Saves the following variables to the working file:

- **Estimated response probabilities.** Model-estimated probabilities of classifying a factor/covariate pattern into the response categories. There are as many probabilities as the number of response categories.

- **Predicted category.** The response category that has the maximum estimated probability for a factor/covariate pattern.

- **Predicted category probability.** Estimated probability of classifying a factor/covariate pattern into the predicted category. This probability is also the maximum of the estimated probabilities of the factor/covariate pattern.

- **Actual category probability.** Estimated probability of classifying a factor/covariate pattern into the actual category.

Print log-likelihood. This controls the display of the log-likelihood. Including the multinomial constant gives you the full value of the likelihood. To compare your results across products that do not include the constant, you may choose to exclude it.

Ordinal Regression Location Model

The Location dialog box allows you to specify the location model for your analysis.

Figure 7-4
Ordinal Regression Location dialog box.

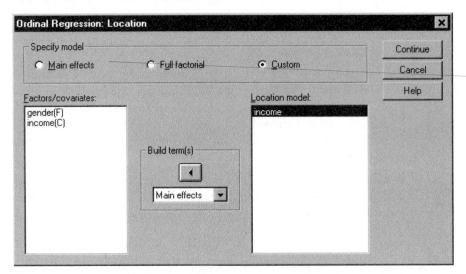

Specify model. A main-effects model contains the covariate and factor main effects but no interaction effects. A full factorial model contains all main effects and all factor-by-factor interactions. It does not contain covariate interactions. You can create a custom model to specify subsets of factor interactions or covariate interactions.

Factors/covariates. The factors and covariates are listed with (F) for factor and (C) for covariate.

Location model. The model depends on the main and interaction effects you select.

Build Terms

For the selected factors and covariates:

Interaction. Creates the highest-level interaction term of all selected variables.

Main effects. Creates a main-effects term for each variable selected.

All 2-way. Creates all possible two-way interactions of the selected variables.

All 3-way. Creates all possible three-way interactions of the selected variables.

All 4-way. Creates all possible four-way interactions of the selected variables.

All 5-way. Creates all possible five-way interactions of the selected variables.

Ordinal Regression Scale Model

The Scale dialog box allows you to specify the scale model for your analysis.

Figure 7-5
Ordinal Regression Scale dialog box.

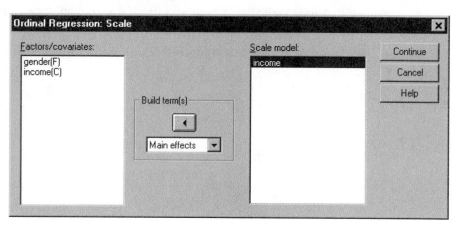

Factors/covariates. The factors and covariates are listed with (F) for factor and (C) for covariate.

Scale model. The model depends on the main effects and interaction effects you select.

Build Terms

For the selected factors and covariates:

Interaction. Creates the highest-level interaction term of all selected variables.

Main effects. Creates a main-effects term for each variable selected.

All 2-way. Creates all possible two-way interactions of the selected variables.

All 3-way. Creates all possible three-way interactions of the selected variables.

All 4-way. Creates all possible four-way interactions of the selected variables.

All 5-way. Creates all possible five-way interactions of the selected variables.

Ordinal Regression Command Additional Features

You can customize your Ordinal Regression if you paste your selections into a syntax window and edit the resulting PLUM command syntax. The SPSS command language also allows you to:

■ Create customized hypothesis tests by specifying null hypotheses as linear combinations of parameters.

See the *SPSS Syntax Reference Guide* for complete syntax information.

Life Tables

There are many situations in which you would want to examine the distribution of times between two events, such as length of employment (time between being hired and leaving the company). However, this kind of data usually includes some cases for which the second event isn't recorded (for example, people still working for the company at the end of the study). This can happen for several reasons: for some cases, the event simply doesn't occur before the end of the study; for other cases, we lose track of their status sometime before the end of the study; still other cases may be unable to continue for reasons unrelated to the study (such as an employee becoming ill and taking a leave of absence). Collectively, such cases are known as **censored cases**, and they make this kind of study inappropriate for traditional techniques such as *t* tests or linear regression.

A statistical technique useful for this type of data is called a follow-up **life table**. The basic idea of the life table is to subdivide the period of observation into smaller time intervals. For each interval, all people who have been observed at least that long are used to calculate the probability of a terminal event occurring in that interval. The probabilities estimated from each of the intervals are then used to estimate the overall probability of the event occurring at different time points.

Example. Is a new nicotine patch therapy better than traditional patch therapy in helping people to quit smoking? You could conduct a study using two groups of smokers, one of which received the traditional therapy and the other of which received the experimental therapy. Constructing life tables from the data would allow you to compare overall abstinence rates between the two groups to determine if the experimental treatment is an improvement over the traditional therapy. You can also plot the survival or hazard functions and compare them visually for more detailed information.

Statistics. Number entering, number leaving, number exposed to risk, number of terminal events, proportion terminating, proportion surviving, cumulative proportion surviving (and standard error), probability density (and standard error), and hazard rate (and standard error) for each time interval for each group; median survival time for each group; and Wilcoxon (Gehan) test for comparing survival distributions between groups. Plots: function plots for survival, log survival, density, hazard rate, and one minus survival.

Data. Your time variable should be quantitative. Your status variable should be dichotomous or categorical, coded as integers, with events being coded as a single value or a range of consecutive values. Factor variables should be categorical, coded as integers.

Assumptions. Probabilities for the event of interest should depend only on time after the initial event—they are assumed to be stable with respect to absolute time. That is, cases that enter the study at different times (for example, patients who begin treatment at different times) should behave similarly. There should also be no systematic differences between censored and uncensored cases. If, for example, many of the censored cases are patients with more serious conditions, your results may be biased.

Related procedures. The Life Tables procedure uses an actuarial approach to this kind of analysis (known generally as Survival Analysis). The Kaplan-Meier Survival Analysis procedure uses a slightly different method of calculating life tables that does not rely on partitioning the observation period into smaller time intervals. This method is recommended if you have a small number of observations, such that there would be only a small number of observations in each survival time interval. If you have variables that you suspect are related to survival time or variables that you want to control for (covariates), use the Cox Regression procedure. If your covariates can have different values at different points in time for the same case, use Cox Regression with Time-Dependent Covariates.

To Create a Life Table

▶ From the menus choose:

Analyze
  Survival
    Life Tables...

Figure 8-1
Life Tables dialog box

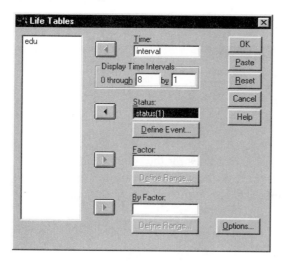

▶ Select one numeric survival variable.

▶ Specify the time intervals to be examined.

▶ Select a status variable to define cases for which the terminal event has occurred.

▶ Click Define Event to specify the value of the status variable that indicates that an event occurred.

Optionally, you can select a first-order factor variable. Actuarial tables for the survival variable are generated for each category of the factor variable.

You can also select a second-order *by factor* variable. Actuarial tables for the survival variable are generated for every combination of the first- and second-order factor variables.

Life Tables Define Event for Status Variable

Figure 8-2
Life Tables Define Event for Status Variable dialog box

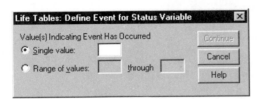

Occurrences of the selected value or values for the status variable indicate that the terminal event has occurred for those cases. All other cases are considered to be censored. Enter either a single value or a range of values that identifies the event of interest.

Life Tables Define Range

Figure 8-3
Life Tables Define Range dialog box

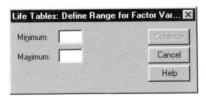

Cases with values for the factor variable in the range you specify will be included in the analysis, and separate tables (and plots, if requested) will be generated for each unique value in the range.

Life Tables Options

Figure 8-4
Life Tables Options dialog box

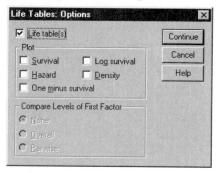

You can control various aspects of your Life Tables analysis.

Life tables. To suppress the display of life tables in the output, deselect Life tables.

Plot. Allows you to request plots of the survival functions. If you have defined factor variable(s), plots are generated for each subgroup defined by the factor variable(s). Available plots are survival, log survival, hazard, density, and one minus survival.

Compare Levels of First Factor. If you have a first-order control variable, you can select one of the alternatives in this group to perform the Wilcoxon (Gehan) test, which compares the survival of subgroups. Tests are performed on the first-order factor. If you have defined a second-order factor, tests are performed for each level of the second-order variable.

SURVIVAL Command Additional Features

The SPSS command language also allows you to:

- Specify more than one dependent variable.
- Specify unequally spaced intervals.
- Specify more than one status variable.
- Specify comparisons that do not include all the factor and all the control variables.
- Calculate approximate, rather than exact, comparisons.

See the *SPSS Syntax Reference Guide* for complete syntax information.

Kaplan-Meier Survival Analysis

There are many situations in which you would want to examine the distribution of times between two events, such as length of employment (time between being hired and leaving the company). However, this kind of data usually includes some censored cases. Censored cases are cases for which the second event isn't recorded (for example, people still working for the company at the end of the study). The Kaplan-Meier procedure is a method of estimating time-to-event models in the presence of censored cases. The Kaplan-Meier model is based on estimating conditional probabilities at each time point when an event occurs and taking the product limit of those probabilities to estimate the survival rate at each point in time.

Example. Does a new treatment for AIDS have any therapeutic benefit in extending life? You could conduct a study using two groups of AIDS patients, one receiving traditional therapy and the other receiving the experimental treatment. Constructing a Kaplan-Meier model from the data would allow you to compare overall survival rates between the two groups to determine whether the experimental treatment is an improvement over the traditional therapy. You can also plot the survival or hazard functions and compare them visually for more detailed information.

Statistics. Survival table, including time, status, cumulative survival and standard error, cumulative events, and number remaining; and mean and median survival time, with standard error and 95% confidence interval. Plots: survival, hazard, log survival, and one minus survival.

Data. The time variable should be continuous, the status variable can be categorical or continuous, and the factor and strata variables should be categorical.

Assumptions. Probabilities for the event of interest should depend only on time after the initial event—they are assumed to be stable with respect to absolute time. That is, cases that enter the study at different times (for example, patients who begin treatment at different times) should behave similarly. There should also be no systematic differences between censored and uncensored cases. If, for example, many of the censored cases are patients with more serious conditions, your results may be biased.

Related procedures. The Kaplan-Meier procedure uses a method of calculating life tables that estimates the survival or hazard function at the time of each event. The Life Tables procedure uses an actuarial approach to survival analysis that relies on partitioning the observation period into smaller time intervals and may be useful for dealing with large samples. If you have variables that you suspect are related to survival time or variables that you want to control for (covariates), use the Cox Regression procedure. If your covariates can have different values at different points in time for the same case, use Cox Regression with Time-Dependent Covariates.

To Obtain a Kaplan-Meier Survival Analysis

▶ From the menus choose:

Analyze
  Survival
    Kaplan-Meier...

Figure 9-1
Kaplan-Meier dialog box

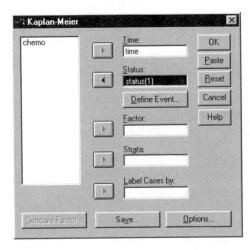

▶ Select a time variable.

▶ Select a status variable to identify cases for which the terminal event has occurred. This variable can be numeric or short string. Then click Define Event.

Optionally, you can select a factor variable to examine group differences. You can also select a strata variable, which will produce separate analyses for each level (stratum) of the variable.

Kaplan-Meier Define Event for Status Variable

Figure 9-2
Kaplan-Meier Define Event for Status Variable dialog box

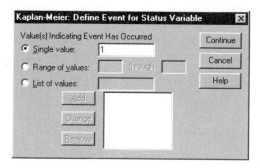

Enter the value or values indicating that the terminal event has occurred. You can enter a single value, a range of values, or a list of values. The Range of Values option is available only if your status variable is numeric.

Kaplan-Meier Compare Factor Levels

Figure 9-3
Kaplan-Meier Compare Factor Levels dialog box

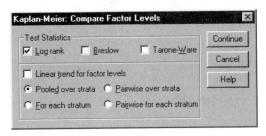

You can request statistics to test the equality of the survival distributions for the different levels of the factor. Available statistics are log rank, Breslow, and Tarone-Ware. Select one of the alternatives to specify the comparisons to be made: pooled over strata, for each stratum, pairwise over strata, or pairwise for each stratum.

Linear trend for factor levels. Allows you to test for a linear trend across levels of the factor. This option is available only for overall (rather than pairwise) comparisons of factor levels.

Kaplan-Meier Save New Variables

Figure 9-4
Kaplan-Meier Save New Variables dialog box

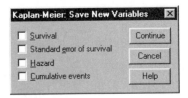

You can save information from your Kaplan-Meier table as new variables, which can then be used in subsequent analyses to test hypotheses or check assumptions. You can save survival, standard error of survival, hazard, and cumulative events as new variables.

Kaplan-Meier Options

Figure 9-5
Kaplan-Meier Options dialog box

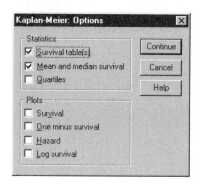

You can request various output types from Kaplan-Meier analysis.

Statistics. You can select statistics displayed for the survival functions computed, including survival table(s), mean and median survival, and quartiles. If you have included factor variables, separate statistics are generated for each group.

Plots. Plots allow you to examine the survival, hazard, log-survival, and one-minus-survival functions visually. If you have included factor variables, functions are plotted for each group.

KM Command Additional Features

The SPSS command language also allows you to:

- Obtain frequency tables that consider cases lost to follow-up as a separate category from censored cases.

- Specify unequal spacing for the test for linear trend.

- Obtain percentiles other than quartiles for the survival time variable.

See the *SPSS Syntax Reference Guide* for complete syntax information.

Cox Regression Analysis

Like Life Tables and Kaplan-Meier survival analysis, Cox Regression is a method for modeling time-to-event data in the presence of censored cases. However, Cox Regression allows you to include predictor variables (covariates) in your models. For example, you could construct a model of length of employment based on educational level and job category. Cox Regression will handle the censored cases correctly, and it will provide estimated coefficients for each of the covariates, allowing you to assess the impact of multiple covariates in the same model. You can also use Cox Regression to examine the effect of continuous covariates.

Example. Do men and women have different risks of developing lung cancer based on cigarette smoking? By constructing a Cox Regression model, with cigarette usage (cigarettes smoked per day) and gender entered as covariates, you can test hypotheses regarding the effects of gender and cigarette usage on time-to-onset for lung cancer.

Statistics. For each model: $-2LL$, the likelihood-ratio statistic, and the overall chi-square. For variables in the model: parameter estimates, standard errors, and Wald statistics. For variables not in the model: score statistics and residual chi-square.

Data. Your time variable should be quantitative and your status variable can be categorical or continuous. Independent variables (covariates) can be continuous or categorical; if categorical, they should be dummy or indicator coded (there is an option in the procedure to recode categorical variables automatically). Strata variables should be categorical, coded as integers or short strings.

Assumptions. Observations should be independent, and the hazard ratio should be constant across time; that is, the proportionality of hazards from one case to another should not vary over time. The latter assumption is known as the **proportional hazards assumption**.

Related procedures. If the proportional hazards assumption does not hold (see above), you may need to use the Cox with Time-Dependent Covariates procedure. If you have no covariates, or if you have only one categorical covariate, you can use the Life Tables or Kaplan-Meier procedure to examine survival or hazard functions for your sample(s). If you have no censored data in your sample (that is, every case experienced the terminal event), you can use the Linear Regression procedure to model the relationship between predictors and time-to-event.

To Obtain a Cox Regression Analysis

▶ From the menus choose:

Analyze
  Survival
    Cox Regression...

Figure 10-1
Cox Regression dialog box

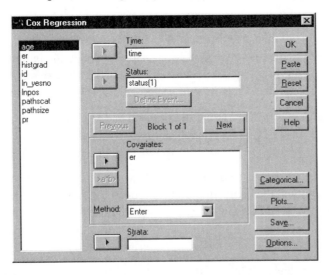

▶ Select a time variable.

▶ Select a status variable, and then click Define Event.

▶ Select variables to use as covariates.

Optionally, you can compute separate models for different groups by defining a strata variable.

Cox Regression Define Categorical Variables

Figure 10-2
Cox Regression Define Categorical Covariates dialog box

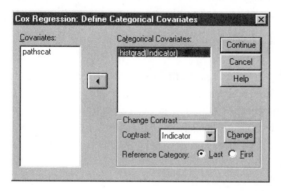

You can specify details of how the Cox Regression procedure will handle categorical variables.

Covariates. Contains a list of all of the covariates specified in the main dialog box, either by themselves or as part of an interaction, in any layer. If some of these are string variables or are categorical, you can use them only as categorical covariates.

Categorical Covariates. Lists variables identified as categorical. Each variable includes a notation in parentheses indicating the contrast coding to be used. String variables (denoted by the symbol < following their names) are already present in the Categorical Covariates list. Select any other categorical covariates from the Covariates list and move them into the Categorical Covariates list.

Change Contrast. Allows you to change the contrast method. Available contrast methods are:

■ **Indicator.** Contrasts indicate the presence or absence of category membership. The reference category is represented in the contrast matrix as a row of zeros.

■ **Simple.** Each category of the predictor variable except the reference category is compared to the reference category.

- **Difference.** Each category of the predictor variable except the first category is compared to the average effect of previous categories. Also known as reverse Helmert contrasts.

- **Helmert.** Each category of the predictor variable except the last category is compared to the average effect of subsequent categories.

- **Repeated.** Each category of the predictor variable except the first category is compared to the category that precedes it.

- **Polynomial.** Orthogonal polynomial contrasts. Categories are assumed to be equally spaced. Polynomial contrasts are available for numeric variables only.

- **Deviation.** Each category of the predictor variable except the reference category is compared to the overall effect.

If you select Deviation, Simple, or Indicator, select either First or Last as the reference category. Note that the method is not actually changed until you click Change.

String covariates *must* be categorical covariates. To remove a string variable from the Categorical Covariates list, you must remove all terms containing the variable from the Covariates list in the main dialog box.

Cox Regression Plots

Figure 10-3
Cox Regression Plots dialog box

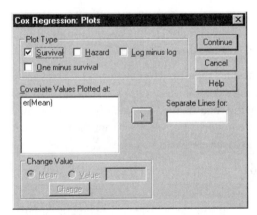

Plots can help you to evaluate your estimated model and interpret the results. You can plot the survival, hazard, log-minus-log, and one-minus-survival functions.

Because these functions depend on values of the covariates, you must use constant values for the covariates to plot the functions versus time. The default is to use the mean of each covariate as a constant value, but you can enter your own values for the plot using the Change Value control group.

You can plot a separate line for each value of a categorical covariate by moving that covariate into the Separate Lines For text box. This option is available only for categorical covariates, which are denoted by (Cat) after their names in the Covariate Values Plotted At list.

Cox Regression Save New Variables

Figure 10-4
Cox Regression Save New Variables dialog box

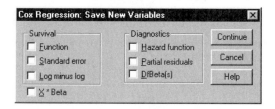

You can save various results of your analysis as new variables. These variables can then be used in subsequent analyses to test hypotheses or to check assumptions.

Survival. Allows you to save the survival function, standard error, and log-minus-log estimates as new variables.

Diagnostics. Allows you to save the hazard function, partial residuals, and DfBeta(s) for the regression as new variables.

If you are running Cox with a time-dependent covariate, DfBeta(s) are the only variables that you can save. You can also save the linear predictor variable X*Beta.

Cox Regression Options

Figure 10-5
Cox Regression Options dialog box

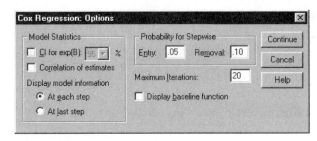

You can control various aspects of your analysis and output.

Model Statistics. You can obtain statistics for your model parameters, including confidence intervals for exp(*B*) and correlation of estimates. You can request these statistics either at each step or at the last step only.

Probability for Stepwise. If you have selected a stepwise method, you can specify the probability for either entry or removal from the model. A variable is entered if the significance level of its *F*-to-enter is less than the Entry value, and a variable is removed if the significance level is greater than the Removal value. The Entry value must be less than the Removal value.

Maximum Iterations. Allows you to specify the maximum iterations for the model, which controls how long the procedure will search for a solution.

Display baseline function. Allows you to display the baseline hazard function and cumulative survival at the mean of the covariates. This display is not available if you have specified time-dependent covariates.

Cox Regression Define Event for Status Variable

Enter the value or values indicating that the terminal event has occurred. You can enter a single value, a range of values, or a list of values. The Range of Values option is available only if your status variable is numeric.

COXREG Command Additional Features

The SPSS command language also allows you to:

- Obtain frequency tables that consider cases lost to follow-up as a separate category from censored cases.

- Select a reference category, other than first or last, for the deviation, simple, and indicator contrast methods.

- Specify unequal spacing of categories for the polynomial contrast method.

- Specify additional iteration criteria.

- Control the treatment of missing values.

- Specify the names for saved variables.

- Write output to an external SPSS system file.

- Hold data for each split-file group in an external scratch file during processing. This can help conserve memory resources when running analyses with large data sets. This is not available with time-dependent covariates.

See the *SPSS Syntax Reference Guide* for complete syntax information.

11

Computing Time-Dependent Covariates

There are certain situations in which you would want to compute a Cox Regression model but the proportional hazards assumption does not hold. That is, hazard ratios change across time; the values of one (or more) of your covariates are different at different time points. In such cases, you need to use an extended Cox Regression model, which allows you to specify **time-dependent covariates**.

In order to analyze such a model, you must first define your time-dependent covariate. (Multiple time-dependent covariates can be specified using command syntax.) To facilitate this, a system variable representing time is available. This variable is called T_-. You can use this variable to define time-dependent covariates in two general ways:

- If you want to test the proportional hazards assumption with respect to a particular covariate or estimate an extended Cox regression model that allows nonproportional hazards, you can do so by defining your time-dependent covariate as a function of the time variable T_- and the covariate in question. A common example would be the simple product of the time variable and the covariate, but more complex functions can be specified as well. Testing the significance of the coefficient of the time-dependent covariate will tell you whether the proportional hazards assumption is reasonable.

- Some variables may have different values at different time periods but aren't systematically related to time. In such cases, you need to define a **segmented time-dependent covariate**, which can be done using **logical expressions**. Logical expressions take the value 1 if true and 0 if false. Using a series of logical expressions, you can create your time-dependent covariate from a set of measurements. For example, if you have blood pressure measured once a week for the four weeks of your study (identified as *BP1* to *BP4*), you can define your time-dependent covariate as

$$(T\_ < 1) * BP1 + (T\_ \geq 1 \ \& \ T\_ < 2) * BP2 + (T\_ \geq 2 \ \& \ T\_ < 3) * BP3 + (T\_ \geq 3 \ \& \ T\_ < 4) * BP4$$

Notice that exactly one of the terms in parentheses will be equal to 1 for any given case and the rest will all equal 0. In other words, this function means that if time is less than one week, use *BP1*; if it is more than one week but less than two weeks, use *BP2*, and so on.

For segmented time-dependent covariates, cases that are missing any values are removed from the analysis. Therefore, you must be sure that all cases have values for all measured time points on the covariate, even for time points after the case is removed from the risk set (due to event or censoring). These values are not used in the analysis, but they must be valid SPSS values to prevent the cases from being dropped. For example, with the definition given above, a case censored at the second week must still have values for *BP3* and *BP4* (they can be 0 or any other number, since they are not used in the analysis).

In the Compute Time-Dependent Covariate dialog box, you can use the function-building controls to build the expression for the time-dependent covariate, or you can enter it directly in the Expression for T_COV_ text area. Note that string constants must be enclosed in quotation marks or apostrophes, and numeric constants must be typed in American format, with the dot as the decimal delimiter. The resulting variable is called *T_COV_* and should be included as a covariate in your Cox Regression model.

To Compute a Time-Dependent Covariate

▶ From the menus choose:

Analyze
  Survival
    Cox w/ Time-Dep Cov...

Figure 11-1

Compute Time-Dependent Covariate dialog box

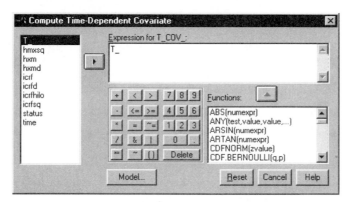

▶ Enter an expression for the time-dependent covariate.

▶ Click Model to proceed with your Cox Regression.

Note: Be sure to include the new variable *T_COV_* as a covariate in your Cox Regression model.

For more information about the model-building process, see Chapter 10.

Cox Regression with Time-Dependent Covariates Additional Features

The SPSS command language also allows you to specify multiple time-dependent covariates.

Other command syntax features are available for Cox Regression with or without time-dependent covariates.

See the *SPSS Syntax Reference Guide* for complete syntax information.

GLM Multivariate Examples

Multivariate analysis of variance considers the effects of factors on several dependent variables at once, using a general linear model. The factors divide the cases (or subjects) into groups. The hypotheses tested are similar to those in univariate analysis, except that in multivariate analysis, a vector of means replaces the individual means.

In addition to the output in univariate analysis, multivariate F tests are available. You can also display the hypothesis and error sums-of-squares and cross-product (SSCP) matrices for each effect in the design, the transformation coefficient table (**M** matrix), Box's M test for equality of covariance matrices, and Bartlett's test of sphericity.

This chapter includes the following examples:

Example 1: Multivariate ANOVA: Multivariate two-way fixed-effects model with interaction. The effects of two measurements, the amount of an additive and the rate of extrusion of plastic film, are studied simultaneously on three properties of the manufactured plastic film. The SSCP (sums-of-squares and cross-products) matrices are displayed for the main effects and the interaction effect. These values are used by SPSS to calculate the F values for hypothesis testing on the three dependent variables. The conclusion is that the main effects of amount of additive and rate of extrusion are significant, but their interaction is not.

Example 2: Profile analysis: Setting up custom linear hypotheses. In a survey, 30 couples were given questions designed to rate companionate and passionate love on a five-point scale. A plot of the mean answers of husbands and wives is used to set up hypotheses that will investigate the differences between groups. The **L** and **M** matrices are used together in the model to define contrasts, where **LBM = 0**. The conclusion is that the parallelism and the coincidence of the profiles of husbands and wives is not rejected. However, the equality of means of the four answers is rejected.

Example 1
Multivariate ANOVA: Multivariate Two-Way Fixed-Effects Model with Interaction

How can the optimum conditions for extruding plastic film be evaluated by using a statistical technique called evolutionary operation? A study was conducted to examine how the amount of an additive and the rate of extrusion affected the conditions for extruding plastic film. The data are from Johnson and Wichern (1988). The amount of additive and rate of extrusion are two fixed factors that may interact so that the model is a two-way fixed-effects model with interaction. Three properties of the extruded film were measured: tear resistance, gloss, and opacity. These are the three dependent variables in this multivariate model. Evolutionary operation, the statistical method for process improvement used here, was described by Box and Draper (1969).

Figure 12-1

Effects of rate of extrusion and amount of additive on plastic film

Independent Factors		Dependent Variables		
Change in rate of extrusion	Amount of additive	Tear resistance	Gloss	Opacity
1	1	6.5	9.5	4.4
1	1	6.2	9.9	6.4
1	1	5.8	9.6	3.0
1	1	6.5	9.6	4.1
1	1	6.5	9.2	0.8
1	2	6.9	9.1	5.7
1	2	7.2	10.0	2.0
1	2	6.9	9.9	3.9
1	2	6.1	9.5	1.9
1	2	6.3	9.4	5.7
2	1	6.7	9.1	2.8
2	1	6.6	9.3	4.1
2	1	7.2	8.3	3.8
2	1	7.1	8.4	1.6
2	1	6.8	8.5	3.4
2	2	7.1	9.2	8.4
2	2	7.0	8.8	5.2
2	2	7.2	9.7	6.9
2	2	7.5	10.1	2.7
2	2	7.6	9.2	1.9

The data are recorded in the SPSS file *plastic*, in the order shown in Figure 12-1. There are two independent factors in the model: the change in rate of extrusion (*extrusn*) and the amount of additive (*additive*). The *extrusn* factor has two levels: low and high (indicated by 1 and 2, respectively, in the data). The *additive* factor has two levels: 1.0% and 1.5% (indicated by 1 and 2, respectively, in the data). In addition to these two main factors, their interaction *extrusn*additive* is included in the model. Since three dependent variables are studied at the same time, multivariate analysis of variance is used.

SSCP Matrices

In univariate fixed-effects analysis of variance, the total sum of squares of the model is partitioned into sums of squares due to the effects in the model and the error sum of squares. Each effect in the model is then evaluated by using an *F* statistic, which is the ratio of the sum of squares due to the effect and the error sum of squares. In a multivariate model, there is more than one dependent variable; hence, the sums of squares due to the effects in the model and the error sums of squares are no longer scalars. Instead, they are replaced by square matrices. For each of these square matrices, the dimension is equal to the number of dependent variables. In univariate analysis, there is only one dependent variable, and the matrix reduces to a scalar, which is the same as the sum of squares of the corresponding effect.

In a multivariate model, these square matrices are called the sums-of-squares and cross-products (**SSCP**) matrices. Analogous to the univariate test of an effect, the "ratio" of the SSCP matrix due to the effect being tested (**H**) and the SSCP matrix of the appropriate error (**E**) is used to evaluate the effect of interest. Since **H** and **E** are matrices, this "ratio" in a multivariate model is evaluated by the determinant of $\mathbf{HE}^{-1}$, where $\mathbf{E}^{-1}$ is the inverse of **E**. The **H** matrix, which is the SSCP matrix of the effect being tested, is called the hypothesis SSCP matrix, and the **E** matrix, which is the SSCP matrix of the appropriate error, is called the error SSCP matrix. In a fixed-effects multivariate analysis of variance, the hypothesis SSCP matrix for testing any effect in the model is its own SSCP matrix due to that effect, and the error SSCP matrix for all tests in the model is always the SSCP matrix due to error in the model.

Running the Tests

To produce the output shown in this example, from the menus choose:

Analyze
  General Linear Model
    Multivariate...

▶ Dependent variables: tear_res, gloss, opacity
▶ Fixed Factor(s): extrusn, additive

Options...
  ☑ Hypothesis and error SSCP matrices

 Activate the multivariate tests table and drag the Effect icon from the row tray to the layer tray. Click the arrows on the Effect icon to cycle through the layers.

The hypothesis SSCP matrices for testing the effects in the model are shown in Figure 12-2. These are the matrices that are used in calculating the *F* values.

Figure 12-2
Between-subjects SSCP matrix

			TEAR_RES	GLOSS	OPACITY
Hypothesis	Intercept	TEAR_RES	920.724	1264.05	533.979
		GLOSS	1264.045	1735.38	733.090
		OPACITY	533.979	733.090	309.684
	EXTRUSN	TEAR_RES	1.740	-1.505	.855
		GLOSS	-1.505	1.301	-.740
		OPACITY	.855	-.740	.421
	ADDITIVE	TEAR_RES	.760	.682	1.930
		GLOSS	.682	.612	1.732
		OPACITY	1.930	1.732	4.900
	EXTRUSN*ADDITIVE	TEAR_RES	.000	.016	.044
		GLOSS	.016	.544	1.468
		OPACITY	.044	1.468	3.960
Error		TEAR_RES	1.764	.020	-3.070
		GLOSS	.020	2.628	-.552
		OPACITY	-3.070	-.552	64.924

Based on Type III Sum of Squares

The results of the multivariate analysis of variance are shown in Figure 12-3. Each effect is shown as a layer.

Figure 12-3
Multivariate tests

Effect: Intercept

	Value	F	Hypothesis df	Error df	Sig.	Noncent. Parameter	Observed Power[1]
Pillai's Trace	.999	5950.906^2	3.000	14.000	.000	17852.717	1.000
Wilks' Lambda	.001	5950.906^2	3.000	14.000	.000	17852.717	1.000
Hotelling's Trace	1275.194	5950.906^2	3.000	14.000	.000	17852.717	1.000
Roy's Largest Root	1275.194	5950.906^2	3.000	14.000	.000	17852.717	1.000

[1]. Computed using alpha = .05
[2]. Exact statistic

Effect: EXTRUSN

	Value	F	Hypothesis df	Error df	Sig.	Noncent. Parameter	Observed Power[1]
Pillai's Trace	.618	7.554^2	3.000	14.000	.003	22.663	.948
Wilks' Lambda	.382	7.554^2	3.000	14.000	.003	22.663	.948
Hotelling's Trace	1.619	7.554^2	3.000	14.000	.003	22.663	.948
Roy's Largest Root	1.619	7.554^2	3.000	14.000	.003	22.663	.948

[1]. Computed using alpha = .05
[2]. Exact statistic

Effect: ADDITIVE

	Value	F	Hypothesis df	Error df	Sig.	Noncent. Parameter	Observed Power[1]
Pillai's Trace	.477	4.256^2	3.000	14.000	.025	12.767	.744
Wilks' Lambda	.523	4.256^2	3.000	14.000	.025	12.767	.744
Hotelling's Trace	.912	4.256^2	3.000	14.000	.025	12.767	.744
Roy's Largest Root	.912	4.256^2	3.000	14.000	.025	12.767	.744

[1]. Computed using alpha = .05
[2]. Exact statistic

Multivariate tests (Continued)

Effect: EXTRUSN * ADDITIVE

	Value	F	Hypothesis df	Error df	Sig.	Noncent. Parameter	Observed Power[1]
Pillai's Trace	.223	1.339[2]	3.000	14.000	.302	4.016	.280
Wilks' Lambda	.777	1.339[2]	3.000	14.000	.302	4.016	.280
Hotelling's Trace	.287	1.339[2]	3.000	14.000	.302	4.016	.280
Roy's Largest Root	.287	1.339[2]	3.000	14.000	.302	4.016	.280

[1]. Computed using alpha = .05

[2]. Exact statistic

Above the upper left corner in each of these layer tables is the effect in the model being tested, and the first column lists the names of the test statistics. Four commonly used test statistics for multivariate analysis are displayed in the output: Pillai's trace, Wilks' lambda, Hotelling's trace, and Roy's largest root. The next column displays the value of the test statistics, followed by the F statistic, which is a transformed value of the corresponding test statistic and has an approximate F distribution. The hypothesis and error degrees of freedom of the F distribution are shown. The noncentrality parameter estimate of the F distribution and observed power of detecting an effect of observed magnitude are displayed in the last two columns.

Of the four test statistics, Wilks' lambda has the virtue of being convenient and related to the likelihood-ratio criterion. However, for some practical situations (see Olsen, 1976), Pillai's trace may be the most robust and powerful criterion among the others. Choice of these multivariate statistics may depend on the situation. Their F statistics may sometimes, although not necessarily, be the same. Whenever the F statistic has an exact F distribution, a footnote is displayed as a reminder.

In the test of the interaction effect *extrusn*additive*, the four F statistics are all the same, with a value of 1.339. Since the F value is not significant at the 0.05 alpha level, we conclude that there is no interaction effect. The F statistics for testing *extrusn* and *additive* are 7.554 and 4.256, respectively. Both are significant at $\alpha = 0.05$, indicating that changes in both the rate of extrusion and the amount of additive affect the three dependent variables.

Example 2
Profile Analysis: Setting Up Custom Linear Hypotheses

Do husbands and wives share the same point of view on love and marriage? An investigation was performed to study the points of view of married couples on love and marriage. A set of four questions was answered by a sample of 30 couples. The first two questions concerned the feeling of passionate love, while the second two questions were about the feeling of companionate love. All four questions were rated on a five-point scale, ranging from "None at all" to "A tremendous amount." The data are taken from Johnson and Wichern (1988).

Figure 12-4 shows a plot of the means of the answers to the four questions. The mean rating by husbands and the mean rating by wives for each question are plotted on separate lines.

Figure 12-4
Plot of husbands' and wives' profiles

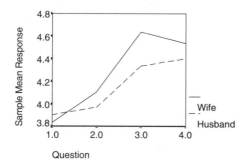

The plot suggests three queries:

■ Parallelism of profiles: Are the population mean profiles of husbands and wives parallel to each other?

■ Equality of husbands' and wives' profiles: Assuming parallelism, are the profiles of husbands and wives equal?

■ Equality of answer means: Assuming parallelism, are the answer means equal?

In order to satisfy parallelism of profiles, the two profile plots should be parallel to each other for each line segment between adjacent questions. This query can be viewed as testing the hypothesis of no response by group interaction. Testing the equality of the two profiles is equivalent to testing whether there is any difference between the husbands' and wives' answers. Testing the equality of answer means is equivalent to testing for any differences between husbands and wives in each of the four survey questions. In the next section, we will study each of the three queries related to the plot by specifying the **L** matrix and the **M** matrix, using a multivariate linear model.[*]

Setting Up Contrast Matrices

In the SPSS data file *love*, *Q1*, *Q2*, *Q3*, and *Q4* are variables that represent the answers to the four love and marriage questions, on a five-point scale. The variable *spouse* divides the cases into two groups, husbands and wives. You can form a multivariate linear model with *Q1*, *Q2*, *Q3*, and *Q4* as the dependent variables and *spouse* as the factor.

To answer the three queries listed in the previous section, you can use the LMATRIX and the MMATRIX syntax subcommands, which correspond to the **L** matrix and **M** matrix of the general multivariate linear hypothesis **LBM = 0**. The **B** matrix is the parameter matrix in which each column corresponds to the parameter vector for the linear model on each of the dependent variables. In this example, the four dependent variables correspond to the four columns of **B**. Since there is only one factor, *spouse*, in the model, and it has only two levels, *husband* and *wife*, each column of **B** has three parameters to be estimated: the overall intercept and the two parameters for each level of *spouse*. The **L** matrix sets up contrasts for the factor in the model, and the **M** matrix sets up contrasts for the dependent variables.

Testing Parallelism

To test for parallelism, you must set up both the **L** matrix and the **M** matrix. Since the first query asks whether the line segments between adjacent answers are parallel, the **M** matrix should be set for contrasts, which can compare adjacent answers. In other words, comparisons should be made of the mean of *Q1* against *Q2*, *Q2* against *Q3*, and *Q3* against *Q4*. The **M** matrix will be a 4×3 matrix of the following form:

$$\begin{bmatrix} 1 & 0 & 0 \\ -1 & 1 & 0 \\ 0 & -1 & 1 \\ 0 & 0 & -1 \end{bmatrix}$$

*This problem would normally be handled by using a repeated measures effect. However, the example here is used to illustrate the use of LMATRIX and MMATRIX subcommands.

Because the **M** matrix is used to test whether the line segments of the husband group and the wife group are parallel, the **L** matrix compares the husband group with the wife group. The **L** matrix will be a 1×3 matrix of the following form:

$$\begin{bmatrix} 0 & 1 & -1 \end{bmatrix}$$

where the first value, 0, corresponds to the overall intercept parameter in the linear model, and the pair 1 and -1 compares the husband group with the wife group.

To produce the output in this section, from the menus choose:

Analyze
  General Linear Model
    Multivariate...

▶ Dependent variables: q1, q2, q3, q4
▶ Fixed Factor(s): spouse
Model...
  ⊙ Custom
  ▶ Model: spouse

Paste

To the pasted syntax, add the LMATRIX and MMATRIX subcommands as shown:

```
GLM q1 q2 q3 q4 BY spouse
 /METHOD = SSTYPE(3)
 /INTERCEPT = INCLUDE
 /CRITERIA = ALPHA(.05)
 /DESIGN spouse
 /LMATRIX = spouse 1 -1
 /MMATRIX = q1 1 q2 -1;
           q2 1 q3 -1;
           q3 1 q4 -1.
```

To run the GLM command, click the Run Current tool. The syntax indicates that there are four dependent variables, *Q1, Q2, Q3,* and *Q4*, in the model, and one factor, *spouse*. The DESIGN subcommand indicates the model. The subcommands METHOD, INTERCEPT, and CRITERIA are default specifications (with which we are not concerned here).

    The **L** matrix is specified by using the LMATRIX subcommand, followed by the factor name *spouse* and the contrast for the factor. The **M** matrix is specified by the MMATRIX subcommand, followed by an equals sign, the name of one dependent variable, its coefficient, the name of the dependent variable being compared with the first, and its coefficient. Each of the three comparisons is listed in a similar manner. If a dependent variable and its coefficient are not specified, the coefficient of that dependent variable is assumed to be 0. A semicolon (;) is used to indicate the end of one column in the **M** matrix.

Parallelism Test Results

The results of the custom hypothesis test of parallelism are shown in Figure 12-5.

Figure 12-5
Multivariate test results

	Value	F	Hypothesis df	Error df	Sig.	Noncent. Parameter	Observed Power[1]
Pillai's trace	.121	2.580[2]	3.000	56.000	.063	7.740	.604
Wilks' lambda	.879	2.580[2]	3.000	56.000	.063	7.740	.604
Hotelling's trace	.138	2.580[2]	3.000	56.000	.063	7.740	.604
Roy's largest root	.138	2.580[2]	3.000	56.000	.063	7.740	.604

1. Computed using alpha = .05
2. Exact statistic

With $p = 0.063$, the test is not significant at $\alpha = 0.05$. Parallelism of the mean profiles of husbands and wives will be assumed.

Testing for Equality of Profiles

To test the equality of husbands' and wives' profiles, the means of the four answers for the husband group and the wife group are compared. In this case, the **M** matrix corresponds to the average of the four answers, and the **L** matrix corresponds to the contrast used to compare husbands and wives.

To produce the output in this section, recall the GLM Multivariate dialog box and paste, or from the menus choose:

Analyze
  General Linear Model
    Multivariate...

▶ Dependent variables: q1, q2, q3, q4
▶ Fixed Factor(s): spouse
Model...
    ⊙ Custom
    ▶ Model: spouse

Paste

To the pasted syntax, add the LMATRIX and MMATRIX subcommands as shown:

```
GLM q1 q2 q3 q4 BY spouse
 /METHOD = SSTYPE(3)
 /INTERCEPT = INCLUDE
 /CRITERIA = ALPHA(.05)
 /DESIGN spouse
 /LMATRIX = spouse 1 -1
 /MMATRIX = q1 .25 q2 .25 q3 .25 q4 .25.
```

To run the GLM command, click the **Run Current** tool. The results are shown in Figure 12-6.

Figure 12-6
Univariate test results

Source	Transformed Variable	Type III Sum of Squares	df	Mean Square	F	Sig.	Noncentrality Parameter	Observed Power
Contrast	T1	.234	1	.234	1.533	.221	1.533	.230
Error	T1	8.869	58	.153				

Since the **M** matrix has only one column, the univariate result is used. The p value for the test is 0.221, which is not significant at $\alpha = 0.05$. This means that equality of the husbands' and wives' profiles can be assumed. That is, the answers from the husbands and the wives to the four questions can be assumed to be the same.

Testing for Equality of Answer Means

To test the equality of answer means, the means of the husbands' group and wives' group for the four answers are compared with each other. In this case, the **M** matrix is the one used in testing parallelism, while the **L** matrix corresponds to taking the average of each group. It is [1 0.5 0.5]. The value 1 corresponds to the intercept, and the two values of 0.5 correspond to the husbands' group and the wives' group, respectively.

To produce the output in this section, recall the GLM Multivariate dialog box and paste, or from the menus choose:

Analyze
  General Linear Model
    Multivariate...

▶ Dependent variables: q1, q2, q3, q4
▶ Fixed Factor(s): spouse
Model...
    ⊙ Custom
    ▶ Model: spouse

Paste

To the pasted syntax, add the LMATRIX and MMATRIX subcommands as shown:

```
GLM Q1 Q2 Q3 Q4 BY spouse
 /DESIGN spouse
 /METHOD = SSTYPE(3)
 /INTERCEPT = INCLUDE
 /CRITERIA = ALPHA(.05)
 /LMATRIX = INTERCEPT 1 spouse .5 .5
 /MMATRIX = Q1 1 Q2 -1;
            Q2 1 Q3 -1;
            Q3 1 Q4 -1.
```

The contrast coefficients are specified in the **L** matrix, and the transformation coefficients are specified in the **M** matrix. The results are displayed in Figure 12-7.

Figure 12-7
Multivariate test results

	Value	F	Hypothesis df	Error df	Sig.	Noncent. Parameter	Observed Power[1]
Pillai's trace	.305	8.188[2]	3.000	56.000	.000	24.564	.988
Wilks' lambda	.695	8.188[2]	3.000	56.000	.000	24.564	.988
Hotelling's trace	.439	8.188[2]	3.000	56.000	.000	24.564	.988
Roy's largest root	.439	8.188[2]	3.000	56.000	.000	24.564	.988

[1]. Computed using alpha = .05
[2]. Exact statistic

For each test, $p < 0.0005$, which is significant. It means that the equality of answers cannot be assumed.

Figure 12-8
Univariate test results for each individual contrast on the dependent variables

Source	Transformed Variable	Type III Sum of Squares	df	Mean Square	F	Sig.	Noncentrality Parameter	Observed Power
Contrast	T1	1.667	1	1.667	2.433	.124	2.433	.335
	T2	12.150	1	12.150	13.973	.000	13.973	.957
	T3	1.667E-02	1	1.7E-02	.212	.647	.212	.074
Error	T1	39.733	58	.685				
	T2	50.433	58	.870				
	T3	4.567	58	7.9E-02				

Figure 12-8 displays the univariate results for this custom hypothesis on each difference of adjacent answers. The three columns in the **M** matrix each correspond to one contrast (or transformation) on the dependent variables. The right side of the first column in Figure 12-8 displays the name of the transformed variable. The first transformed variable, *T1*, corresponds to the first column of the **M** matrix, which compares *q1* with *q2*. The second transformed variable, *T2,* corresponds to the second column of the **M** matrix, which compares *q2* with *q3*. The last transformed variable,

T3, corresponds to the last column of the **M** matrix, which compares *q3* with *q4*. The three contrast results, taken as a set, imply that the first two population means are the same, but differ from the last two, which do not differ from each other.

GLM Repeated Measures Examples

Repeated measures analysis applies to situations where the same measurement is made multiple times on each subject or case. A within-subjects factor that encompasses each set of repeated measurements is defined. Between-subjects factors that divide the cases into groups can be specified as well as covariates.

This chapter includes the following examples:

Example 1: Repeated measures analysis of variance. Twelve students were each tested four times on a learning task. They were also rated for high anxiety or low anxiety. The data are arranged with four trial variables so that the four scores are recorded in one case for each student. A within-subjects factor, *trial,* is defined, and the *anxiety* factor is specified as a between-subjects factor because it divides the group of subjects into two groups. The *anxiety* factor is shown to be not significant, while the *trial* effect is significant. In checking assumptions, Box's *M* and Mauchly's test of sphericity are used.

Example 2: Doubly multivariate repeated measures analysis of variance. A new drug is tested against a placebo in its effects on respiration and pulse. Half of the patients receive the new drug, and half receive the placebo. The variable *drug* divides the subjects into the new-drug group and the placebo group and is used as a between-subjects factor. Both effects, respiration and pulse, are measured together at three different times, making six variables in the data file. The newly defined within-subjects variable is called *time*, with three levels for the three times.

Example 1
Repeated Measures Analysis of Variance

Does the anxiety of a person affect performance on a learning task? Twelve subjects were assigned to one of two anxiety groups on the basis of an anxiety test, and the number of errors made in four blocks of trials on a learning task was measured. In this example, we use a repeated measures analysis-of-variance technique to study the data.

In the data file *anxiety2*, there is one case for each subject (*subject*). Four trial variables (*trial1*, *trial2*, *trial3*, and *trial4*) contain the scores for all of the subjects (see Figure 13-1).

Figure 13-1
Data arrangement

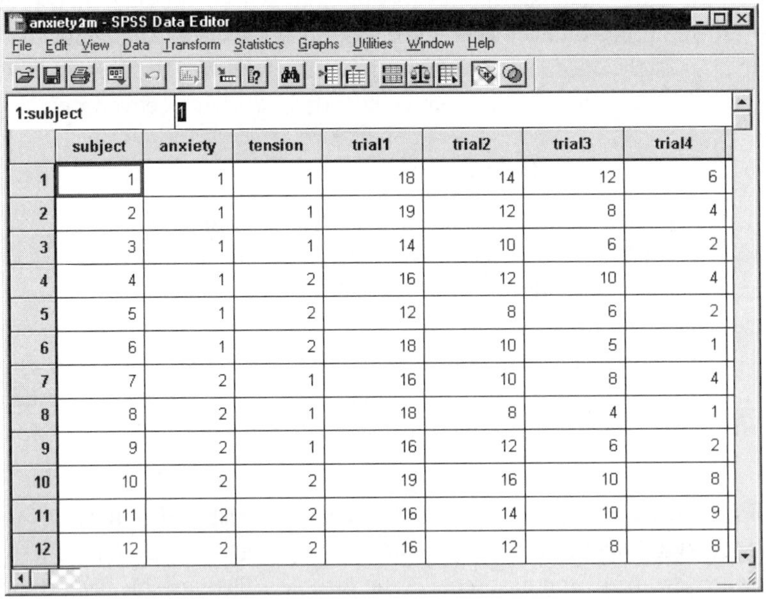

	subject	anxiety	tension	trial1	trial2	trial3	trial4
1	1	1	1	18	14	12	6
2	2	1	1	19	12	8	4
3	3	1	1	14	10	6	2
4	4	1	2	16	12	10	4
5	5	1	2	12	8	6	2
6	6	1	2	18	10	5	1
7	7	2	1	16	10	8	4
8	8	2	1	18	8	4	1
9	9	2	1	16	12	6	2
10	10	2	2	19	16	10	8
11	11	2	2	16	14	10	9
12	12	2	2	16	12	8	8

To use the repeated measures analysis-of-variance technique, we distinguish two types of factors in the model: between-subjects factors and within-subjects factors. A **between-subjects factor** is any factor that divides the sample of subjects or cases into discrete subgroups. For example, the factor *anxiety* is a between-subjects factor because it divides the 12 subjects into two groups: one with high anxiety measurement scores and one with low anxiety measurement scores. A **within-subjects factor** is any factor that distinguishes measurements made on the same subject or case rather than distinguishing different subjects or cases. For example, the factor *trial* is a within-subjects factor in this analysis because it distinguishes the four measurements of error taken for each of the subjects.

A repeated measures analysis consists of the analysis of a within-subjects model, which describes the model for the within-subjects factors, plus the analysis of a between-subjects model, which describes the model for the between-subject factors. For example, in the current repeated measures analysis, the within-subjects part of the model consists of the within-subjects factor *trial* and the interaction, and the between-subjects part of the model consists of the between-subjects factor *anxiety*.

In the data file *anxiety2*, the variables *trial1*, *trial2*, *trial3,* and *trial4* contain the number of errors made at each of the four trials by each subject.

To produce the output in this example, from the menus choose:

Analyze
  General Linear Model
    Repeated Measures...

Within-Subject Factor Name: trial
Number of Levels: 4

Click Add and click Define.

▶ Within-Subjects Variables (trial): trial1, trial2, trial3, trial4
▶ Between-Subjects Factor(s): anxiety

Options...
    ☑ Homogeneity tests

 Activate the tests of within-subjects effects table and drag the Epsilon Corrections icon from the row tray to the layer tray.

In the above choices, for the within-subjects factor, a new name, *trial*, is typed, which designates the measurements made on the same subject. The number of levels is the number of measurements made on each subject (4). Each of the four within-subjects variables, *trial1*, *trial2*, *trial3,* and *trial4,* corresponds to one measurement for each subject.

Between-Subjects Tests

For repeated measures analysis, the results for testing the effects in the model from a multivariate approach and a univariate approach are both provided. For testing the between-subjects effects in the model, both approaches yield the same results. This test is constructed by summing all of the within-subjects variables in the model and dividing by the square root of the number of within-subjects variables. Then an analysis of variance is performed on the result. In this example, since there is only one between-subjects factor, *anxiety*, the test for the between-subjects effects is performed by a one-way analysis of variance using

$$\frac{\text{trial}_1 + \text{trial}_2 + \text{trial}_3 + \text{trial}_4}{\sqrt{4}}$$

as the dependent variable. The results from testing the between-subjects effect, *anxiety*, are shown in Figure 13-2. The significance $p = 0.460$ indicates that this effect is not significant at $\alpha = 0.05$.

Figure 13-2

Test of between-subjects effects

Measure: MEASURE_1

Transformed Variable: Average

Source	Type III Sum of Squares	df	Mean Square	F	Sig.	Eta Squared	Noncent. Parameter	Observed Power[1]
Intercept	4800.000	1	4800.000	280.839	.000	.966	280.839	1.000
ANXIETY	10.083	1	10.083	.590	.460	.056	.590	.107
Error	170.917	10	17.092					

1. Computed using alpha = .05

Multivariate Tests

The multivariate table contains tests of the within-subjects factor, *trial*, and the interaction of the within-subjects factor and the between-subjects factor, *trial*anxiety*. The results are shown in Figure 13-3.

Figure 13-3
Multivariate tests

Effect		Value	F	Hypothesis df	Error df	Sig.	Noncent. Parameter	Observed Power[1]
TRIAL	Pillai's Trace	.961	64.854[2]	3.000	8.000	.000	194.561	1.000
	Wilks' Lambda	.039	64.854[2]	3.000	8.000	.000	194.561	1.000
	Hotelling's Trace	24.320	64.854[2]	3.000	8.000	.000	194.561	1.000
	Roy's Largest Root	24.320	64.854[2]	3.000	8.000	.000	194.561	1.000
TRIAL * ANXIETY	Pillai's Trace	.479	2.451[2]	3.000	8.000	.138	7.354	.408
	Wilks' Lambda	.521	2.451[2]	3.000	8.000	.138	7.354	.408
	Hotelling's Trace	.919	2.451[2]	3.000	8.000	.138	7.354	.408
	Roy's Largest Root	.919	2.451[2]	3.000	8.000	.138	7.354	.408

1. Computed using alpha = .05
2. Exact statistic

Four test statistics—Pillai's trace, Wilks' lambda, Hotelling's trace and Roy's largest root—are provided. In this example, the F statistics for all four tests are the same. The p value for testing the *trial* effect is less than 0.001, which is significant at $\alpha = 0.05$, while the p value for testing the *trial*anxiety* effect is 0.138, which is not significant at $\alpha = 0.05$.

Checking Assumptions

The assumption for the multivariate approach is that the vector of the dependent variables follows a multivariate normal distribution, and the variance-covariance matrices are equal across the cells formed by the between-subject effects. Box's M test for this assumption is shown in Figure 13-4. The significance is 0.315, indicating that the null hypothesis (that the observed variance-covariance matrices are equal across the two levels of the *anxiety* effect) is not rejected.

Figure 13-4
Test for equality of covariance matrices

Box's Test of Equality of Covariance Matrices [a]

Box's M	21.146
F	1.161
df1	10
df2	478
Sig.	.315

Tests the null hypothesis that the observed
covariance matrices of the dependent variables
are equal across groups.

a. Design: Intercept+ANXIETY
   Within Subjects Design: TRIAL

Testing for Sphericity

To use the univariate results for testing the within-subjects factor, *trial,* and the interaction of the within-subjects factor and the between-subjects factor, *trial*anxiety,* some assumptions about the variance-covariance matrices of the dependent variables should be checked. The validity of the F statistic used in the univariate approach can be assured when the variance-covariance matrix of the dependent variables is *circular* in form (Huynh and Mandeville, 1979). Mauchly (1940) derived a test that verifies this variance-covariance matrix structure by performing a test of sphericity on the orthonormalized transformed dependent variable. This test, which is automatically performed when a repeated measures analysis is used, is shown in Figure 13-5. The significance of this test is 0.053, which is slightly larger the 0.05 alpha level, indicating that the variance-covariance matrix assumption is just barely satisfied.

Figure 13-5
Mauchly's test of sphericity

Mauchly's Test of Sphericity[1]

Measure: MEASURE_1

Within Subjects Effect	Mauchly's W	Approx. Chi-Square	df	Sig.	Epsilon[2]		
					Greenhouse-Geisser	Huynh-Feldt	Lower-bound
TRIAL	.283	11.011	5	.053	.544	.701	.333

Tests the null hypothesis that the error covariance matrix of the orthonormalized transformed dependent variables is proportional to an identity matrix.

[1]. Design: Intercept+ANXIETY
   Within Subjects Design: TRIAL

[2]. May be used to adjust the degrees of freedom for the averaged tests of significance. Corrected tests are displayed in the layers (by default) of the Tests of Within Subjects Effects table.

What if the significance indicated rejection? If the above sphericity test were to be rejected, sphericity could not be assumed. Then an adjustment value, called epsilon, would be needed for multiplying the numerator and denominator degrees of freedom in the F test. The significance of the F test would then be evaluated with the new degrees of freedom. The last three columns in Figure 13-5 display three possible values of epsilon, based on three different criteria: Greenhouse-Geisser, Huynh-Feldt, and lower-bound. The Greenhouse-Geisser epsilon is conservative, especially for a small sample size. The Huynh-Feldt epsilon is an alternative that is not as conservative as the Greenhouse-Geisser epsilon; however, it may be a value greater than 1. When its calculated value is greater than 1, the Huynh-Feldt epsilon is displayed as 1.000, and this value is used in calculating the new degrees of freedom and significance. The lower-bound epsilon takes the reciprocal of the degrees of freedom for the within-subjects factor. This represents the most conservative approach possible, since it indicates the most extreme possible departure from sphericity. SPSS displays results for each of the values of epsilon.

Testing Hypotheses

The univariate tests for the within-subjects factor, *trial,* and the interaction term, *trial*anxiety,* are shown in Figure 13-6, with all layers displayed.

Figure 13-6
Tests of within-subjects effects

Source	Measure		Type III Sum of Squares	df	Mean Square	F	Sig.	Eta Squared	Noncent. Parameter	Observed Power[1]
TRIAL	MEASURE_1	Sphericity Assumed	991.500	3	330.500	128.627	.000	.928	385.881	1.000
		Greenhouse-Geisser	991.500	1.632	607.468	128.627	.000	.928	209.943	1.000
		Huynh-Feldt	991.500	2.102	471.773	128.627	.000	.928	270.329	1.000
		Lower-bound	991.500	1.000	991.500	128.627	.000	.928	128.627	1.000
TRIAL * ANXIETY	MEASURE_1	Sphericity Assumed	8.417	3	2.806	1.092	.368	.098	3.276	.265
		Greenhouse-Geisser	8.417	1.632	5.157	1.092	.346	.098	1.782	.194
		Huynh-Feldt	8.417	2.102	4.005	1.092	.357	.098	2.295	.220
		Lower-bound	8.417	1.000	8.417	1.092	.321	.098	1.092	.157
Error(TRIAL)	MEASURE_1	Sphericity Assumed	77.083	30	2.569					
		Greenhouse-Geisser	77.083	16.322	4.723					
		Huynh-Feldt	77.083	21.016	3.668					
		Lower-bound	77.083	10.000	7.708					

[1.] Computed using alpha = .05

The significance for each test when sphericity is assumed, or when any of the three epsilons is used, is displayed. The third column indicates what type of epsilon is used in evaluating the significance of the test. For example, the row labeled *Sphericity Assumed* indicates that the assumption about the variance-covariance matrix is assumed and that the significance is evaluated using the original degrees of freedom. The row labeled *Greenhouse-Geisser* indicates that the Greenhouse-Geisser epsilon is used and that the significance in this row is evaluated using the Greenhouse-Geisser epsilon adjustment. In this example, because the variance-covariance matrix assumption is assumed to be satisfied (by the result of the Mauchly's test), the conclusion can be drawn based on the row labeled *Sphericity Assumed.* The *trial* effect is significant, with a p value of less than 0.001, and the *trial*anxiety* interaction effect is not significant, with a p value of 0.368. Notice that the same conclusion can be drawn using any three of the epsilons.

Contrasts

It is sometimes useful to introduce contrasts among the within-subjects variables in order to study the levels of the within-subjects factors. To specify contrasts for the within-subjects variables, recall the dialog box for Repeated Measures and choose:

Contrasts...
    Factors: trial
    Contrast: Repeated (Click Change)

This set of contrasts does not affect the results of the univariate and multivariate analyses. It is useful only for comparing the levels of the within-subjects factor. The tests of within-subjects contrasts are shown in Figure 13-7.

Figure 13-7
Within-subjects contrasts

Tests of Within Subjects Contrasts

Measure: MEASURE_1

Source	Transformed Variable	Type III Sum of Squares	df	Mean Square	F	Sig.	Noncentrality Parameter	Observed Power[1]
TRIAL	TRIAL_1	300.000	1	300.000	52.023	.000	52.023	1.000
	TRIAL_2	168.750	1	168.750	83.678	.000	83.678	1.000
	TRIAL_3	147.000	1	147.000	78.750	.000	78.750	1.000
TRIAL*ANXIETY	TRIAL_1	.333	1	.333	.058	.815	.058	.055
	TRIAL_2	4.083	1	4.083	2.025	.185	2.025	.252
	TRIAL_3	16.333	1	16.333	8.750	.014	8.750	.760
Error(TRIAL)	TRIAL_1	57.667	10	5.767				
	TRIAL_2	20.167	10	2.017				
	TRIAL_3	18.667	10	1.867				

1. Computed using alpha = .050

A repeated contrast compares one level of *trial* with the subsequent level. The first column indicates the effect being tested. For example, the label *TRIAL* tests the hypothesis that, averaged over the two anxiety groups, the mean of the specified contrast is 0.

The transformed variable names under the repeated contrast are in the second column. The first name, *TRIAL_1*, represents the contrast that compares the first level of *trial* with the second level of *trial*. Notice that the first dependent variable, *trial1*, corresponds to the observation of the first level of *trial* and that the second dependent variable, *trial2*, corresponds to the observation of the second level of *trial*, and so on. The first contrast, *TRIAL_1*, corresponds to the transformation $trial1 - trial2$.

Similarly, the second contrast, *TRIAL_2*, represents the transformation $trial2 - trial3$, which compares the second level of *trial* with the third level. The third contrast, *TRIAL_3,* represents the transformation $trial3 - trial4$, which compares the third level with the fourth level. In the above table, all three specified contrasts—*TRIAL_1*, *TRIAL_2,* and *TRIAL_3*—are significant at $\alpha = 0.01$.

The label *TRIAL*ANXIETY* tests the hypothesis that the mean of the specified contrast is the same for the two anxiety groups. Except for the last specified contrast, *TRIAL_3,* which may be significant at $\alpha = 0.05$, all others are not significant at $\alpha = 0.01$.

Example 2
Doubly Multivariate Repeated Measures Analysis of Variance

Can a new drug improve respiratory and pulse scores? A study was performed to determine whether a new drug has any effect on the respiratory score and pulse score of a patient. Twelve randomly selected patients having similar medical conditions were randomly divided into two groups. Patients in one group were treated with the new drug, and patients in another group were treated with a placebo. The respiratory score and the pulse were measured at three different times. The data, created for this example, are shown in Figure 13-8.

Figure 13-8
Respiratory and pulse measurements

Drug	Respiratory Score			Pulse		
	Time 1	Time 2	Time 3	Time 1	Time 2	Time 3
New Drug	3.4	3.3	3.3	77	77	73.5
New Drug	3.4	3.4	3.3	77	77	77
New Drug	3.3	3.4	3.4	80.5	80.5	80.5
New Drug	3.4	3.4	3.4	80.5	80.5	80.5
New Drug	3.3	3.4	3.3	77	77	84
New Drug	3.3	3.3	3.3	70	70	84
Placebo	3.3	3.3	3.3	98	98	94.5
Placebo	3.2	3.3	3.4	91	91	94.5
Placebo	3.2	3.2	3.2	94.5	94.5	94.5
Placebo	3.2	3.2	3.2	91	91	101.5
Placebo	3.2	3.3	3.3	94.5	94.5	101.5
Placebo	3.3	3.2	3.1	91	91	98

The data are stored in the file *new drug*, with one case for each subject. The respiratory scores are stored in three variables (*resp1, resp2,* and *resp3*), one for each time. The pulses are stored in three variables (*pulse1, pulse2,* and *pulse3*), again, one for each time. The variable *drug* has two values, 1 for the group that received the new drug and 2 for the group that received the placebo.

The type of drug divides the patients into two groups; therefore, it is a between-subjects factor. The three time points distinguish measurements taken on the same patient, making *time* a within-subjects factor. Notice that two measurements, respiratory score and pulse score, are taken for all patients at each factor combination—this is a doubly multivariate repeated measures design.

To produce the output shown in this example, from the menus choose:

Analyze
  General Linear Model
    Repeated Measures...

Within-Subject Factor Name: time
Number of Levels: 3 (Click Add)

Measure>>
  Measure Name: resp pulse (Click Add for each measure)

Click Define.

▶ Within-Subjects Variables (time): resp1, resp2, resp3, pulse1, pulse2, pulse3
▶ Between-Subjects Factor(s): drug

The within-subjects factor name is a new name that you specify to designate groups of measurements made on the same subject—in this example, *time* for the three times. The number of levels indicates the number of groups for the within-subjects factor. A measure name is a new name that you specify to designate the group of like scores measured at different times. In this example, the measure names indicate the respiratory score and the pulse. Notice the order of the within-subjects variables. All three respiratory score names appear first, and then the three pulse names, matching the order on Measure Name.

The multivariate results of the analysis are shown in Figure 13-9 and Figure 13-10. In this example, the *TIME* effect and the *TIME*DRUG* effect are not significant. However, the *DRUG* effect is significant at $p < 0.0005$, indicating that the new drug has an effect on the respiratory and pulse scores.

Figure 13-9
Multivariate tests

Multivariate Tests[1]

Effect			Value	F	Hypothesis df	Error df	Sig.	Noncent. Parameter	Observed Power[2]
Between Subjects	Intercept	Pillai's Trace	1.000	32480.4[3]	2.000	9.000	.000	64960.841	1.000
		Wilks' Lambda	.000	32480.4[3]	2.000	9.000	.000	64960.841	1.000
		Hotelling's Trace	7217.871	32480.4[3]	2.000	9.000	.000	64960.841	1.000
		Roy's Largest Root	7217.871	32480.4[3]	2.000	9.000	.000	64960.841	1.000
	DRUG	Pillai's Trace	.956	98.177[3]	2.000	9.000	.000	196.354	1.000
		Wilks' Lambda	.044	98.177[3]	2.000	9.000	.000	196.354	1.000
		Hotelling's Trace	21.817	98.177[3]	2.000	9.000	.000	196.354	1.000
		Roy's Largest Root	21.817	98.177[3]	2.000	9.000	.000	196.354	1.000
Within Subjects	TIME	Pillai's Trace	.612	2.761[3]	4.000	7.000	.114	11.044	.464
		Wilks' Lambda	.388	2.761[3]	4.000	7.000	.114	11.044	.464
		Hotelling's Trace	1.578	2.761[3]	4.000	7.000	.114	11.044	.464
		Roy's Largest Root	1.578	2.761[3]	4.000	7.000	.114	11.044	.464
	TIME * DRUG	Pillai's Trace	.496	1.722[3]	4.000	7.000	.249	6.887	.301
		Wilks' Lambda	.504	1.722[3]	4.000	7.000	.249	6.887	.301
		Hotelling's Trace	.984	1.722[3]	4.000	7.000	.249	6.887	.301
		Roy's Largest Root	.984	1.722[3]	4.000	7.000	.249	6.887	.301

[1]. Design: Intercept+DRUG
   Within Subjects Design: TIME

[2]. Computed using alpha = .05

[3]. Exact statistic

Figure 13-10

Between-subjects effects

Tests of Between-Subjects Effects

Transformed Variable: Average

Source	Measure	Type III Sum of Squares	df	Mean Square	F	Sig.	Noncent. Parameter	Observed Power[1]
Intercept	RESP	391.380	1	391.380	69750.941	.000	69750.941	1.000
	PULSE	224.001	1	224.001	14197.254	.000	14197.254	1.000
DRUG	RESP	.100	1	.100	17.871	.002	17.871	.967
	PULSE	2.454	1	2.454	155.563	.000	155.563	1.000
Error	RESP	5.611E-02	10	5.611E-03				
	PULSE	.158	10	1.578E-02				

1. Computed using alpha = .05

14

Variance Components Examples

What components contribute to variation in the absorption of calcium by turnip leaves? Can you estimate the size of the individual components? Is variance in testing of ovens due to their nonhomogeneity? These questions can be investigated by using the Variance Components procedure. In this chapter, you can find illustrations of four different methods as well as technical background information.

Factors, Effects, and Models

A key concept in the variance components model is the idea of fixed and random effects. Factors make up the effects, and then the effects are combined into a model.

Types of Factors

Since effects in the model are composed of factors, first consider the types of factors. When the levels of a factor are all of the possible values in the entire population or all of the levels of interest to the researchers, then it is a **fixed factor**. For example, imagine that researchers for a computer magazine conduct a study to compare the lifetimes of five types of laptop computer batteries: Nickel Cadmium (*NiCad*), Nickel Metal Hydride (*NiMH*), Lead Acid, and Lithium Ion (*LiIon*). The variable labeled *Type of battery* is treated as a fixed factor either when these five types are the only ones on the market or when the researchers are interested in making inferences about only these five types.

A factor is said to be **random** when the levels of the factor represent a random sample of all possible values from a population and inferences will be made on the entire population. Suppose, in the above example, that the study of battery types is conducted using batteries from five different manufacturers. It is not unreasonable to think of those manufacturers as a randomly chosen sample from a population of battery manufacturers. The lifetime of batteries from any one of these five manufacturers may have no particular interest in and of itself to the researchers. The five manufacturers are chosen with the objective of treating them as representative of the population of all laptop computer battery manufacturers, and inferences can and will be made about the whole population. Thus, *Manufacturer* is treated as a random factor.

Types of Effects

Effects are made up of factors, and in the Variance Components procedure, they also inherit the random nature of the composing factors. An effect is treated as a **fixed effect** when all of its composing factors are fixed factors; otherwise, the effect is treated as a **random effect**.

In the laptop computer battery example, the main effect *Type of Battery* is a fixed effect, and the nested effect *Manufacturer within Type of Battery* is a random effect.

Types of Models

If all effects in a model are random effects, the model is called a **random-effects model**. Similarly, a model with only fixed effects and the residual term is called a **fixed-effects model**. It is common to find models where some effects are random and some are fixed. In this case, the model is a **mixed model**. Since the intercept is generally treated as a fixed effect, a model including the intercept and one or more random factors is by default a mixed model. Using the above laptop computer battery example, an example of a mixed model is:

Intercept + Type of Battery + Manufacturer within Type of Battery + Residual

while an example of a fixed-effects model is:

Intercept + Type of Battery + Residual

Model for One-Way Classification

For a first example of variance components, classification by one factor provides a simple model. This section deals with the one-way classification model generally, using one data set to demonstrate two methods of variance component estimation. Consider the turnip leaf data that appeared in Table 13.3.1 of Snedecor and Cochran (1980). As mentioned in the authors' book, the data presented here are a small subset of the original data collected from a larger experiment on the precision of estimation of calcium concentration in percentage dry weight of turnip greens. Four determinations were made on each of the four leaves from a single plant. The data are shown in Figure 14-1.

Figure 14-1

Calcium concentration in turnip greens (% dry weight)

Leaf	% Calcium Determination			
	1	2	3	4
1	3.28	3.09	3.03	3.03
2	3.52	3.48	3.38	3.38
3	2.88	2.80	2.81	2.76
4	3.34	3.38	3.23	3.26

In the SPSS data file, each measurement is one case. The variables are leaf (*leaf*), percentage of calcium (*pctca*), and determination (*determ*).

Consider how the mean calcium concentration varies with *leaf*. You can use the Summarize (Case Summaries) procedure to compute the observed means and the observed standard deviations for each level of *leaf*. The results are shown in Figure 14-2.

Figure 14-2

Case summaries

Percentage of Calcium

Leaf	Mean	Std. Deviation
1	3.1075	.1184
2	3.4400	.0712
3	2.8125	.0499
4	3.3025	.0695
Total	3.1656	.2540

It is apparent that the means vary among these four leaves; thus, *leaf* is a plausible effect. Now the question is: Are you really interested in (1) the different percentages of calcium in the four specific leaves chosen, or (2) the variation in all leaves from which the four leaves may have been drawn? Since the leaf i ($i = 1, 2, 3, 4$) is just one from among randomly picked leaves, the answer should be (2), and the *leaf* effect must be treated as a random effect.

Let y_{ij} be the jth determination on leaf i. The mathematical model that relates the expected percentage on leaf i to the grand mean and the *leaf* effect is

$$y_{ij} = \mu + \alpha_i + \varepsilon_{ij} \qquad \text{for } j = 1, 2, 3, 4$$

where μ is the grand mean, α_i are the main effects ($i = 1, 2, 3, 4$), and ε_{ij} are residual errors. The errors are independent, and each follows a distribution with a mean of 0 and variance *Var(Error)*. For readers who are familiar with the general linear model, this equation looks exactly like the one for a one-way ANOVA model. However, some underlying assumptions are different: the main effects (α_i) are random variables whose values depend on which four leaves are picked. Thus, they follow certain probability distributions. It is usually assumed that the α_i are independent, and each has a mean of 0 and the same variance *Var(LEAF)*. Moreover, the main effects and the residuals are also assumed to be independent. It follows from these assumptions that

$$\mathrm{Var}(y_{ij}) = \mathrm{Var}(\mathrm{LEAF}) + \mathrm{Var}(\mathrm{Error})$$

The total variance, then, of y_{ij} is the sum of the two components, *Var(LEAF)* and *Var(Error)*—hence the name **variance components**. If *leaf* has no effects on the percentage of calcium, then the component *Var(LEAF)* equals 0. You can use the GLM Univariate procedure to test this null hypothesis (discussed in the *SPSS Base User's Guide.*) However, GLM cannot estimate the variance *Var(LEAF)*, while the Variance Components procedure does estimate the variance.

Estimation Methods

Four estimation methods are available in the Variance Components procedure: ANOVA, minimum norm quadratic unbiased estimator (MINQUE), maximum likelihood (ML), and restricted maximum likelihood (REML). For illustration purposes, both the ANOVA method using Type I sums of squares and the maximum likelihood method are used in this example.

ANOVA Method

The ANOVA method does not require any knowledge of the distributions of the random effect *leaf* and the residual error other than their means and the variances. This method estimates the variance components by equating the expected mean squares of the random effects and the residual to their observed mean squares. The expected and the observed mean squares vary depending on the type of sum of squares used. The Variance Components procedure offers two types of sums of squares: Type I and Type III. If you are new to these types, see Chapter 3 for general information. For a one-way classification model (one factor), both types produce the same sums of squares. For the sake of simplicity, only Type I results are shown here.

To produce the output, from the menus choose:

Analyze
  General Linear Model
    Variance Components...

▶ Dependent variable: pctca
▶ Random factor: leaf

Options...
  Method
  ⊙ ANOVA
  Sum of Squares
  ⊙ Type I
  Display
  ☑ Sums of squares
  ☑ Expected mean squares

The expected mean squares table is shown in Figure 14-3 and the ANOVA table, in Figure 14-4.

Figure 14-3
Expected mean squares

Source	Variance Components		Quadratic Term
	Var(LEAF)	Var(Error)	
Intercept	4.000	1.000	Intercept
LEAF	4.000	1.000	
Error	.000	1.000	

Figure 14-4
ANOVA table

Source	Type I Sum of Squares	df	Mean Square
Corrected Model	.888	3	.296
Intercept	160.339	1	160.339
LEAF	.888	3	.296
Error	7.923E-02	12	6.602E-03
Total	161.306	16	
Corrected Total	.968	15	

Dependent Variable: PCTCA

Since the Variance Components procedure does not perform hypothesis testing, only the sums of squares, degrees of freedom, and mean squares are reported in the ANOVA table.

Reading from the expected mean squares table (Figure 14-3), the expected mean squares of *LEAF* and *Error* are:

$$\text{EMS(LEAF)} = 4 \times \text{Var(LEAF)} + \text{Var(Error)}$$
$$\text{EMS(Error)} = \text{Var(Error)}$$

Equating these expected mean squares with the corresponding observed mean squares in the ANOVA table produces the following two equations:

$$0.296 = 4 \times \text{Var(LEAF)} + \text{Var(Error)}$$
$$0.006602 = \text{Var(Error)}$$

Solving for the variances yields:

$$\text{Var(Error)} = 0.006602$$
$$\text{Var(LEAF)} = \left(\frac{0.296 - 0.006602}{4}\right) = 0.0723$$

These solutions are the ANOVA Type I variance estimates. SPSS calculates these variances and displays full precision values of the estimates in the variance estimates table (Figure 14-5).

Figure 14-5
Variance estimates

Component	Estimate
Var(LEAF)	7.238E-02
Var(Error)	6.602E-03

The ANOVA Type I variance estimates are $Var(LEAF) = 0.07238$ and $Var(Error) = 0.006602$, which agree with the estimates given in Table 13.3.1 in Snedecor and Cochran (1980).

Maximum Likelihood Method

The maximum likelihood method requires distributional assumptions other than those on the means and the variances of the main effects *leaf* and the residual error, which were the assumptions required for the ANOVA method. Maximum likelihood assumes that the data are normally distributed. Although this is a considerably strong assumption, it is unlikely to be seriously violated in many situations. Moreover, the likelihood principle behind the maximum likelihood method is known to give estimates with useful statistical properties and estimates superior to those computed by the ANOVA method, when the data are approximately normally distributed.

Under the normality assumption, the likelihood function is maximized with respect to a set of parameters. In practice, the natural logarithm of the likelihood function (called the log-likelihood function) is maximized. The parameters include all of the fixed effects and all of the variance components. In the turnip-leaf example, there are three parameters: the intercept term, the variance *Var(LEAF)*, and the residual variance *Var(Error)*. The set of parameter values at which the log-likelihood function attains its maximum value are called the maximum likelihood estimates. The Variance Components procedure adopts an iterative algorithm that combines the rapid convergence property of the Newton-Raphson method with the robustness property of the Fisher scoring method to find the maximum likelihood estimates (robustness against the initial estimate).

Although the complete set of parameters includes the intercept term, its estimate is not displayed. The variance estimates table in Figure 14-6 displays the maximum likelihood estimates for the two variance components.

To produce this output, recall the dialog box and choose:

Options...
   Method
     ⊙ Maximum likelihood
   Display
     ☑ Iteration history

Figure 14-6
Variance estimates

Component	Estimate
Var(LEAF)	5.387E-02
Var(Error)	6.602E-03

The maximum likelihood variance estimates are $Var(LEAF) = 0.05387$ and $Var(Error) = 0.006602$. Comparing with the ANOVA Type I estimates, we find that the two methods give different estimates for $Var(LEAF)$. This difference is expected, primarily because the maximum likelihood method assumes normality in addition to the assumptions required by the ANOVA method.

Another reason that the maximum likelihood method is sometimes preferred to the ANOVA method is that it readily gives an asymptotic variance-covariance matrix of the variance estimates as a by-product of the iteration procedure. In contrast, the sampling variance-covariance matrix of the ANOVA method estimates is often very difficult to derive.

The Variance Components procedure always displays the asymptotic covariance matrix table along with the variance estimates table. Using the asymptotic normality property of the maximum likelihood estimators, the asymptotic variance-covariance matrix can be used in establishing confidence intervals and testing hypotheses about the variance components.

Figure 14-7
Asymptotic covariance matrix

	Var(LEAF)	Var(Error)
Var(LEAF)	1.542E-03	-1.816E-06
Var(Error)	-1.816E-06	7.265E-06

Dependent Variable: PCTCA
Method: Maximum Likelihood Estimation

For example, variance for the estimated $Var(LEAF)$, as read from Figure 14-7, is 0.001542. Taking the positive square root of this number gives the standard error for $Var(LEAF)$, which is 0.03927. Thus, an asymptotic 95% confidence interval can be constructed. To calculate the upper 2.5% point of the standard normal distribution, from the Transform menu, choose Compute and enter

$$Z = \text{IDF.NORMAL}(0.975, 0, 1)$$

The *z* value, found in the Data Editor, is 1.9600. The confidence interval, then, is

$$\text{Var(LEAF)} \pm 1.9600 \times \text{standard error of Var(LEAF)}$$

Since the estimate of *Var(LEAF)* is 0.05387 and the standard error of *Var(LEAF)* is 0.03927, the asymptotic 95% confidence interval for *Var(LEAF)* is (−0.02310, 0.1308). Often the interval is reported as (0, 0.1308) because *Var(LEAF)* is a non-negative quantity by definition. For more about negative variances, see "Negative Variance Estimates" on p. 132.

Similarly, the asymptotic 95% confidence interval for *Var(Error)* is (0.001319, 0.01188).

You can examine the estimates at various stages of the iteration by requesting the iteration history table. It helps to identify problems when the iteration fails to converge within the maximum number of iterations or is terminated because iteration cannot be continued. For this example, the iteration table (Figure 14-8) does not indicate any problems, and the iteration converged at the seventh iteration with the desired precision.

Figure 14-8
Iteration history

Iteration	Log-likelihood	Var(LEAF)	Var(Error)
0	10.071	7.403E-02	4.952E-03
1	10.319	3.893E-02	6.602E-03
2	10.414	4.785E-02	6.743E-03
3	10.428	5.253E-02	6.632E-03
4	10.429	5.380E-02	6.604E-03
5	10.429	5.387E-02	6.602E-03
6	10.429	5.387E-02	6.602E-03
7	10.429[1]	5.387E-02	6.602E-03

Dependent Variable: PCTCA
Method: Maximum Likelihood Estimation
[1] Convergence achieved.

Negative Variance Estimates

Variances by definition are non-negative quantities. Indeed, you might think that estimates for the variance components are always non-negative; but computationally, the ANOVA method and the minimum normal quadratic unbiased estimation method sometimes produce negative estimates. There is no mechanism in the ANOVA method or the minimum normal quadratic unbiased estimation method that will prevent negative variance estimates from occurring. However, such occurrences do not imply that the computational algorithms are incorrect.

When a negative variance estimate is obtained, an immediate question is: What does a negative variance estimate indicate? There seems to be no definite answer to this question. Such negative variance estimates are associated with the data or the model. Some possible explanations are:

- The variation of observations may be too large for the sample size, producing negative variance estimates even though the true variances are positive. Try to collect more data in the hope that a larger sample size will then yield positive estimates.

- Outliers or erroneously recorded observations are in the data. Identify these observations and handle them appropriately.

- The true value of the variance component may be small or 0. This is usually the case when the negative estimate has a large absolute value. Taking the variance component to be 0 is equivalent to dropping the corresponding random effects from the model.

- The method of estimation is not appropriate. For example, using the ANOVA method on a highly unbalanced data set with empty cells is more likely to produce negative variance estimates. You may want to use the maximum likelihood or the restricted maximum likelihood methods.

- The specified model is not correct. The covariance structure of data assumed under the variance components model may not be appropriate for your data. Sometimes a negative variance estimate indicates that observations in your data are negatively correlated.

The above reasons are some of the common possibilities, and they are in no way exhaustive. Users interested in the problem of negative estimates can find more information in LaMotte (1973) and Hocking (1985). Although it is hard to predict when a negative estimate will occur, one thing is sure—such occurrences lead to some embarrassment: a variance that by definition is non-negative is being estimated as a negative number.

Nested Design Model for Two-Way Classification

A more complicated model can include more than one factor, and the factors can be crossed or nested. Consider the data about test ovens described in Bowker and Lieberman (1972). A quality assurance engineer for an electronics components manufacturing firm claims that the 36 ovens used by this firm for testing the life of the various components are not homogeneous. To determine whether or not the claim can be justified, the engineer conducted an experiment using a single type of electronic component. Three randomly selected ovens were used for the experiment. The electronic component was tested at the two temperatures normally used for life testing of that component. Each component was operated in an oven until it failed. Then the lifetime, in minutes, of the component was recorded. Three components were tested per oven-temperature combination. The original data are shown in Figure 14-9.

Figure 14-9
Lifetimes of electronic components in minutes

Temperature	Oven 1	Oven 2	Oven 3
550°F	237, 254, 246	208, 178, 187	<u>192</u>, 186, 183
600°F	178, 179, <u>183</u>	146, 145, 141	142, 125, 136

Hemmerle and Hartley (1973) deliberately excluded two values (underlined in the above table) in the oven data to introduce a set of unbalanced data. This new set of data is analyzed in this section.

The factor *oven* is clearly a random factor because the three ovens used in the experiment are just a sample of the larger population of 36 ovens. Temperature is also treated as a random factor because 550° F and 600° F were just two of the many temperatures that could be used for testing. Since there is no information on whether or not the ranges of temperature for testing were the same for all of the ovens, we further assume that temperature is nested within oven. Hence, a nested design model is used.

The SPSS data file contains four variables: *oven*, *tempture*, *lifetime*, and *qusehh*, with one case for each lifetime recorded. *Lifetime* is the lifetime of a component that is the dependent variable, *oven* is the oven factor with three levels, *tempture* is the temperature factor with two levels, *tempture(oven)* is the temperature within the oven, and *qusehh* is the SPSS weight variable that is used to exclude the two cases not considered in Hemmerle and Hartley (1973) by assigning zero weights to them and unit weights to all other cases. Using these variables, the nested design model is represented as:

LIFETIME = Constant + OVEN + TEMPTURE(OVEN) + Residual

where both *OVEN* and *TEMPTURE(OVEN)* are random effects.

SPSS offers several methods to estimate the variance components *Var(OVEN)*, *Var(TEMPTURE(OVEN))* and *Var(Error)*. However, not all of them are suitable for unbalanced data; for example, the ANOVA Type I method is not suitable. The minimum norm quadratic unbiased estimation (MINQUE) method is used here because it involves no normality assumption. Without any knowledge of what prior values should be used, estimates using both prior values schemes, MINQUE(0) and MINQUE(1), are computed.

To produce the output, from the menus choose:

Data
  Weight Cases...

⊙ Weight cases by: qusehh

Analyze
  General Linear Model
    Variance Components...

▶ Dependent Variable: lifetime
▶ Random Factor(s): oven tempture

Model...
  ⊙ Custom
  ▶ Model: oven tempture

Options...
  Method:
  ⊙ MINQUE
  Random Effect Priors
  ⊙ Zero

Paste

In the syntax window, at the end of the DESIGN subcommand, type (oven) to specify the nesting effect, TEMPTURE(OVEN). The modified syntax is

```
VARCOMP LIFETIME BY OVEN TEMPTURE
  /RANDOM = OVEN TEMPTURE
  /METHOD = MINQUE(0)
  /DESIGN = OVEN TEMPTURE(OVEN)
  /INTERCEPT = INCLUDE.
```

Run the syntax by clicking the Run Current tool. For MINQUE with the other prior values scheme, change the method to

```
/METHOD = MINQUE(1)
```

and run the syntax again. The results for both methods are shown in Figure 14-10.

Figure 14-10

Variance estimates for the MINQUE(0) and MINQUE(1) methods

Component	Estimate
Var(OVEN)	85.923
Var(TEMPTURE(OVEN))	1940.664
Var(Error)	-157.119[1]

Dependent Variable: LIFETIME
Method: Minimum Norm Quadratic Unbiased
Estimation (Weight = 0 for Random Effects, 1 for
Residual)

[1]. For the ANOVA and MINQUE methods, negative variance component estimates may occur. Some possible reasons for their occurrence are: (a) the specified model is not the correct model, or (b) the true value of the variance equals zero.

Component	Estimate
Var(OVEN)	102.839
Var(TEMPTURE(OVEN))	1545.921
Var(Error)	70.067

Dependent Variable: LIFETIME
Method: Minimum Norm Quadratic
Unbiased Estimation (Weight = 1 for
Random Effects and Residual)

Estimates of the residual variance based on the two prior value schemes contradict each other. In order to decide which scheme gives a more reasonable answer, estimates based on another method are computed. The ANOVA Type III method is used, since Type III sums of squares are suitable for unbalanced data. Also, the ANOVA method does not require any normality assumption. The results are shown in Figure 14-11.

Figure 14-11

Variance estimates for the ANOVA Type III method

Component	Estimate
Var(OVEN)	9.750
Var(TEMPTURE(OVEN))	1475.803
Var(Error)	78.633

Dependent Variable: LIFETIME
Method: ANOVA (Type III Sum of Squares)

The first finding is that the signs of the MINQUE(1) estimates and the ANOVA Type III estimates do agree. Second, values of the corresponding variance estimates are close except that of *Var(OVEN)*. Based on these findings, it seems that the second scheme of prior values is more appropriate than the first scheme for this data.

Based on the MINQUE(1) estimates (using the uniform scheme of prior values) in Figure 14-10, the variability among the ovens is about one and a half times the size of the residual variance, and it contributes

$$102.839/(102.839 + 1545.921 + 70.067) = 5.98\%$$

to the total variance. This result supports the engineer's claim, and efforts should be spent on improving homogeneity of the ovens. Notice that the variance of the temperature-within-oven effect is substantially larger than the residual variance—22 times, to be exact. This effect alone explained

$$1545.921/(102.839 + 1545.921 + 70.067) = 89.94\%$$

of total variance. This strongly suggests that a very significant and important part of the variance of an electronic component's lifetime is attributed to the temperature used for testing.

Univariate Repeated Measures Analysis Using a Mixed Model Approach

A notable property of longitudinal studies and repeated measures experiments is that each subject is observed at several different times (not necessarily equally spaced) or under different experimental conditions. A classical technique is to apply a univariate mixed model to the data (see Winer, Brown, and Michels, 1991). This model assumes that observations from the same subject have a constant variance and a common correlation. In other words, the variance-covariance matrix of observations from each subject exhibits the **compound symmetry** structure. The common correlation is often called the **intra-class correlation**. In this example, we show how to estimate this intra-class correlation using the Variance Components procedure.

A study was designed to investigate whether boys and girls have different growth rates. Using the distance, in millimeters, from the center of the pituitary to the pteryo-maxillary fissure as a measure of growth, data were collected from each of 11 girls and 16 boys at ages 8, 10, 12 and 14 by investigators at the University of North Carolina Dental School. Occasionally, this distance decreases with age because the distance represents the relative position of two points. The data appeared in Potthoff and Roy

(1964) and were again analyzed by Jennrich and Schluchter (1986). The complete data are shown in Figure 14-12.

Figure 14-12
Data for growth study

		Girl				Boy			
		8	10	12	14	8	10	12	14
Distance (mm) from center of pituitary to pteryo-maxillary fissure	1	21.0	20.0	21.5	23.0	26.0	25.0	29.0	31.0
	2	21.0	21.5	24.0	25.5	21.5	22.5	23.0	26.5
	3	20.5	24.0	24.5	26.0	23.0	22.5	24.0	27.5
	4	23.5	24.5	25.0	26.5	25.5	27.5	26.5	27.0
	5	21.5	23.0	22.5	23.5	20.0	23.5	22.5	26.0
	6	20.0	21.0	21.0	22.5	24.5	25.5	27.0	28.5
	7	21.5	22.5	23.0	25.0	22.0	22.0	24.5	26.5
	8	23.0	23.0	23.5	24.0	24.0	21.5	24.5	25.5
	9	20.0	21.0	22.0	21.5	23.0	20.5	31.0	26.0
	10	16.5	19.0	19.0	19.5	27.5	28.0	31.0	31.5
	11	24.5	25.0	28.0	28.0	23.0	23.0	23.5	25.0
	12	.	.	.	.	21.5	23.5	24.0	28.0
	13	.	.	.	.	17.0	24.5	26.0	29.5
	14	.	.	.	.	22.5	25.5	25.5	26.0
	15	.	.	.	.	23.0	24.5	26.0	30.0
	16	.	.	.	.	22.0	21.5	23.5	25.0

You may need to rearrange data so that it is most convenient to specify a univariate mixed model using SPSS. In this example, a categorical variable named *subject* is created to give each individual a unique identification. Girls 1 to 11 in Figure 14-12 are assigned subject values 1 to 11. Boys 1 to 16 are assigned values 12 to 27. A second categorical variable called *age* is created with four levels that correspond to the four ages (8, 10, 12, and 14). A third categorical variable called *gender* uses the characters *F* for female and *M* for male. Finally, *distance* is the dependent variable. There is one case for each distance.

Using repeated measures terminology, *gender* is a between-subjects factor and *age* is a within-subjects factor because each subject is observed at these four ages. Both *gender* and *age* are fixed factors. The variable *subject*, on the other hand, is a random factor because its levels are arbitrarily chosen solely for identification purpose.

The following design uses a common technique (for example, see Winer, Brown, and Michels, 1991) to formulate a repeated measures analysis as a mixed model:

$$\text{DISTANCE} = \text{Constant} + \text{GENDER} + \text{SUBJECT(GENDER)} + \text{AGE}$$
$$+ \text{AGE*GENDER} + \text{Residual}$$

with the effect *SUBJECT(GENDER)* being random. The corresponding mathematical model is:

$$d_{ijk} = \mu + g_i + s_{k(i)} + a_j + (ag)_{ij} + e_{ijk}$$

$$k = 1, \ldots, n_i, j = 1, 2, 3, 4 \text{ and } i = 1, 2$$

where $n_1 = 11$, $n_2 = 16$, d_{ijk} is the distance of the kth individual observed for the ith level of *gender* and the jth level of *age*, and g_i is the fixed-effect parameter corresponding to the ith level of *gender*. Similarly, a_j and $(ag)_{ij}$ are the fixed-effect parameters that correspond respectively to the jth level of *age* and the (i,j)th level of the interaction effect *age*gender*. $s_{k(i)}$ is a random-effect parameter that corresponds to the kth individual within the ith level of *gender*, and e_{ijk} is the residual. The usual assumptions are: $s_{k(i)}$ are uncorrelated, each has zero mean and variance σ_s^2, and the residuals are also uncorrelated, while each has zero mean and variance σ_e^2. Furthermore, the random-effect parameters and the residuals are uncorrelated also.

Consider, for example, the distance observed from the first boy at age 10 (that is, d_{221}). It follows from the above distributional assumptions that the variance of this observation is $\sigma_s^2 + \sigma_e^2$. Next consider the distance observed from the same boy at age 14 (that is, d_{241}). Its variance also equals $\sigma_s^2 + \sigma_e^2$. The covariance between these two distances is σ_s^2 because the two corresponding residuals are uncorrelated. In general, all distances observed from any boy or girl have equal variances and the common value is $\sigma_s^2 + \sigma_e^2$. Also, the covariance between any two distances observed at two different ages is equal to σ_s^2. Therefore, the correlation between any two distances observed at two different ages is the same. The common correlation value is called the intra-class correlation. In this example, it is equal to $\sigma_s^2/(\sigma_s^2 + \sigma_e^2)$. Since both the numerator and the denominator are positive, the intra-class correlation is also positive.

All estimation methods except the maximum likelihood method give the same variance component estimates. For purposes of illustration, only estimates based on the maximum likelihood method and those based on the restricted maximum likelihood method are displayed here. In order to obtain maximum precision, the tables are edited and up to eight decimal points are shown.

To produce the output, from the menus choose:

Analyze
  General Linear Model
    Variance Components...

Dependent Variable: distance
Fixed Factor(s): gender age
Random Factor(s): subject

Model...
  ⊙ Custom
  Model: gender age subject age*gender

Options...
  Method
  ⊙ Maximum likelihood
  Display
  ☑ Iteration history

Paste

After you paste the syntax, indicate nesting by adding (**gender**) after subject. The modified syntax is

```
VARCOMP distance  BY gender age  subject
 /RANDOM = subject
 /METHOD = ML
 /CRITERIA = ITERATE(50)
 /CRITERIA = CONVERGE(1.0E-8)
 /PRINT = HISTORY (1)
 /DESIGN = gender subject(gender) age age*gender
 /INTERCEPT = INCLUDE .
```

 Double-click the variance estimates table, highlight the cells containing numbers, and change the format (Cell Properties) to eight decimal places. You may need to drag the right boundary of the cells to display this larger number of decimal places.

Change the method to REML and run the command again. The variance estimates are shown in Figure 14-13 and Figure 14-14.

Figure 14-13
Variance estimates for ML

Component	Estimate
Var(SUBJECT(GENDER))	3.04202616
Var(Error)	1.82873878

Dependent Variable: DISTANCE
Method: Maximum Likelihood Estimation

Figure 14-14
Variance estimates for REML

Component	Estimate
Var(SUBJECT(GENDER))	3.28538826
Var(Error)	1.97503788

Dependent Variable: DISTANCE
Method: Restricted Maximum Likelihood Estimation

Based on the maximum likelihood estimates, the estimate for intra-class correlation is

$$\rho = \frac{3.04202616}{(3.04202616 + 1.82873878)} = 0.62454793$$

whereas the correlation estimate based on the restricted maximum likelihood estimates is

$$\rho = \frac{3.28538826}{(3.28538826 + 1.97503788)} = 0.62454793$$

Although the variance component estimates are different, the two intra-class correlation estimates are surprisingly close (up to eight decimal points). In order to compute the asymptotic standard errors for these two correlation estimates, you need the asymptotic variance-covariance matrices for the variance component estimates. They are shown in Figure 14-15 and Figure 14-16.

Figure 14-15
Asymptotic covariance matrix for ML

	Var(SUBJECT(GENDER))	Var(Error)
Var(SUBJECT(GENDER))	.91215920	-.02064374
Var(Error)	-.02064374	.08257495

Dependent Variable: DISTANCE
Method: Maximum Likelihood Estimation

Figure 14-16
Asymptotic covariance matrix for REML

	Var(SUBJECT(GENDER))	Var(Error)
Var(SUBJECT(GENDER))	1.14905789	-.02600516
Var(Error)	-.02600516	.10402066

Dependent Variable: DISTANCE
Method: Restricted Maximum Likelihood Estimation

Using the delta method (see Johnson, Kotz, and Kemp, 1992), the variance of the intra-class correlation is approximated by

$$\text{var}(\rho) = \text{var}(\sigma_s^2/(\sigma_s^2 + \sigma_e^2))$$

$$= (\sigma_e^4 \text{var}(\sigma_s^2) + \sigma_s^4 \text{var}(\sigma_e^2) - 2\sigma_s^2\sigma_e^2\text{cov}(\sigma_s^2, \sigma_e^2))/(\sigma_s^2 + \sigma_e^2)^4$$

With the maximum likelihood method,

$$\text{var}(\sigma_s^2) = 0.91215920, \text{var}(\sigma_e^2) = 0.08257495 \text{ and}$$

$$\text{cov}(\sigma_s^2, \sigma_e^2) = -0.02064374$$

The approximate variance of the intra-class correlation is

$$\text{var}(\rho) \approx \frac{\left(1.82873878^2 \times 0.91215920 + 3.04202616^2 \times 0.08257495 - 2 \times 3.04202616 \times 1.82873878 \times \left(-0.02064374\right)\right)}{\left(3.04202616 + 1.82873878\right)^4}$$

$$= 0.00718555$$

Taking the square root of $\text{var}(\rho)$ gives the standard error of the intra-class correlation. Based on the maximum likelihood estimates, the standard error equals 0.08476761.

Since the maximum likelihood variance estimates are asymptotically normally distributed, it follows that the intra-class correlation is also asymptotically normal. Thus, you can compute an asymptotic 95% confidence interval for this intra-class correlation as $\rho \pm Z_{0.025} \times \text{se}(\rho)$ where Z is the upper 2.5% point of the standard normal distribution. From the Transform menu, choose Compute and enter

$$Z_{0.025} = \text{IDF.NORMAL}(0.975, 0, 1)$$

The $Z_{0.025}$ value is 1.95996400. Hence, the asymptotic 95% confidence interval is (0.45840647, 0.79068939).

Similarly, based on the restricted maximum likelihood variance estimates, the standard error of the intra-class correlation is 0.08809308. The asymptotic 95% confidence interval for the intra-class correlation is (0.45188866, 0.79720720). Although both the maximum likelihood and the restricted maximum likelihood methods give very close estimates for the intra-class correlation, the maximum likelihood method does produce a narrower confidence interval.

For an intra-class correlation estimate based on the ANOVA method, see Searle, Casella and McCulloch (1992).

Background Information

The following sections include technical background information about variance components models and the types of estimation methods. For readers who are interested in a thorough discussion of this subject, see Rao and Kleffe (1988) and Searle, Casella, and McCulloch (1992).

Model

A variance components model analyzes the contribution of each random effect to the total variation in each cross-classification category. Each cross-classification constitutes a cell and each categorical variable is called a factor. A variance components model formulates the value of the dependent variable in each cell as the sum of a linear combination of parameters and a residual error term. The parameters are identified by association with the categorical variables and the covariates in the model. The parameters are then classified into fixed-effects parameters and random-effects parameters. The classification is based on the nature (fixed or random) of the effects with which the parameters are associated. The residual error term is assumed to have a zero mean and a constant variance across all the cells. The mathematical model for the observed value of the dependent variable in a cell is given by

$$y_{ik} = \mathbf{x}_{io}\beta_o + \sum_{s=1}^{m} \mathbf{x}_{is}\beta_s + \varepsilon_{ik}, \quad k = 1,\dots,n_i \text{ and } i = 1,\dots,r$$

where y_{ik} is the kth repetition within the ith cell, x_{io} is the portion of the ith row of the design matrix associated with the fixed effects, β_o is the vector of fixed-effects parameters, $\mathbf{x}_{is}$ is the portion of the ith row of the design matrix associated with the sth random effect, β_s is the vector of the sth random-effect parameters, ε_{ik} is the residual error associated with the value y_{ik}, n_i is the number of repetitions within the ith cell, m is the number of random effects, and r is the number of cells.

When there are no random effects (that is, $m = 0$) this equation corresponds to a general linear model with fixed effects only.

Distribution Assumptions

Various assumptions are made when you use variance components analysis.

Random Effects

Under a variance components model, the vectors $\beta_1, \ldots, \beta_m$ are random vectors. In other words, elements of these vectors are random variables. Therefore, these random vectors have their expected values and variance-covariance matrices.

For the sth random effect:

- Each element of the vector β_s has zero expected value.

- Variances of the elements of the vector β_s are the same. Denote the common variance as σ_s^2.

- Elements of the vector β_s are uncorrelated. In other words, covariance between *any* two elements is 0.

It is further assumed that the random vectors $\beta_1, \ldots, \beta_m$ are mutually uncorrelated. Thus, covariance between an element from a random vector and an element from a different random vector is always 0.

Residual Error Term

It is often assumed that:

- The residual error term has zero expectation and constant variance across all cells. Denote the constant variance as σ_ε^2.

- The residuals from different cells are uncorrelated.

- The residual error term is uncorrelated with all elements of the random-effect vectors.

Variance Decomposition

With the above assumptions, the total variance of an observation in the *i*th cell is

$$\text{var}(y_{ik}) = \sum_{s=1}^{m} \sigma_s^2 \|\mathbf{x}_{is}\|^2 + \sigma_\varepsilon^2, \quad k = 1, \dots, n_i \text{ and } i = 1, \dots, r$$

where $\|\mathbf{x}_{is}\|^2$ is the sum of squares of all elements of the row vector $\mathbf{x}_{is}$. Hence the data variance is decomposed into a weighted sum of the variances of the random effects and the residual variance. Variance of a random effect is called a **variance component**.

A logical conclusion from the above assumptions is that observations in a variance components model are correlated. This correlation clearly distinguishes between a variance components model and a general linear model. Because the observations are correlated, special estimation methods are used to estimate the variance components.

Estimation Methods

The following four estimation methods are available in the Variance Components procedure:

- ANOVA
- Minimum norm quadratic unbiased estimation (MINQUE)
- Maximum likelihood (ML)
- Restricted maximum likelihood (REML)

ANOVA Method

The ANOVA method first computes sums of squares and expected mean squares for all effects following the general linear model approach. Then a system of linear equations is established by equating the sums of squares of the random effects to their expected mean squares. The variables in the equations are the variance components and the residual variance. Any solution, if one exists, to this system of linear equations constitutes a set of estimates for the variance components.

This method is computationally less laborious and the estimates are statistically unbiased. However, negative variance estimates can happen and the variance-covariance matrix of the estimates is difficult to obtain even asymptotically.

The Variance Components procedure offers two types of sums of squares: Type I and Type III. For detailed descriptions of these two types of sums of squares, see Chapter 3. A discussion of choosing the appropriate type can be found in Speed (1979).

MINQUE Method

The MINQUE method requires a set of *a priori* values for the variance components or the ratios of the components to the residual variance. The estimators are then functions of the data and of the prior values. When the prior values are proportional to the true but unknown values of each variance component (or ratios of each component to the residual variance), the estimates achieve minimum variance in the class of all unbiased, translation invariant quadratic estimators. Since the variance components are unknown, the correct prior values are seldom found. Therefore, the estimators are unlikely to possess the above optimal properties in reality. Despite this fact, the MINQUE method is popular because of its considerable flexibility with respect to the form of models that can be fitted. For a summary of the method, see Rao (1973). For an in-depth discussion of the method, see Rao and Kleffe (1988).

The Variance Components procedure offers two schemes of prior values. The first scheme, MINQUE(0), assigns zero prior values to ratios of variance components to the residual variance. The second scheme, MINQUE(1), gives the ratios unit prior values. With either scheme, a system of linear equations is established based on the prior values and the data. The variables are the ratios of the variance components to the residual variance, and the residual variance itself. The system of linear equations is then solved to obtain the MINQUE estimates. Details of the estimation procedure can be found in Giesbrecht (1983).

Maximum Likelihood Method

The maximum likelihood method finds a set of values, called the maximum likelihood estimates, at which the log-likelihood function attains its local maximum. The estimators are the fixed-effects parameters, the variance components, and the residual variance. The maximum likelihood estimates are obtained by an iterative procedure that uses both the Newton-Raphson method and the Fisher scoring method. Although the fixed-effects parameters are part of the estimators, their values are not displayed. As a by-product of the iterative procedure, the asymptotic variance-covariance matrix of the variance component estimates are also obtained.

For technical details of computing the maximum likelihood estimates, see Hemmerle and Hartley (1973), Jennrich and Sampson (1976), and Searle, Casella and McCulloch (1992).

Restricted Maximum Likelihood Method

The restricted maximum likelihood method is basically the same as the maximum likelihood method except for one difference: the restricted maximum likelihood method takes into account the degrees of freedom used for estimating fixed effects when estimating variance components, while the maximum likelihood method does not. Instead of using the original data vector, the restricted maximum likelihood method operates on linear combinations of the observations, chosen in such a way that those combinations are invariant to the values of the fixed-effect parameters. These linear combinations turn out to be equivalent to residuals calculated after fitting by ordinary least squares (weighted least squares if a regression weight is specified) only the fixed effects part of the model. Thus, the method performs maximization over a restricted vector space.

For balanced data, the restricted maximum likelihood estimates are identical to the ANOVA estimates, although their variance-covariance matrices are different. Because of this property, the restricted maximum likelihood method is preferred to the maximum likelihood method for balanced data. Also, computational burdens are smaller for the restricted maximum likelihood method, since it maximized with respect to a smaller number of variables.

For more information about this method, see Patterson and Thompson (1971), Corbeil and Searle (1976), and Searle, Casella and McCulloch (1992).

Model Selection
Loglinear Analysis Examples

When examining the relationship between two categorical variables, the straightforward approach, familiar to most researchers, is to construct a contingency table and compute the appropriate chi-square statistic to test the hypothesis of independence. But what happens when you have more than two categorical variables? One approach would be to construct a series of two-way tables and compute corresponding chi-square statistics for each one. However, this strategy is flawed in the sense that results will be confounded by interactions between variables. Interpretation also becomes more difficult as the number of variables increases. The ideal solution would allow you to examine the relationships among all of the variables simultaneously, including interactions among groups of variables.

The Loglinear Model

By using a structured kind of model called a **loglinear model**, we can do just that. Loglinear models attempt to predict cell frequencies based on values of the categorical variables in the model. It is analogous to factorial ANOVA in that it allows you to partition variance in your cell frequencies into subsets attributable to main effects and interaction effects of the variables of interest.

Figure 15-1
Exposure and sickness

		Exposed to event?		
		No	Yes	
Got sick?	No	A	B	P
	Yes	C	D	Q
		R	S	N

For example, let's assume that we're investigating the relationship between exposure to a traumatic event and sickness. Given the contingency table shown in Figure 15-1, we can build a model of the cell frequencies (which we can call F), including a parameter θ, representing the overall sample size (this corresponds to the "grand mean" in ANOVA), a parameter λ_x, representing the effect of exposure to the event (X), a parameter λ_y for the effect of getting sick (Y), and a parameter λ_{xy} for the joint effect of being exposed to the event *and* getting sick (the interaction term):

$$\ln F \ = \ \theta + \lambda_x + \lambda_y + \lambda_{xy}$$

This gives us a linear model, which allows us to compute values for the parameters. Using this model allows us to isolate effects of each of the variables from each other and from their combined effect. (The natural log of cell frequency is used to simplify both computation and interpretation of parameter estimates.)

Notice that in this model there are four parameters (θ and the three λ parameters), and there are four cell frequencies to be estimated (A, B, C, and D). Because there are as many parameters as there are values to be estimated, this model will always reproduce the original contingency table values perfectly. Models such as this, which include all possible effects of individual variables and combinations of variables, are called **saturated models**.

It is also possible to analyze a particular contingency table with a model that omits one or more possible effects. For example, we could use the following model for Figure 15-1:

$$\ln F \ = \ \theta + \lambda_x + \lambda_y$$

Notice that this model does not include the interaction term. That is, it assumes that exposure and sickness do *not* have a joint influence on cell frequency. Notice also that the model contains only three parameters but is still used to estimate four values (the cell frequencies). Because of this, unless exposure and sickness are perfectly independent, there will be some discrepancies between the estimated values we get from the model and the observed values. We can measure these discrepancies and determine whether the model estimates are significantly different from the observed values. If we have a good model, the estimates will be close to the observed values.

There are three procedures in SPSS for handling loglinear models: General Loglinear Analysis, Model Selection Loglinear Analysis, and Logit Loglinear Analysis. Use General Loglinear Analysis if you have a specific model with specific effects in mind that you want to test. Use Model Selection Loglinear Analysis if you need to explore many possible models to determine the best model to use for your data.

Use Logit Loglinear Analysis if you have one variable in your set that you want to define as a dependent variable (outcome) to be predicted based on the other variables.

The Likelihood-Ratio Chi-Square

To test the discrepancy between an unsaturated model and the data we are modeling, we use the **likelihood-ratio chi-square** instead of the traditional Pearson chi-square. It is computed using the following formula:

$$G^2 = 2 \sum_i O_i \ln\left(\frac{O_i}{E_i}\right)$$

where O_i is the observed frequency for cell i and E_i is the expected frequency for cell i. The likelihood-ratio chi-square statistic has the desirable property that it is additive, in the same sense that sums of squares in simple ANOVA are additive—the sum of the chi-square values for the individual effects in the model equals the chi-square for the total model. Therefore, if you take the difference between two likelihood-ratio chi-square statistics for related models, the result is another likelihood-ratio chi-square statistic. This property allows you to make two important inferences in your analysis: you can *compare nested models,* and you can *assess individual effects.*

Nested Models

One model is said to be nested within another model if the effects in the nested model are a subset of the effects in the more complex model. For example, the model

$$\ln F = \theta + \lambda_x + \lambda_y \qquad\qquad \text{Equation 15-1}$$

is nested within the model

$$\ln F = \theta + \lambda_x + \lambda_y + \lambda_{xy} \qquad\qquad \text{Equation 15-2}$$

Notice that all of the effects in Equation 15-1, plus the interaction term, are included in Equation 15-2. By computing likelihood-ratio chi-square statistics for each of these models and then taking the difference, we get another likelihood-ratio chi-square statistic that tests the relative advantage of the more complex model (Equation 15-2) over the simpler model (Equation 15-1) in predicting cell frequencies. If the resulting value is not statistically significant, we can conclude that the models are equivalent in their predictive ability. In such cases, we would usually choose the simpler model (that is, the more parsimonious model) that still explains the observed data.

Individual Effects

Each model is an attempt to capture the variability of cell frequencies in terms of the variables involved. The total variability of cell frequencies can be measured by the difference in likelihood-ratio chi-squares for the full model and a baseline model. This baseline model assumes that no effects are present, and cases are expected to be evenly distributed across all cells of the contingency table. The complete independence model is given by the following equation:

$$\ln F = \theta$$

where θ is simply the natural log of the average number of cases per cell.

The total variability, as measured by the likelihood-ratio chi-square, can be partitioned into effect variance in a manner similar to the partitioning of the sum of squares in ANOVA. As explained above, taking the difference between the likelihood-ratio chi-square values for two nested models allows you to test how much better the saturated model (Equation 15-2) fits the data than the simpler model (Equation 15-1). This can also be thought of as a test of the contribution of the interaction term, λ_{xy}, to the model. In fact, all of the effects in the model can be tested this way, each in turn, to give a relative index of each effect's contribution to the model. In each case, the nested model omitting the effect of interest is compared to the model including that effect (but no higher-level interactions) to compute a likelihood-ratio chi-square, called the **partial chi-square** (see Figure 15-2). This statistic can be used as an indicator of the relative importance of each effect, and it can also be used to test the hypothesis that the effect is 0.

Figure 15-2
Testing effects

To test this effect:	Compare this model...	To this model
λ_x	$\ln F = \theta + \lambda_y$	$\ln F = \theta + \lambda_x + \lambda_y$
λ_y	$\ln F = \theta + \lambda_x$	$\ln F = \theta + \lambda_x + \lambda_y$
λ_{xy}	$\ln F = \theta + \lambda_x + \lambda_y$	$\ln F = \theta + \lambda_x + \lambda_y + \lambda_{xy}$

Note that this strategy can be generalized to test effects within unsaturated models as well. For example, in the model given in Equation 15-1, there are two effects that can be tested: the effect of X is tested by comparing the model $\ln F = \theta + \lambda_y$ to the baseline (Equation 15-1), and the effect of Y is tested by comparing the model $\ln F = \theta + \lambda_x$ to the baseline.

Hierarchical Model Selection

As Einstein said, "Things should be made as simple as possible, but no simpler." If we include only the main effects and exclude any interactions among variables, we risk overlooking some important effects, and our model probably won't fit the data very well. On the other hand, if we include every possible effect and interaction, we will have a complicated model with as many parameters as there are table cells. Thus, we will not have simplified anything. Sometimes it can be difficult to find the right compromise between the two extremes. A strategy of testing a series of nested models can help you identify the appropriate amount of complexity for your model. The strategy is based on sequentially considering orders of complexity to select the simplest model that provides reasonable prediction of cell frequencies. Suppose that we have three categorical variables, X, Y, and Z. There are three orders of complexity involved: the main effects (simplest), the two-way interactions (more complex), and the three-way interaction (most complex). We can start with the most complex model, the saturated model:

$$\ln F = \theta + \lambda_x + \lambda_y + \lambda_z + \lambda_{xy} + \lambda_{xz} + \lambda_{yz} + \lambda_{xyz}$$

and then compare this third-order model with the second-order model:

$$\ln F = \theta + \lambda_x + \lambda_y + \lambda_z + \lambda_{xy} + \lambda_{xz} + \lambda_{yz}$$

which, in turn, is compared to the first-order model:

$$\ln F = \theta + \lambda_x + \lambda_y + \lambda_z$$

which is finally compared to the zero-order model:

$$\ln F = \theta$$

At each stage, we assess the change in fit, using the likelihood-ratio chi-square. If the change is not significant, then we conclude that we can simplify the model at that level without sacrificing much predictive ability, and we proceed to the next stage. We continue through the levels until the change is significant; this tells us that we have found the point of "diminishing returns"—the point at which the loss of predictive power becomes too large to ignore.

Notice that if a higher-level effect is in the model, then the corresponding lower-level effects are also in the model. That is, with three variables X, Y, and Z, if λ_{xy} is in the model, then λ_x and λ_y are also in the model (although λ_z may or may not be). Models that meet this requirement are called **hierarchical loglinear models**. For models that operate under this constraint, we can identify a model simply by specifying the effects at the highest level of complexity at which they appear. For example, if we specify that λ_{xy} is included in the model, then we know that λ_x and λ_y are also included. Thus, we can abbreviate this model using the shorthand $X*Y$. This specification is called the **generating class** of the model. Figure 15-3 shows some more examples of generating classes and the corresponding models.

Figure 15-3
Generating classes and corresponding models

Generating Class	Model
X,Y	$\ln F = \theta + \lambda_x + \lambda_y$
X*Y,Z	$\ln F = \theta + \lambda_x + \lambda_y + \lambda_z + \lambda_{xy}$
X*Y*Z	$\ln F = \theta + \lambda_x + \lambda_y + \lambda_z + \lambda_{xy} + \lambda_{xz} + \lambda_{yz} + \lambda_{xyz}$
X*Y, X*Z	$\ln F = \theta + \lambda_x + \lambda_y + \lambda_z + \lambda_{xy} + \lambda_{xz}$

The Model Selection Loglinear procedure can analyze only hierarchical models. If you need to analyze nonhierarchical models, use the General Loglinear procedure.

Strategy for Using Model Selection

In an ideal world, you would have specific expectations about relationships among your variables, based on theory or prior research. However, in many situations, you may not have such bases for developing specific hypotheses about your data. In such cases, you must take an exploratory approach to finding an appropriate model for your data. Model Selection Loglinear Analysis is designed to help you explore a range of models in an organized fashion in order to find a model that maximizes predictive ability while minimizing model complexity. Here is a useful approach to exploring relationships in your categorical data:

■ Select your variables carefully. Don't just include everything—include only the variables that will be most interesting or useful.

■ Identify a specific model using Model Selection Loglinear Analysis. Use this procedure to find the appropriate level of complexity for your model and to identify which effects should be included and which should be excluded.

■ Test the resulting model using the General Loglinear Model procedure. This procedure lets you test a specific model more thoroughly (for example, by printing parameter estimates for unsaturated models) and allows you to save residuals and predicted values as new variables for further analysis.

Example 1: Examining a saturated model. This is a model of the relationships among exposure to a traumatic event, health, and gender. The saturated model is used to examine the relationships and interactions among these variables.

Example 2: Using backward elimination to select a suitable model. A method using automatic elimination of extraneous effects is demonstrated here. We examine the same set of variables, with the goal of reducing the complexity of the model without sacrificing predictive validity.

Example 1
Examining a Saturated Model

Is it true that exposure to a traumatic event can cause adverse effects on health? Are there differences in this effect between males and females? In this first example, we will look at a saturated model of the relationships among these variables.

The variables involved were measured as follows (all variables are based on responses to questionnaire items):

Exposure to traumatic event. The event studied was a crowd accident at a college football stadium. Students trying to rush onto the field after a football game were crushed against a metal gate by the mass of the crowd, causing difficulty in breathing and injury in some students. Each student was assigned to one of four categories:

■ Control (coded as 1): The student was not at the football game and was not exposed to the event at all.

■ Witness (coded as 2): The student was at the football game and witnessed the event but was not directly involved.

■ Non-injured (coded as 3): The student was involved in the crush (was part of the crowd moving toward the gate) but was not injured.

■ Injured (coded as 4): The student was in the crowd and was injured as a result of the crush.

Gender. Student gender was recorded as *Male* (coded as 0) or *Female* (coded as 1).

Health effect. This was assessed by asking students to indicate the number of colds they had experienced in the two months following the stadium incident. The assumption is that an adverse impact on health will be reflected in an increased number of colds reported. The variable is coded as zero colds in the last two months, one cold, two colds, or three or more colds (coded as 0, 1, 2, or 3, respectively).

Notice that the variables are coded numerically. All variables used in the Model Selection Loglinear Analysis procedure must be coded numerically. If you have string variables that you want to use in this procedure, you will need to recode them using Recode or Automatic Recode (on the Transform menu) before you begin your model selection loglinear analysis.

To produce this output, from the menus choose:

Analyze
  Loglinear
    Model Selection...

Click Reset to restore dialog box defaults, and then select:

▶ Factor(s): group, ncold, sex
  Define Range for each variable

⊙ Enter in single step

Model...
  ⊙ Saturated

Options...
  Display for Saturated Model
  ☑ Parameter estimates
  ☑ Association table
  Model Criteria
  Delta: 0

The first table presented in the output (Figure 15-4) is the table of observed and expected frequencies for all cells. Because this is a saturated model, the observed and expected values are equal, and residuals are all equal to 0.

Figure 15-4
Observed and expected frequencies and residuals

Factor	Code	OBS count	EXP count	Residual	Std Resid
GROUP	CONTROL				
NCOLD	0				
SEX	MALE	18.0	18.0	.00	.00
SEX	FEMALE	29.0	29.0	.00	.00
NCOLD	1				
SEX	MALE	43.0	43.0	.00	.00
SEX	FEMALE	70.0	70.0	.00	.00
NCOLD	2				
SEX	MALE	19.0	19.0	.00	.00
SEX	FEMALE	37.0	37.0	.00	.00
NCOLD	3				
SEX	MALE	12.0	12.0	.00	.00
SEX	FEMALE	32.0	32.0	.00	.00
GROUP	WITNESS				
NCOLD	0				
SEX	MALE	14.0	14.0	.00	.00
SEX	FEMALE	15.0	15.0	.00	.00
NCOLD	1				
SEX	MALE	20.0	20.0	.00	.00
SEX	FEMALE	34.0	34.0	.00	.00
NCOLD	2				
SEX	MALE	15.0	15.0	.00	.00
SEX	FEMALE	16.0	16.0	.00	.00
NCOLD	3				
SEX	MALE	7.0	7.0	.00	.00
SEX	FEMALE	13.0	13.0	.00	.00
GROUP	NON-INJU				
NCOLD	0				
SEX	MALE	17.0	17.0	.00	.00
SEX	FEMALE	2.0	2.0	.00	.00
NCOLD	1				
SEX	MALE	33.0	33.0	.00	.00
SEX	FEMALE	19.0	19.0	.00	.00
NCOLD	2				
SEX	MALE	22.0	22.0	.00	.00
SEX	FEMALE	19.0	19.0	.00	.00
NCOLD	3				
SEX	MALE	7.0	7.0	.00	.00
SEX	FEMALE	6.0	6.0	.00	.00
GROUP	INJURED				
NCOLD	0				
SEX	MALE	1.0	1.0	.00	.00
SEX	FEMALE	7.0	7.0	.00	.00
NCOLD	1				
SEX	MALE	4.0	4.0	.00	.00
SEX	FEMALE	8.0	8.0	.00	.00
NCOLD	2				
SEX	MALE	5.0	5.0	.00	.00
SEX	FEMALE	8.0	8.0	.00	.00
NCOLD	3				
SEX	MALE	3.0	3.0	.00	.00
SEX	FEMALE	2.0	2.0	.00	.00

Following the observed and expected frequencies and residuals are the goodness-of-fit statistics. Again, because this is a saturated model, the chi-square fit statistics equal 0, indicating perfect fit.

Figure 15-5
Goodness-of-fit test statistics

```
Likelihood ratio chi square =      .00000    DF = 0   P = 1.000
            Pearson chi square =   .00000    DF = 0   P = 1.000
```

The next table helps us assess the level of complexity required in our model. It tests the hypothesis that the *k*-way and higher-order effects are 0. We can see that the third-order effect ($X*Y*Z$) is not significantly different from 0 at the 5% level ($G^2 = 12.999$, $p = 0.1626$) and thus could be omitted from the model without unduly reducing model fit. The second-order effects ($X*Y$, $X*Z$, and $Y*Z$) and first-order effects (X, Y, and Z), however, appear to be significantly different from 0, so we must keep these levels in order to maintain model fit.

Figure 15-6
Tests that k-way and higher-order effects are 0

K	DF	L.R. Chisq	Prob	Pearson Chisq	Prob	Iteration
3	9	12.999	.1626	12.121	.2066	3
2	24	55.247	.0003	51.335	.0010	2
1	31	343.028	.0000	384.788	.0000	0

The next table reports the contribution of each order of effect by itself, as opposed to the previous table, which tests the contribution of all levels at or above the level being tested. For our example, the statistics reported for the second-order effects in Figure 15-6 test whether the model is still accurate, omitting both second- and third-order effects. In Figure 15-7, the statistics given for second-order effects consider the second-order effects by themselves. This can be seen clearly by noting that the sum of G^2 values for the second-order and third-order effects equals the G^2 for the second-order effects from the previous table (within rounding error): 42.247 + 12.999 = 55.246.

Figure 15-7
Tests that k-way effects are 0

```
K     DF   L.R. Chisq   Prob   Pearson Chisq   Prob   Iteration

1      7    287.781    .0000        333.453    .0000         0
2     15     42.247    .0002         39.214    .0006         0
3      9     12.999    .1626         12.121    .2066         0
```

Partial associations allow you to test the significance of each individual effect in the model. There is a term for each effect in the model, giving the degrees of freedom, the partial chi-square, the probability associated with the chi-square, and the number of iterations required to solve for the partial association. In general, terms with partial associations that do not differ from 0 (that is, that have a nonsignificant partial chi-square) can be omitted from the model without sacrificing too much predictive accuracy. In this case, it seems that the *GROUP*NCOLDS* interaction and the *SEX*NCOLDS* interaction could safely be omitted from the model.

Figure 15-8
Tests of partial associations

```
Tests of PARTIAL associations.

Effect Name                       DF   Partial Chisq   Prob   Iter


GROUP*NCOLD                        9          10.806   .2893     2
GROUP*SEX                          3          28.033   .0000     2
NCOLD*SEX                          3           3.147   .3696     2
GROUP                              3         188.705   .0000     2
NCOLD                              3          88.398   .0000     2
SEX                                1          10.679   .0011     2
```

The last section of output reports the parameter estimates for the saturated model. (An excerpt is shown in Figure 15-9.) Each coefficient is reported, along with its standard error, *z* value, and confidence interval. The parameters are reported as follows:

■ For main effects, there will be $k - 1$ parameters, where k is the number of categories for the main effect in question. In our example, the *GROUP* effect has three parameters $(4 - 1)$. They are numbered starting with the first category and ending with the next to the last category. The last category is redundant because of the constraint that the sum of the parameter estimates for a particular effect must equal 1.

■ For interaction effects, there will be $(k_1 - 1) \times (k_2 - 1) \times ... \times (k_n - 1)$ parameters, where $k_1 ... k_n$ are the number of categories for variables $1 ... n$. In this example, for the *GROUP*NCOLD*SEX* interaction, there are

$(4-1) \times (4-1) \times (2-1) = 9$ parameters. As with main effects, the last category of each variable is redundant and is omitted from the parameters table. Parameters are labeled based on the order of categories in each variable involved in the interaction, with categories in the last variable cycling the fastest and those for the first variable cycling slowest. See Figure 15-10 for an example from the current data set for the three-way interaction *GROUP*NCOLD*SEX*. (Don't be confused by the fact that the last variable, *SEX*, has the value *Male* for all parameters; this is because the variable has only two values, so one of them is redundant and only the first category is used.)

Figure 15-9
Estimates for parameters

GROUP*NCOLD*SEX

Parameter	Coeff.	Std. Err.	Z-Value	Lower 95 CI	Upper 95 CI
1	.0192792161	.16651	.11579	-.30707	.34563
2	.1149988198	.11772	.97690	-.11573	.34573
3	.0123338705	.13014	.09478	-.24273	.26740
4	.0572037498	.18066	.31663	-.29689	.41130
5	-.0727088092	.13559	-.53623	-.33847	.19305
6	.1472630100	.14812	.99418	-.14306	.43759
7	.6272222983	.25041	2.50474	.13641	1.11803
8	-.0658713615	.14959	-.44033	-.35908	.22733
9	-.2816769613	.15418	-1.82695	-.58387	.02051

Figure 15-10
Parameters for GROUP*NCOLD*SEX

	Represents cases with these values		
Parameter	**GROUP**	**NCOLD**	**SEX**
1	1 (Control)	0	0 (Male)
2	1 (Control)	1	0 (Male)
3	1 (Control)	2	0 (Male)
4	2 (Witness)	0	0 (Male)
5	2 (Witness)	1	0 (Male)
6	2 (Witness)	2	0 (Male)
7	3 (Non-injured)	0	0 (Male)
8	3 (Non-injured)	1	0 (Male)
9	3 (Non-injured)	2	0 (Male)

Example 2
Using Backward Elimination to Select a Suitable Model

In this example, we use the same data set and examine the same relationships. This time, however, we let the computer make decisions about which effects to include or exclude, and we can evaluate the fit of our final model.

Backward elimination uses a stepwise procedure to find a parsimonious model of cell frequencies. The procedure starts with a saturated model and examines the highest order of effects (interactions) to see if any can be removed without significantly weakening predictive power. If an effect can be removed, a nested model without the effect is evaluated, and the remaining effects are examined to see whether any can be removed. The process repeats until no more effects can be removed without sacrificing predictive power.

To produce this output, from the menus choose:

Analyze
  Loglinear
    Model Selection...

Click Reset to restore dialog box defaults, and then select:

▸ Factor(s): group, ncold, sex
  Define Range for each variable

⊙ Use backward elimination

Model...
⊙ Saturated

Options...
  Model Criteria
  Delta: 0

The first portion of the output, regarding the saturated model, is identical to the output given above and will not be repeated in this discussion. After the table shown in Figure 15-7, you will see the first step of the backward elimination, shown in Figure 15-11.

Figure 15-11
Backward elimination

```
Backward Elimination (p = .050) for DESIGN 1 with generating class

   GROUP*NCOLD*SEX

 Likelihood ratio chi square =       .00000   DF = 0  P = 1.000

 - - - - - - - - - - - - - - - - - - - - - - - - - - - - - - - - - - -


 If Deleted Simple Effect is           DF   L.R. Chisq Change    Prob  Iter

   GROUP*NCOLD*SEX                       9              12.999   .1626    3
```

All of the effects in the saturated model are nested within the third-order interaction, so only that term can be considered for elimination at this point. Since the chi-square change for that term is not significantly different from 0, the computer deletes this term and generates the next model. After omitting the third-order interaction, the second-order effects are no longer nested under another effect, so they can be considered for removal.

Figure 15-12
Step 1

```
   The best model has generating class

       GROUP*NCOLD
       GROUP*SEX
       NCOLD*SEX

 Likelihood ratio chi square =    12.99921   DF = 9  P =  .163

 - - - - - - - - - - - - - - - - - - - - - - - - - - - - - - - - - - -


 If Deleted Simple Effect is           DF   L.R. Chisq Change    Prob  Iter

   GROUP*NCOLD                           9              10.806   .2893    2
   GROUP*SEX                             3              28.033   .0000    2
   NCOLD*SEX                             3               3.147   .3696    2
```

The *NCOLD*SEX* interaction has the least predictive value in this model (as measured by the probability value of the chi-square change statistic), so it is removed.

Figure 15-13
Step 2

```
The best model has generating class

     GROUP*NCOLD
     GROUP*SEX

 Likelihood ratio chi square =    16.14579   DF = 12  P =  .185

- - - - - - - - - - - - - - - - - - - - - - - - - - - - - - - - - - - - - -


If Deleted Simple Effect is           DF   L.R. Chisq Change   Prob  Iter

GROUP*NCOLD                             9              10.937   .2801    2
GROUP*SEX                               3              28.164   .0000    2
```

The next model, with the *NCOLD*SEX* interaction excluded, is evaluated. As we can see from the chi-square change statistic, the *GROUP*NCOLD* interaction term does not improve the model significantly, so it is removed.

Figure 15-14
Step 3

```
 The best model has generating class

     GROUP*SEX
     NCOLD

 Likelihood ratio chi square =    27.08264   DF = 21  P =  .168

- - - - - - - - - - - - - - - - - - - - - - - - - - - - - - - - - - - - - -


If Deleted Simple Effect is          DF   L.R. Chisq Change   Prob  Iter

GROUP*SEX                             3              28.164   .0000    2
NCOLD                                 3              88.398   .0000    2
```

At this point, none of the remaining effects can be excluded without weakening the predictive power of the model. The process stops, and the final model is reported. The output includes observed and expected frequencies, residuals and standardized residuals for each cell, and goodness-of-fit statistics.

Figure 15-15

Observed and expected frequencies and residuals

Observed, Expected Frequencies and Residuals.

Factor	Code	OBS count	EXP count	Residual	Std Resid
GROUP	CONTROL				
NCOLD	0				
SEX	MALE	18.0	17.0	.99	.24
SEX	FEMALE	29.0	31.1	-2.07	-.37
NCOLD	1				
SEX	MALE	43.0	38.2	4.85	.78
SEX	FEMALE	70.0	69.7	.33	.04
NCOLD	2				
SEX	MALE	19.0	23.3	-4.29	-.89
SEX	FEMALE	37.0	42.5	-5.53	-.85
NCOLD	3				
SEX	MALE	12.0	13.5	-1.54	-.42
SEX	FEMALE	32.0	24.7	7.27	1.46
GROUP	WITNESS				
NCOLD	0				
SEX	MALE	14.0	10.4	3.64	1.13
SEX	FEMALE	15.0	14.4	.58	.15
NCOLD	1				
SEX	MALE	20.0	23.2	-3.22	-.67
SEX	FEMALE	34.0	32.3	1.65	.29
NCOLD	2				
SEX	MALE	15.0	14.2	.82	.22
SEX	FEMALE	16.0	19.7	-3.75	-.84
NCOLD	3				
SEX	MALE	7.0	8.2	-1.24	-.43
SEX	FEMALE	13.0	11.5	1.52	.45
GROUP	NON-INJU				
NCOLD	0				
SEX	MALE	17.0	14.6	2.39	.63
SEX	FEMALE	2.0	8.5	-6.51	-2.23
NCOLD	1				
SEX	MALE	33.0	32.8	.24	.04
SEX	FEMALE	19.0	19.1	-.08	-.02
NCOLD	2				
SEX	MALE	22.0	20.0	2.00	.45
SEX	FEMALE	19.0	11.6	7.36	2.16
NCOLD	3				
SEX	MALE	7.0	11.6	-4.63	-1.36
SEX	FEMALE	6.0	6.8	-.77	-.30
GROUP	INJURED				
NCOLD	0				
SEX	MALE	1.0	2.4	-1.40	-.91
SEX	FEMALE	7.0	4.6	2.38	1.11
NCOLD	1				
SEX	MALE	4.0	5.4	-1.39	-.60
SEX	FEMALE	8.0	10.4	-2.37	-.74
NCOLD	2				
SEX	MALE	5.0	3.3	1.71	.94
SEX	FEMALE	8.0	6.3	1.67	.66
NCOLD	3				
SEX	MALE	3.0	1.9	1.09	.79
SEX	FEMALE	2.0	3.7	-1.68	-.88

Figure 15-16
Goodness-of-fit test statistics

```
Likelihood ratio chi square =    27.08264    DF = 21  P =  .168
            Pearson chi square =    25.41861    DF = 21  P =  .229
```

The likelihood-ratio chi-square for this reduced model is not significant, indicating that the model provides a reasonably good fit for the data. Notice also that the three effects that were eliminated from the saturated model (*GROUP*NCOLD*SEX*, *NCOLD*SEX*, and *GROUP*NCOLD*) were the same effects that we would have dropped, based on the partial chi-square statistics reported for the saturated model in "Examining a Saturated Model" on p. 153.

From here, you might examine this final model using the General Loglinear Analysis procedure. That procedure will report parameter estimates for the unsaturated model, as well as allow you to save residuals and predicted values. You can use these saved variables to evaluate your solution in more detail and to look for potential problems, such as outliers or bias in your estimates. You might also consider using the Logit Loglinear Analysis procedure to design a model where one variable is cast as a dependent variable to be predicted by the other variables. In the case of this example, you might want to see if you can predict number of colds (*NCOLD*), based on exposure to the incident (*GROUP*) and sex (*SEX*).

General Loglinear Analysis Examples

The General Loglinear Analysis (Genlog) procedure uses the Generalized Linear Model (GLM) approach to fit loglinear and logit models. Loglinear models are used to study association patterns among categorical variables, sometimes with auxiliary information provided by covariates. For example, you might study the toxicity of various concentrations of a medicine, taking into account the dosage.

Categorical data and loglinear analysis are used extensively in marketing research and the social sciences as well as in medicine and the biological sciences. Table 16-1 illustrates typical data that can be analyzed with loglinear techniques.

Table 16-1
Melanoma occurrence by age group and region

Age group	Melanoma cases, n_{ij}		Estimated population at risk, N_{ij}	
	Northern	Southern	Northern	Southern
less than 35	61	64	2880262	1074246
35–44	76	75	564535	220407
45–54	98	68	592983	198119
55–64	104	63	450740	134084
65–74	63	45	270908	70708
75 +	80	27	161850	34233

In this example, the variables are categorical and the data represent counts. One way to analyze these data would be to use the Crosstabs procedure to display a contingency table and calculate measures of association; this method deals with two variables at a time and does not estimate parameters. Loglinear analysis goes further by allowing models that take into account several variables at once and multiple categories in each variable. Loglinear analysis, in addition to testing hypotheses, also produces estimates of parameters.

In linear regression analysis, the variable to be predicted is continuous. The regression model equation has the form

$$y = B_0 + B_1 x_1 + B_2 x_2 + \dots$$ Equation 16-1

The dependent variable y is expressed as a linear combination of independent factors and covariates.

In loglinear analysis, the variable to be predicted is a count (which appears on the left, as in the regression model), and the original equation is exponential, as in

$$m = e^{B_0 + B_1 x_1 + B_2 x_2 + \dots}$$ Equation 16-2

When the natural logarithm of both sides of the equation is taken, a linear equation results:

$$\ln(m) = B_0 + B_1 x_1 + B_2 x_2 + \dots$$ Equation 16-3

The log of the counts is expressed as a linear combination of factors and covariates. However, it is easy to convert the log values back to counts by calculating the exponentials. This type of conversion is demonstrated in the examples.

Several examples are analyzed in this chapter, and many more are available in the sources cited. Logit loglinear examples are in Chapter 17. The current chapter begins with two examples of parameter estimation and then provides theoretical background information, followed by more examples. The sections appear in the following order:

Parameter Estimation Examples

Example 1: Complete table. Data from a report of automobile accidents in Florida are used to determine the relationship between wearing a seat belt and the type of injury sustained. The odds ratio indicates significant evidence of a relationship.

Example 2: Incomplete table. The severity level of disabilities suffered by stroke patients was recorded at admission and at discharge. Some cells in the table are necessarily empty because of hospital rules on discharge, and these cells are treated as structural zeros. The study indicates that the final state is independent of the initial state.

Background Information

- Distribution assumptions
- Cell structure variable
- Steps in a general loglinear analysis

Model Diagnosis

- Goodness-of-fit statistics
- Residuals

Additional Examples

Example 3: Survival parametric model. The General Loglinear Analysis procedure is used to fit a special case of the proportional hazard (PH) model where survival times have an exponential distribution. The structure variable is used to include an offset term in a study of remission times for leukemia patients.

Example 4: Table standardization. The method of adjustment of marginal tables is applied to estimate population counts whose marginal distributions match those of a previous census.

Example 5: Poisson loglinear regression. The data show new melanoma cases and the population at risk for a two-year period, tabulated by areas and age groups. The generalized log-odds ratio (GLOR) values are calculated and used to compare age groups and areas.

Parameter Estimation

Analyses of a complete table and an incomplete table are illustrated in the next two sections. A complete table has observed counts for every cell, whereas an incomplete table has some empty cells, designated as **structural zeros**. In the example of an incomplete table (Table 16-3 on p. 173), the structural zeros are denoted by hyphens in the cells. For more information on structural zeros, see "Structural Zero Indicator" on p. 181.

In these examples, we are interested in estimating values of the parameters in the loglinear equations. The Genlog procedure first constructs a design matrix of all possible effects in the model equations and then applies a redundancy check to determine which columns in the design matrix are redundant in producing a unique solution to the equations (see "Design Matrix" on p. 182). The Genlog procedure adopts the easy-to-interpret convention of setting the redundant (aliased) parameters to 0.

Odds and the Log-Odds Ratio

The **odds** of an event occurring are defined as the ratio of the probability that the event will occur to the probability that it will not. For example, the odds that an ace will be drawn from a deck of 52 cards are

$$\frac{4/52}{48/52} = \frac{1}{12}$$

whereas the probability of drawing an ace is

$$\frac{4}{52} = \frac{1}{13}$$

The ratio of two odds is called the **odds ratio**. When dealing with equations involving exponentials, it is often useful to take the natural log (ln) of the exponential expression to evaluate the parameters. The log of the odds ratio is called the **log-odds ratio**. Once the natural log of an exponential expression is calculated, you can evaluate the expression by finding the value of e raised to the power you calculated for the log, where $e = 2.718$, approximately. Thus, if the log-odds ratio is 1.98, the odds ratio is

$$e^{1.98} = 7.21$$

Example 1
Complete Table

Consider Table 16-2, which is a two-way classification table showing the type of injury sustained in an automobile accident and whether seat belts were worn. The data are based on the 1988 automobile accident report of the Florida State Department of Highway Safety and Motor Vehicles cited by Agresti (1990). The Genlog procedure can be used to determine the relationship between wearing a seat belt and the type of injury sustained.

Table 16-2
1988 Florida automobile accident data

Wearing a seat belt?	Injury type	
	Fatal	Nonfatal
No	1601	162527
Yes	510	412368

Figure 16-1 shows the same data as they appear in the Data Editor.

Figure 16-1
Data structure for accident data

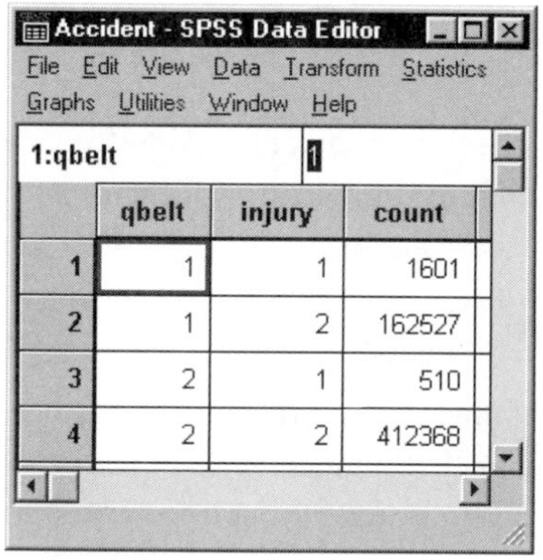

The variables to be analyzed are *qbelt* (whether a seat belt is worn) and *injury* (injury type). The variable *count* gives the number of cases for each combination of *qbelt* and *injury*. The file is weighted by *count*, simulating a data set in which there are 1601 cases with *qbelt* = 1 and *injury* = 1, 162,527 cases with *qbelt* = 1 and *injury* = 2, and so on. This way of entering categorical data using a weight variable is very common and often convenient. The analysis is the same whether the data are entered this way or whether the file actually contains all of the individual cases. To begin the analysis, from the menus choose:

Data
  Weight Cases...
  ▶ Weight cases by: count

Analyze
  Loglinear
    General...

  ▶ Factor(s): qbelt injury

Options...
  Display
      ☑ Frequencies
      ☑ Residuals
      ☑ Estimates
    Plots: deselect all plots
    Criteria
      Delta: 0

The default model is a **saturated design**, which includes all main effects and interactions involving factor variables. The natural logarithm of the expected number of fatal injuries without seat belts is expressed as

$$\ln(m_{11}) = \mu + \alpha_1 + \beta_1 + \gamma_{11}$$

Equation 16-4

where μ is the overall intercept, α_1 is the main-effects term corresponding to the first category of *qbelt* (not wearing a seat belt), β_1 is the main-effects term corresponding to the first category of *injury* (fatal injury), and γ_{11} is the interaction term corresponding to the first category of *qbelt* and the first category of *injury*. Similarly, the natural logarithms of the other expected numbers are expressed as

$$\ln(m_{12}) = \mu + \alpha_1 + \beta_2 + \gamma_{12}$$
$$\ln(m_{21}) = \mu + \alpha_2 + \beta_1 + \gamma_{21}$$
$$\ln(m_{22}) = \mu + \alpha_2 + \beta_2 + \gamma_{22}$$

Equation 16-5

The first design matrix constructed by the Genlog procedure has all of the parameters represented. In the current model, there are nine parameters but only four cells. To get a unique solution to the equations, some constraints must be applied. Before estimating parameters, the Genlog procedure uses a SWEEP process to identify aliased columns. The parameters for these aliased columns are set to 0 (see "Incorporating Cell Structure

Information" on p. 184). In this example, the Genlog procedure identifies the following five parameters as aliased and sets their values to 0:

$$\alpha_2 = 0; \quad \beta_2 = 0; \quad \gamma_{12} = 0; \quad \gamma_{21} = 0; \quad \gamma_{22} = 0 \qquad \text{Equation 16-6}$$

In Figure 16-2, the aliased parameters are indicated by an x in the column labeled *Aliased*.

Figure 16-2
Correspondence between parameters and terms of the design

```
Correspondence Between Parameters and Terms of the Design

Parameter   Aliased   Term

     1                 Constant
     2                 [QBELT = 1]
     3          x      [QBELT = 2]
     4                 [INJURY = 1]
     5          x      [INJURY = 2]
     6                 [QBELT = 1]*[INJURY = 1]
     7          x      [QBELT = 1]*[INJURY = 2]
     8          x      [QBELT = 2]*[INJURY = 1]
     9          x      [QBELT = 2]*[INJURY = 2]

Note: 'x' indicates an aliased (or a redundant) parameter.
      These parameters are set to zero.
```

If 0 is substituted for aliased parameters in Equation 16-5, the model equations become

$$\ln(m_{11}) = \mu + \alpha_1 + \beta_1 + \gamma_{11}$$
$$\ln(m_{12}) = \mu + \alpha_1$$
$$\ln(m_{21}) = \mu + \beta_1 \qquad \text{Equation 16-7}$$
$$\ln(m_{22}) = \mu$$

From Equation 16-7,

$$\mu = \ln(m_{22})$$
$$\alpha_1 = \ln(m_{12}) - \ln(m_{22}) = \ln(m_{12}/m_{22})$$
$$\beta_1 = \ln(m_{21}) - \ln(m_{22}) = \ln(m_{21}/m_{22}) \qquad \text{Equation 16-8}$$
$$\gamma_{11} = \ln(m_{11}) - \ln(m_{12}) - (\ln(m_{21}) - \ln(m_{22})) = \ln\left(\frac{m_{11}m_{22}}{m_{12}m_{21}}\right)$$

By definition of the log-odds, α_1 is the expected log-odds between the first and second categories of *qbelt* within the second category of *injury*, β_1 is the expected log-odds between the first and second categories of *injury* within the second category of *qbelt*, and γ_{11} is the expected log-odds ratio of the table. If *qbelt* and *injury* are independent, the odds ratio is 1, which corresponds to a log-odds ratio equal to 0. Hence, γ_{11} is a measure of the strength of association between *qbelt* and *injury*. Since the design is saturated, the expected counts equal the observed counts. Therefore, the parameter estimates are

$$\hat{\mu} = \ln(412368) = 12.9297$$

$$\hat{\alpha}_1 = \ln\left(\frac{162527}{412368}\right) = -0.9311$$

$$\hat{\beta}_1 = \ln\left(\frac{510}{412368}\right) = -6.6953$$

Equation 16-9

$$\hat{\gamma}_{11} = \ln\left(\frac{1601 \times 412368}{162527 \times 510}\right) = 2.0750$$

By referring to the parameter designations in Figure 16-2, you can compare these calculations with the parameter estimates of the Genlog procedure shown in Figure 16-3.

Figure 16-3
Parameter estimates for the saturated model

```
Parameter Estimates

                                                  Asymptotic 95% CI
Parameter    Estimate       SE    Z-value      Lower      Upper
        1    12.9297     .0016    8302.90      12.93      12.93
        2     -.9311     .0029    -317.90       -.94       -.93
        3     .0000         .          .          .          .
        4    -6.6953     .0443    -151.11      -6.78      -6.61
        5     .0000         .          .          .          .
        6    2.0750      .0509      40.74       1.98       2.17
        7     .0000         .          .          .          .
        8     .0000         .          .          .          .
        9     .0000         .          .          .          .
```

Parameter 1 corresponds to the constant μ, parameter 2 corresponds to α_1, and so on. Parameter 6 is γ_{11}, the interaction term between not wearing a seat belt (*qbelt* 1) and fatal injury (*injury* 1).

The asymptotic 95% confidence limits for the sample log-odds ratio, as shown for parameter 6 in Figure 16-3, are 1.98 and 2.17, corresponding to an odds ratio between 7.21 and 8.80, since

$$e^{1.98} = 7.21 \qquad \text{and} \qquad e^{2.17} = 8.80$$

Equation 16-10

This means that at the 95% confidence level, the odds of fatal injury to nonfatal injury for passengers without seat belts is between 7.21 and 8.80 times the corresponding odds when seat belts are worn. From these data, therefore, there is significant evidence that wearing seat belts does help to avoid fatal injury.

Example 2
Incomplete Table

Bishop and Fienberg (1969) present data collected at Massachusetts General Hospital on the severity of disability suffered by 121 stroke patients. These data are shown in Table 16-3. On admission and again on discharge, each patient was assigned a severity level according to his or her physical disability following a stroke. There are five distinct severity levels, labeled from A through E, with A being the least severe and E, the most severe. Since no patient was discharged who did not show any sign of improvement, cells representing patients whose final states were more severe than their initial states are necessarily 0. These are **structural zeros**, which are different from zero values that just happen to occur in the data. The Genlog procedure can be used to investigate the relationship between the initial state and the final state for stroke patients who are released from the hospital.

Table 16-3
Initial and final severity levels of stroke patients

Initial state	Final state					Totals
	A	**B**	**C**	**D**	**E**	
A	5	-	-	-	-	5
B	4	5	-	-	-	9
C	6	4	4	-	-	14
D	9	10	4	1	-	24
E	11	23	12	15	8	69
Totals	35	42	20	16	8	121

Bishop et al. (1975) fit a quasi-independence model to these data. Under a quasi-independence assumption, the initial state and final state are independent, conditional on the nonstructural zero cells.

The data structure is shown in Figure 16-4. Variables *initial* and *final* are coded with numbers that represent the states *A, B, C, D,* and *E*. Variable *qtake* indicates whether the cell is a structural zero (0) or not (1).

Figure 16-4
Data structure for stroke data

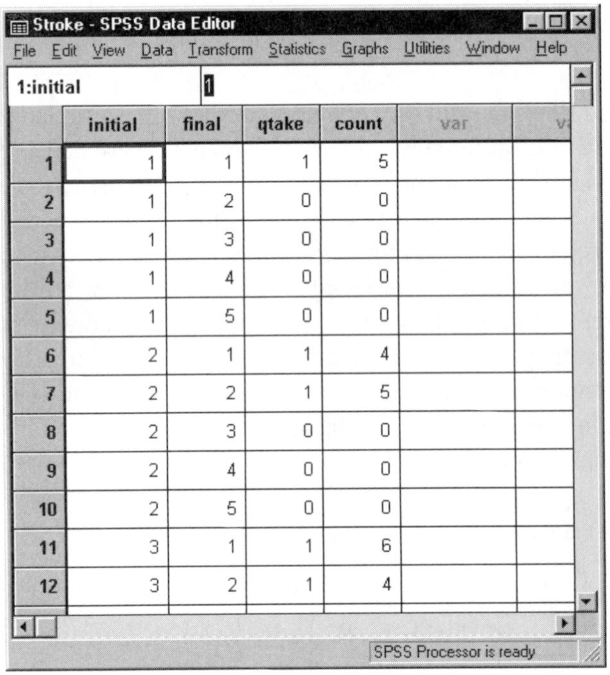

	initial	final	qtake	count	var	v
1	1	1	1	5		
2	1	2	0	0		
3	1	3	0	0		
4	1	4	0	0		
5	1	5	0	0		
6	2	1	1	4		
7	2	2	1	5		
8	2	3	0	0		
9	2	4	0	0		
10	2	5	0	0		
11	3	1	1	6		
12	3	2	1	4		

The data are weighted by *count*. Denoting the expected cell count for the *i*th initial state and the *j*th final state as m_{ij}, the model equations under the quasi-independence model are

$$\ln(m_{ij}) = \mu + \alpha_i + \beta_j; \quad i = 1,2,3,4,5; \text{ and } j = 1,\dots, i \qquad \text{Equation 16-11}$$

where μ is the intercept term, α_i is the main-effects term corresponding to the *i*th category of *initial*, and β_j is the main-effects term corresponding to the *j*th category of *final*. Due to intrinsic aliasing among the model equations, the Genlog procedure identifies the following two parameters as aliased and sets their values to 0:

$$\alpha_5 = 0 \quad \text{and} \quad \beta_5 = 0 \qquad \text{Equation 16-12}$$

The equations represented in Equation 16-11, reexpressed in terms of the nonaliased parameters, can be written as follows:

$$\ln(m_{11}) = \mu + \alpha_1 + \beta_1$$
$$\ln(m_{21}) = \mu + \alpha_2 + \beta_1$$
$$\ln(m_{22}) = \mu + \alpha_2 + \beta_2$$
$$\ln(m_{31}) = \mu + \alpha_3 + \beta_1$$
$$\ln(m_{32}) = \mu + \alpha_3 + \beta_2$$
$$\ln(m_{33}) = \mu + \alpha_3 + \beta_3$$
$$\ln(m_{41}) = \mu + \alpha_4 + \beta_1$$
$$\ln(m_{42}) = \mu + \alpha_4 + \beta_2 \qquad \text{Equation 16-13}$$
$$\ln(m_{43}) = \mu + \alpha_4 + \beta_3$$
$$\ln(m_{44}) = \mu + \alpha_4 + \beta_4$$
$$\ln(m_{51}) = \mu + \beta_1$$
$$\ln(m_{52}) = \mu + \beta_2$$
$$\ln(m_{53}) = \mu + \beta_3$$
$$\ln(m_{54}) = \mu + \beta_4$$
$$\ln(m_{55}) = \mu$$

Under the quasi-independence assumption, the ratio of counts between any two final states, unless prohibited, is the same for all initial states, and vice versa. From Equation 16-13, you can derive the following:

$$\frac{m_{41}}{m_{51}} = \frac{m_{42}}{m_{52}} = \frac{m_{43}}{m_{53}} = \frac{m_{44}}{m_{54}} = e^{\alpha_4} \qquad \text{Equation 16-14}$$

and

$$\frac{m_{21}}{m_{22}} = \frac{m_{31}}{m_{32}} = \frac{m_{41}}{m_{42}} = \frac{m_{51}}{m_{52}} = e^{\beta_1 - \beta_2} \qquad \text{Equation 16-15}$$

Equation 16-14 implies that the ratios of the number of patients with initial state D (*initial* = 4) to initial state E (*initial* = 5) are the same across all possible final states. Similarly, Equation 16-15 signifies that the ratios of the number of patients with final state A (*final* = 1) to final state B (*final* = 2) are the same for all initial states.

To fit this quasi-independence model, from the menus choose:

Data
  Weight Cases...
  ▶ Weight cases by: count

Next, choose:

Analyze
  Loglinear
    General...

▶ Factor(s): initial final

Cell Structure: qtake

Model...
  ⊙ Custom
  ▶ Terms in Model (Main effects): final initial

Options...
  Display
    ☑ Frequencies
    ☑ Estimates
  Plots: deselect all plots

The fitted values are shown in Figure 16-5.

Figure 16-5

Table information for stroke data

```
Table Information
                      Observed              Expected
Factor    Value     Count        %         Count        %
INITIAL     A
FINAL       A        5.00  (    4.13)        5.00  (    4.13)
FINAL       B         .00  (     .00)         .00  (     .00)
FINAL       C         .00  (     .00)         .00  (     .00)
FINAL       D         .00  (     .00)         .00  (     .00)
FINAL       E         .00  (     .00)         .00  (     .00)
INITIAL     B
FINAL       A        4.00  (    3.31)        3.75  (    3.10)
FINAL       B        5.00  (    4.13)        5.25  (    4.34)
FINAL       C         .00  (     .00)         .00  (     .00)
FINAL       D         .00  (     .00)         .00  (     .00)
FINAL       E         .00  (     .00)         .00  (     .00)
INITIAL     C
FINAL       A        6.00  (    4.96)        4.43  (    3.66)
FINAL       B        4.00  (    3.31)        6.20  (    5.12)
FINAL       C        4.00  (    3.31)        3.37  (    2.79)
FINAL       D         .00  (     .00)         .00  (     .00)
FINAL       E         .00  (     .00)         .00  (     .00)
INITIAL     D
FINAL       A        9.00  (    7.44)        6.16  (    5.09)
FINAL       B       10.00  (    8.26)        8.63  (    7.13)
FINAL       C        4.00  (    3.31)        4.69  (    3.88)
FINAL       D        1.00  (     .83)        4.52  (    3.73)
FINAL       E         .00  (     .00)         .00  (     .00)
INITIAL     E
FINAL       A       11.00  (    9.09)       15.66  (   12.94)
FINAL       B       23.00  (   19.01)       21.92  (   18.12)
FINAL       C       12.00  (    9.92)       11.93  (    9.86)
FINAL       D       15.00  (   12.40)       11.48  (    9.49)
FINAL       E        8.00  (    6.61)        8.00  (    6.61)
```

To test the goodness of fit of the model, the Genlog procedure calculates chi-square statistics, as shown in Figure 16-6. The chi-square statistics are derived from comparing the fitted cell counts with the observed cell counts. Since the significance is above 0.05, the quasi-independence model fits the data fairly well.

Figure 16-6

Goodness-of-fit statistics for stroke data

```
Goodness-of-fit Statistics

                    Chi-Square      DF       Sig.

Likelihood Ratio      9.5958         6       .1427
        Pearson       8.3691         6       .2123
```

Therefore, a patient's final state at discharge is independent of his or her initial state, given the fact that a patient is discharged only if the current state is better than the initial state.

Figure 16-7 shows the parameter reference table, and Figure 16-8 shows the parameter estimates.

Figure 16-7

Parameter reference table for stroke data

```
Correspondence Between Parameters and Terms of the Design
Parameter   Aliased   Term
     1                 Constant
     2                 [FINAL = 1]
     3                 [FINAL = 2]
     4                 [FINAL = 3]
     5                 [FINAL = 4]
     6          x      [FINAL = 5]
     7                 [INITIAL = 1]
     8                 [INITIAL = 2]
     9                 [INITIAL = 3]
    10                 [INITIAL = 4]
    11          x      [INITIAL = 5]
Note:  'x' indicates an aliased (or a redundant) parameter.
       These parameters are set to zero.
```

Figure 16-8

Parameter estimates for stroke data under a quasi-independence model

Parameter Estimates

Parameter	Estimate	SE	Z-value	Asymptotic 95% CI Lower	Upper
1	2.0794	.3536	5.88	1.39	2.77
2	.6717	.4091	1.64	-.13	1.47
3	1.0082	.3973	2.54	.23	1.79
4	.3998	.4267	.94	-.44	1.24
5	.3614	.4383	.82	-.50	1.22
6	.0000	.	.	.	.
7	-1.1417	.4923	-2.32	-2.11	-.18
8	-1.4294	.3661	-3.90	-2.15	-.71
9	-1.2633	.3009	-4.20	-1.85	-.67
10	-.9328	.2410	-3.87	-1.41	-.46
11	.0000	.	.	.	.

From Figure 16-7, α_4 is parameter 10. Its value is -0.9328. Thus, under the quasi-independence assumption, the number of patients with initial state D is

$$e^{-0.9328} = 0.39$$ Equation 16-16

times the number of patients with initial state E.

Again from Figure 16-7, β_1 is parameter 2 and β_2 is parameter 3. Using the values in Figure 16-8,

$$e^{\beta_1 - \beta_2} = e^{0.6717 - 1.0082} = 0.71$$ Equation 16-17

This calculation indicates that the number of patients with final state A is 0.71 times the number of patients with final state B, given that the initial state is B or lower.

Background Information

The following sections (p. 179 through p. 184) include technical background information about loglinear analysis and the types of data distributions. You may be able to follow the examples in this chapter without reading this material.

Distribution Assumptions

The Genlog procedure can be used to fit a model under either of two distribution assumptions—the **Poisson loglinear model** or the **multinomial loglinear model**. The multinomial loglinear model is a special case of the **product multinomial loglinear model** (logit model), which has its own dialog box in SPSS. For a detailed explanation of these distribution assumptions, see Agresti (1990).

A general loglinear analysis analyzes the frequency counts of observations falling into each cross-classification category. Each cross-classification constitutes a **cell**, and each categorical variable is called a **factor**. Thus, the dependent variable is the number of cases (frequency) in a cell of the crosstabulation, and the explanatory variables are factors and covariates. A general loglinear model formulates each cell count as the product of a cell-specific constant and the exponential of a linear combination of parameters. The parameters are identified by association with the categorical variables and the covariates in a design matrix (see "Design Matrix" on p. 182). The mathematical model for the expected count in a cell is given by

$$m_i = z_i e^{x_i \beta}; \qquad i = 1\dots, r \qquad \text{Equation 16-18}$$

where m_i is the expected cell count for the ith cell, z_i is the cell-specific constant, x_i is the ith row of the design matrix, β is the vector of parameters, and r is the number of cells.

Poisson Distribution

Under the Poisson distribution assumption:

- The total sample size is not fixed before the study, or the analysis is not conditional on the total sample size.

- The event of an observation being in a cell is statistically independent of the cell counts of other cells.

The joint probability density function of the cell counts (n_i) under the Poisson assumption is given by

$$\prod_{i=1}^{r} e^{-m_i} \frac{m_i^{n_i}}{n_i!}$$

Equation 16-19

Multinomial Distribution

Under the multinomial distribution assumption:

- The total sample size is fixed, or the analysis is conditional on the total sample size.
- The cell counts are not statistically independent.

For a multinomial distribution, the joint probability density function is given by

$$\frac{N!}{\prod_{i=1}^{r} n_i!} \prod_{i=1}^{r} \pi_i^{n_i}$$

Equation 16-20

where $\pi_i = m_i / N$.

Product Multinomial Distribution (Logit Model)

A special case of the **logit model** is the multinomial model. This model is appropriate when it is natural to regard one or more categorical variables as the response variables and the others as the explanatory variables. At each setting or combination of the categories of the explanatory variables, the subtotal sample size is fixed and the cell counts of the response variables follow a multinomial distribution. Furthermore, it is assumed that the collection of cell counts at different settings are statistically independent; thus, the joint distribution for the entire sample is the product of these independent multinomial distributions. Therefore, logit models are also called product multinomial loglinear models in this context.

The joint probability function for the product multinomial loglinear (logit) model is given by

$$\prod_{j=1}^{c}\prod_{i=1}^{r}\frac{N_j}{\prod_{i=1}^{r}n_{ij}!}\;\pi_{ij}^{n_{ij}}$$

Equation 16-21

where $\pi_{ij} = \dfrac{m_{ij}}{N_j}$, $N_j = \sum_{i=1}^{r} m_{ij}$, n_{ij} is the cell count, and c is the number of settings.

Cell Structure Variable

The cell structure variable is used to assign weights to the cells. It can be used for the following purposes:

- To suppress cells that you don't want to estimate by specifying structural zeros in the table (see "Incomplete Table" on p. 173).

- To include an offset term that appears in models for survival data, as illustrated in McCullagh and Nelder, 1989 (see "Survival Parametric Model" on p. 187).

- To adapt the General Loglinear Analysis procedure to fit the log-rate model described in Agresti, 1990 (see "Poisson Loglinear Regression" on p. 196).

- To implement the method of adjustment of marginal tables, as discussed in Haberman, 1979 (see "Table Standardization" on p. 192).

Details on fitting these models using the General Loglinear Analysis procedure are described in the sections cited.

Structural Zero Indicator

If the value of the cell structure variable is not positive for a cell, that particular cell is treated as a **structural zero** (called a "necessarily empty cell" by McCullagh and Nelder, 1989). Both the observed and expected counts for a structural zero are fixed as zeros. Although the cell still constitutes part of the contingency table, it is not used during the estimation.

If the cell count is 0 due to chance variation but its expected count is positive, the cell is treated as a **sampling zero** (called an "accidentally empty cell" by McCullagh and Nelder, 1989). A sampling zero is used in the estimation, and its expected cell count is estimated from the model. All cells whose cell structure values are positive are used in the estimation.

Structural zeros can occur when some combination of levels of the factors is *a priori* impossible. The subset of vegetarians who eat meat represent an example of this. In other situations, structural zeros are imposed to keep certain cells from entering into the analysis. An example is the fitting of a quasi-independence model to a square contingency table. A typical method of applying structural zeros is to declare the diagonal cells to be structural zeros and to use a cell structure variable to fit an independence model using only the off-diagonal cells.

Steps in a General Loglinear Analysis

A general loglinear analysis in SPSS performs the following steps:

- Constructs a design matrix from the user's specifications. It creates an over-parameterized design matrix, incorporates cell structure information, and identifies and removes the aliased columns.

- Estimates parameters.

- Checks the model.

Design Matrix

The Genlog procedure displays the design matrix if you specify Design Matrix in the General Loglinear Analysis Options dialog box (not shown). Each column of the matrix is indexed by a unique parameter number that corresponds to a term of the design. The mapping of the parameter numbers to the terms of the design is shown in the correspondence table in Figure 16-9.

Figure 16-9
Correspondence between parameters and terms of the design

```
Correspondence Between Parameters and Terms of the Design

  Parameter   Aliased   Term

        1               Constant
        2               [QBELT = 1]
        3         x     [QBELT = 2]
        4               [INJURY = 1]
        5         x     [INJURY = 2]
        6               [QBELT = 1]*[INJURY = 1]
        7         x     [QBELT = 1]*[INJURY = 2]
        8         x     [QBELT = 2]*[INJURY = 1]
        9         x     [QBELT = 2]*[INJURY = 2]

  Note: 'x' indicates an aliased (or a redundant) parameter.
        These parameters are set to zero.
```

Each **aliased** (or redundant) term is indicated by an x in the table. The rows of the matrix are indexed by the factor combinations that define the contingency table.

Over-parameterized design matrix. The General Loglinear Analysis procedure uses a regression approach to represent the model in terms of parameters. In this approach, a dummy coding scheme is used.

First, the Genlog procedure forms an identity matrix for each factor variable, with dimension equal to the number of categories of the factor. Then, a constant vector is formed for each factor variable. Each element of the constant vector is equal to 1, and the length of the constant vector is equal to the number of categories of the factor. These identity matrices and constant vectors form the basis for the construction of the final design matrix.

For each effect, the Genlog procedure constructs the columns of the design matrix as the **Kronecker products** of the identity matrices and constant vectors. Effects involving a covariate are treated as regressor variables in the usual sense. If the effect involves a single covariate, the column of the design matrix is the covariate vector, and the associated parameter is the usual regression coefficient. Similarly, if the effect involves a factor-by-covariate interaction, multiple regression coefficients are computed—one for each combination of the categories of the factors involved (see the *SPSS Syntax Reference Guide* for a comparison of the GENLOG and LOGLINEAR commands). The columns are constructed using the algorithm that applies to multiple slopes in the usual regression procedure.

The Genlog procedure does not allow an interaction term between covariates. To specify an interaction effect involving more than one covariate, the products of the covariates must be calculated by a data transformation before using the Genlog procedure. You can choose Compute from the Transform menu to specify the product as a new variable, which can then be specified as a single covariate (see "Two Response Variables with Two Categories Each" on p. 213 in Chapter 17).

Logit model. For the logit model, there is one constant term for every value of the explanatory (factor) variable. The algorithm works in the same way as in the general loglinear model except for some modifications in generating the constant terms. The logit model is discussed in Chapter 17.

Incorporating Cell Structure Information

In some cases, the presence of structural zeros is the cause of aliasing in the design matrix. These aliased columns must be identified.

For each combination of values of the factors, the value of the cell structure variable is checked. If it is not positive, all elements in the corresponding row of the over-parameterized design matrix are assigned a value of 0. Otherwise, the row remains unchanged.

Identifying the aliased columns. To identify the aliased columns in the design matrix, the **cross-product matrix** (the matrix product of the transpose of the matrix multiplied by itself) is calculated. The SWEEP operations are then applied to all rows and columns sequentially. After each SWEEP operation, the diagonal elements are inspected. If the ratio of a diagonal element after the SWEEP to its original value (before the first SWEEP operation) is less than a predetermined threshold value, the corresponding column in the over-parameterized design matrix is declared to be aliased. Aliased columns are then removed from the over-parameterized design matrix. The remaining columns form a **full rank design matrix** that is subsequently used in the estimation stage.

To keep the sum of the expected cell counts equal to the sum of the observed cell counts, the constant term in a general loglinear model and the intercept-like terms in a logit model are not subjected to the redundancy test after the SWEEP operations. Therefore, these terms always stay in the model equation.

Model Diagnosis

Before conclusions or inferences are made based on the results of a selected model, it is important to check whether the model assumptions are satisfied. We usually look for two kinds of indications that the model does not fit:

- The data as a whole show systematic departures from the predicted values. This implies that the model alone is not adequate to explain the behavior of the data.

- Some isolated discrepancies are due to several particular data values, while the rest of the data agree with the predicted values. This implies that there is something unusual about these data values. They may be in areas where the model does not apply, or perhaps they are outliers or the result of typographic errors.

Goodness-of-Fit Statistics

The first step in model diagnosis is the examination of goodness of fit. Two goodness-of-fit statistics are reported in the General Loglinear and Logit Loglinear procedures—the Pearson chi-square statistic and the likelihood-ratio chi-square statistic. Using O to denote the observed value and E to denote the fitted value, the Pearson chi-square statistic is

$$\chi^2 = \sum \frac{(O-E)^2}{E}$$

Equation 16-22

For the Poisson model, the likelihood-ratio chi-square statistic is

$$G^2 = \sum (O \ln(O/E) - (O-E))$$

Equation 16-23

and for the multinomial model, it is

$$G^2 = 2\sum O \ln(O/E)$$

Equation 16-24

where the sum is over all cells that are not structural zeros and do not have zero-fitted values. It should be noted that the G^2 from Equation 16-23 and G^2 from Equation 16-24 are identical because the sum of residuals $(O-E)$ is 0 when an intercept term is included for the Poisson model (the General Loglinear Analysis procedure does include an intercept). Both χ^2 and G^2 have asymptotic chi-square distributions. The degrees of freedom depend on the number of cells excluding structural zeros, the number of non-aliased parameters, and the number of fitted values that are equal to 0. Sometimes, χ^2 is preferred to G^2, and vice versa. χ^2 provides more direct interpretation, while G^2 is useful for comparing nested models. In most cases, both χ^2 and G^2 will lead to the same conclusion.

The likelihood-ratio statistic compares how well the selected model fits the data to the fit of a corresponding saturated model. A saturated model always produces a perfect fit using the greatest number of parameters leaving zero degrees of freedom. However, by the principle of parsimony, we want to use a model with the least number of parameters that can describe the data almost as well as the saturated model. Therefore, the likelihood-ratio statistic and its p value tell us whether the selected model is statistically different from a saturated model. A small p value (labeled *Sig.* in the output) indicates that the selected model cannot adequately describe the data as the saturated model does and should include more parameters in the model.

Also, the likelihood-ratio statistic has a definite advantage because it is additive for nested models, whereas the Pearson statistic in general is not. When one model is nested within another model, the difference in G^2 statistics indicates whether the two models are different from a statistical point of view. It is known that difference has an asymptotic chi-square distribution with degrees of freedom equal to the difference of models' degrees of freedom.

If the selected model is correct, then O has mean E for both Poisson and multinomial models. In a correct model, O also has variance E under the Poisson model and variance $E(1 - E/N)$ under the multinomial model, where N is the total sample size. When N is large, the ratio E/N becomes negligible. Thus, the expression

$$\frac{O - E}{\sqrt{E}}$$

Equation 16-25

has a mean equal to 0 and a variance equal to 1 when the sample size is large. Thus, the order of magnitude of the Pearson statistic χ^2 should be at most that of the degrees of freedom. If the value of χ^2 is too large relative to the degrees of freedom, the model does not fit.

Residuals

Another step in model diagnosis is the examination of residuals. This step helps to evaluate the fit for each observation, to identify possible outliers, and sometimes to provide hints to improve the model. The General Loglinear Analysis procedure provides four types of residuals—raw, standardized, adjusted, and deviance.

Plots are selected in the General Loglinear Analysis Options dialog box. A matrix scatterplot of adjusted residuals versus observed values and adjusted residuals versus fitted values can be generated. A similar matrix scatterplot is available for deviance residuals. Furthermore, all of these residuals, along with the fitted values, can be saved in the working data file for further analyses, as selected in the General Loglinear Analysis Save dialog box. The SPSS system-missing value will be assigned if the corresponding cell contains a structural zero or an otherwise prohibited value.

A **raw residual** (or **residual**) is the difference obtained by subtracting the fitted value from the observed value. Therefore, the sum of all raw residuals is 0 because the sum of all fitted values must be equal to the sum of observed values, as one of the assumptions of the General Loglinear Analysis procedure. Raw residuals do not play an important role in model diagnosis because their magnitudes can be misleading without considering the sizes of the fitted and observed values.

A **standardized residual**, on the other hand, does take into account the size of the fitted values. For the Poisson model, the standardized residual is the raw residual divided by $\sqrt{E}$. For the multinomial model, the denominator is $\sqrt{E(1 - E/N)}$. For the Poisson model, the sum of squares of the standardized residuals is the Pearson chi-square statistic; thus, they are also known as Pearson residuals. Therefore, standardized residuals can be used to check the individual contributions to the Pearson chi-square statistic. The standardized residuals are asymptotically normal with the means equal to 0 and the variances less than 1 if the selected model is correct.

The **adjusted residual** is the standardized residual divided by its estimated standard error (Haberman, 1973). Its asymptotic distribution is standard normal with the mean equal to 0 and the variance equal to 1 under the correct model. Because of this property, the adjusted residual is preferred over the standardized residual for checking normality.

The **deviance residual** is the individual contribution to the likelihood-ratio chi-square statistic. Its sign is the same as that of the raw residual. For both the Poisson and multinomial models, the sum of squares of the deviance residuals equals the likelihood-ratio chi-square statistic. Like adjusted residuals, deviance residuals also have an asymptotic standard normal distribution.

For an example of model diagnosis, see "Model Diagnosis: Coal Miner Data Revisited" on p. 226 in Chapter 17.

Additional Examples

This section contains three examples illustrating various applications of general loglinear analysis. For applications of logit loglinear analysis, see Chapter 17.

Example 3
Survival Parametric Model

McCullagh and Nelder (1989) and Agresti (1990) discuss how to use loglinear models to analyze survival data for various parametric survival models. Detailed descriptions of the equivalence between parametric survival models and loglinear models can be found in their books. This example illustrates how to use the General Loglinear Analysis procedure to fit a special case of the proportional hazard (PH) model where survival times have an exponential distribution.

For survival data, the response is the length of time until the occurrence of some event. With an exponential assumption for survival time, the hazard rate is a constant at all time points. Using λ as the constant hazard rate, the hazard function for a PH model is expressed as

$$h(x) = \lambda e^{\beta'x} \qquad\qquad \text{Equation 16-26}$$

where x denotes a set of explanatory variables and β' is the transposed matrix. For subject i, the product of time at risk (t_i) and the hazard function gives the expected number of events:

$$m_i = t_i \lambda e^{\beta'x_i} \qquad\qquad \text{Equation 16-27}$$

Taking natural logarithms on both sides of Equation 16-27 gives

$$\ln(m_i) - \ln(t_i) = \ln(\lambda) + \beta'x_i \qquad\qquad \text{Equation 16-28}$$

The term $\ln(t_i)$ is referred to as an **offset** in most loglinear analysis literature. In this example, the structure variable is used to include the offset term.

An example of a proportional hazard model is found in data from Freireich et al. (1963), which measured the remission time of leukemia patients. The patients were divided into two groups. The treatment group received an experimental drug and the control group received a placebo. The remission time was measured in weeks. Since the observations can be assumed to be independent, the Poisson distribution is appropriate. The data structure is shown in Figure 16-10.

Figure 16-10
Data structure for leukemia data

	case	time	group	qcensor
1	1	6	1	0
2	2	6	1	1
3	3	6	1	1
4	4	6	1	1
5	5	7	1	1
6	6	9	1	0
7	7	10	1	0
8	8	10	1	1
9	9	11	1	0
10	10	13	1	1
11	11	16	1	1
12	12	17	1	0
13	13	19	1	0
14	14	20	1	0
15	15	22	1	1

	case	time	group	qcensor
20	20	34	1	0
21	21	35	1	0
22	1	1	2	1
23	2	1	2	1
24	3	2	2	1
25	4	2	2	1
26	5	3	2	1
27	6	4	2	1
28	7	4	2	1
29	8	5	2	1
30	9	5	2	1
31	10	8	2	1
32	11	8	2	1
33	12	8	2	1
34	13	8	2	1

The data are recorded in individual cases. Each case number has two entries, one for each group. The variable *group* indicates treatment (1) or control (2). Figure 16-10 shows two views of the data. Note that the entries for the controls (group 2) start with case 1 again. Thus, each case has two entries, one for each group. In the contingency table of *case* by *group*, each cell has one case. The status of each case (censored or not) is in *qcensor*. Weighting the data by *qcensor* (by using the Data menu prior to analysis) causes the cell counts to be 1 for uncensored cases and 0 for censored cases. To identify each case as an individual cell, the ID variable *case* is specified as a factor in the loglinear analysis.

By comparing Equation 16-27 with Equation 16-18, you can see that with an exponential assumption for survival time, *time* is the cell structure variable (cell-specific constant) in the General Loglinear Analysis procedure. Since the group effect is the main interest, *group* is the only explanatory variable in this model. A model with *group* as the only explanatory factor in the custom model is fitted.

From the menus choose:

Data
  Weight Cases...
  ▶ Weight cases by: qcensor

Analyze
  Loglinear
    General...

  ▶ Factor(s): case group

Cell Structure: time

Model...
  ⊙ Custom
  ▶ Terms in Model (Main effects): group

Options...
  Display
    ☑ Frequencies
    ☑ Estimates
  Plots: deselect all plots

Since *qcensor* is a status variable, the estimated cell counts and the goodness of fit are meaningless in this example. The parameter correspondence table is shown in Figure 16-11.

Figure 16-11
Parameter correspondence table

```
Correspondence Between Parameters and Terms of the Design

Parameter   Aliased   Term

       1               Constant
       2               [GROUP = 1.00000]
       3        x      [GROUP = 2.00000]

Note: 'x' indicates an aliased (or a redundant) parameter.
      These parameters are set to zero.
```

The parameter estimates, shown in Figure 16-12, are the items of interest. The parameter estimate for group 1 (parameter 2) is −1.5266 with a standard error of 0.3984. Since the parameter for group 2 (parameter 3) is identified as aliased in the parameter correspondence table, its value is 0.

Figure 16-12
Parameter estimates for leukemia data

```
Parameter Estimates

                                           Asymptotic 95% CI
Parameter   Estimate      SE    Z-value    Lower     Upper
       1    -2.1595    .2182     -9.90     -2.59     -1.73
       2    -1.5266    .3984     -3.83     -2.31      -.75
       3      .0000       .         .         .         .
```

Thus, the estimated hazard ratio for the treatment group as compared to the control group is

$$e^{-1.5266} = 0.2172$$

Equation 16-29

The 95% confidence limits for the log-hazard difference are $(-2.31, -0.75)$, corresponding to hazard ratio limits of $(0.10, 0.47)$.

You can also use the Cox Regression procedure to analyze the same data (see Chapter 21). To use the Cox Regression procedure, from the menus choose:

Data
  Weight Cases...
  ⊙ Do not weight cases

Analyze
  Survival
    Cox Regression...

▸ Time: time

Status: qcensor(1)

Covariates: group(Cat)l

Categorical...
    Categorical Covariates: group
    Contrast: Indicator   (Click Change)

In the Cox Regression procedure output (not shown), the parameter estimate for group 1 is -1.5092 with a standard error of 0.4096. These numbers are close to, but not the same as, those of the General Loglinear Analysis procedure because the Cox Regression procedure fits Cox's proportional hazard model, which does not assume any underlying distribution for the survival time.

Example 4
Table Standardization

Occasionally, researchers want to calculate a set of fitted values that have specified marginal totals or the required marginal distributions. Haberman (1979) discussed the method of adjustment of marginal tables. The method is applied to estimate the population counts whose marginal distributions matched those of a previous census. A similar process, called table standardization (or *raking* the table), is presented in Agresti (1990). In this process, the estimated counts are standardized so that the marginal totals are all equal to 100. In both cases, the purpose is to make the pattern of association more visible and to facilitate comparisons.

Both the adjustment of marginal tables and the table standardization can be done by using the iteratively proportional fitting (IPF) technique (available in the Model Selection Loglinear Analysis procedure). However, the same results can be obtained by specifying a suitable cell structure variable in the General Loglinear Analysis procedure.

The following example is taken from Haberman (1979). Both tables show the classification of number of years of husband's education versus that of wife's education. The first data set is a sample gathered from the 1972 General Social Survey, and the second data set is from the 1970 United States census data. In this example, the 1970 marginal totals will be used to estimate the 1972 census counts using the 1972 sample under a saturated design. The variables are *yrhusb* (years of education of husband), *yrwife* (years of education of wife), *gsscnt* (GSS count), *marhusb* (census marginal count for *yrhusb*), and *marwife* (census marginal count for *yrwife*). The data are shown in Figure 16-13.

Figure 16-13
Data structure for education data

Educathw - SPSS Data Editor

File Edit View Data Transform Statistics Graphs Utilities Window Help

1:yrhusb 1

	yrhusb	yrwife	gsscnt	marhusb	marwife
1	1.00	1.00	283.00	19933782	18052065
2	1.00	2.00	141.00	19933782	17859905
3	1.00	3.00	25.00	19933782	5101589
4	1.00	4.00	4.00	19933782	3584015
5	2.00	1.00	82.00	13275913	18052065
6	2.00	2.00	180.00	13275913	17859905
7	2.00	3.00	43.00	13275913	5101589
8	2.00	4.00	14.00	13275913	3584015
9	3.00	1.00	20.00	5186966	18052065
10	3.00	2.00	104.00	5186966	17859905
11	3.00	3.00	43.00	5186966	5101589
12	3.00	4.00	20.00	5186966	3584015
13	4.00	1.00	4.00	6200883	18052065
14	4.00	2.00	52.00	6200883	17859905
15	4.00	3.00	41.00	6200883	5101589
16	4.00	4.00	69.00	6200883	3584015

Variables *yrhusb* and *yrwife* have four values, each one corresponding to a level of education ranging from grade school through high school, college, and graduate school. An initial estimate of the joint distribution is needed (like the initial estimate in the iteratively proportional fitting algorithm). Since only the marginal totals are available, the model closest to the saturated model is the independence model. Thus, the estimated values from the independence model are used as the initial values. Haberman (1979) contains examples of choosing the initial values under various scenarios.

In the independence model, the estimated cell count is the product of the corresponding marginal totals divided by the total sample size, which is 44,597,744 in this example. (The total sample size is the sum of the four unique values of *marhusb*.)

$$wgt = \frac{marhusb \times marwife}{44597774}$$

Equation 16-30

The *wgt* variable is added to the data by using the Compute Variable dialog box, accessed from the Transform menu. Then, the estimated cell counts are specified as weights by weighting cases by *wgt* (using the Data menu). The 1972 observations are specified as cell structure values. Finally, an independence model is fitted. To carry out the analysis, from the menus choose:

Transform
  Compute...
    wgt=marhusb*marwife/44597774

Data
  Weight Cases...
▶ Weight cases by: wgt

Analyze
  Loglinear
    General...

▶ Factor(s):yrhusb yrwife

Cell Structure: gsscnt

Model...
  ⊙ Custom
  ▶ Terms in Model (Main effects): yrhusb yrwife

Options...
  Display
      ☑ Frequencies
      ☑ Estimates
  Plots: deselect all plots

The fitted values are the estimated 1972 population census counts. The General Loglinear Analysis procedure displays both the observed and the fitted values by default. The output is shown in Figure 16-14.

Figure 16-14
Table information for education data

```
Table Information
```

Factor	Value	Observed Count	%	Expected Count	%
YRHUSB	0-11				
YRWIFE	0-11	8068697.07	(18.09)	13284910.3	(29.79)
YRWIFE	12	7982807.68	(17.90)	5599667.30	(12.55)
YRWIFE	13-15	2280247.51	(5.11)	909085.84	(2.04)
YRWIFE	16+	1601940.35	(3.59)	141029.18	(.32)
YRHUSB	12				
YRWIFE	0-11	5373757.99	(12.05)	3914816.89	(8.78)
YRWIFE	12	5316555.60	(11.92)	7268812.44	(16.30)
YRWIFE	13-15	1518646.46	(3.41)	1590225.64	(3.57)
YRWIFE	16+	1066893.41	(2.39)	501998.52	(1.13)
YRHUSB	13-15				
YRWIFE	0-11	2099554.28	(4.71)	663722.05	(1.49)
YRWIFE	12	2077205.02	(4.66)	2919328.37	(6.55)
YRWIFE	13-15	593342.81	(1.33)	1105394.76	(2.48)
YRWIFE	16+	416840.62	(.93)	498497.57	(1.12)
YRHUSB	16+				
YRWIFE	0-11	2509962.56	(5.63)	188522.67	(.42)
YRWIFE	12	2483244.60	(5.57)	2073004.77	(4.65)
YRWIFE	13-15	709325.91	(1.59)	1496856.45	(3.36)
YRWIFE	16+	498322.13	(1.12)	2442471.42	(5.48)

To check whether the 1972 fitted marginal totals have the same distribution (not the same values) as the 1970 census counts, you can compute generalized residuals by using the GRESID subcommand in a syntax window.

From the menus choose:

Transform
  Compute...

In the Compute Variable dialog box, set up eight new variables:

husb1=0
husb1 = 1 if yrhusb = 1
husb2=0
husb2 = 1 if yrhusb = 2
husb3=0
husb3 = 1 if yrhusb = 3
...
wife1=0
wife1 = 1 if yrwife = 1
...

and so on, for all of the values of *yrhusb* and *yrwife*. (You could also use Transform/Recode to set up the eight variables.) These are the coefficients for the generalized residuals. Then paste the syntax from the previous General Loglinear Analysis dialog box and type the following line before the period at the end of the command:

```
/GRESID = HUSB1, HUSB2, HUSB3, HUSB4, WIFE1, WIFE2, WIFE3, WIFE4
```

You can run the command by clicking the Run Current syntax tool on the toolbar. The generalized residuals are shown in Figure 16-15.

Figure 16-15
Generalized residuals

```
Generalized Residual
                 Observed     Expected                    Std.       Adj.
                 Value        Value        Resid.         Resid.     Resid.
HUSB1    19933692.61   19933692.61   1.18092E-06    2.64500E-10     .
HUSB2    13275853.46   13275853.46   8.66130E-07    2.37712E-10     .
HUSB3     5186942.74    5186942.74   2.11410E-07    9.28261E-11     .
HUSB4     6200855.19    6200855.19   3.33413E-07    1.33893E-10     .
WIFE1    18051971.90   18051971.90   1.26660E-06    2.98110E-10     .
WIFE2    17859812.89   17859812.89   8.30740E-07    1.96574E-10     .
WIFE3     5101562.69    5101562.69   2.68221E-07    1.18752E-10     .
WIFE4     3583996.52    3583996.52   2.27243E-07    1.20035E-10     .
```

The 1972 fitted marginal totals have the same distribution as the 1970 census counts. For example, the ratio of the 1972 marginal totals between the first two categories of *yrhusb* is

$$\frac{19,933,692.61}{13,275,853.48} = 1.5015 \qquad \text{Equation 16-31}$$

which is the same as that for the 1970 census counts:

$$\frac{19,933,782}{13,275,913} = 1.5015 \qquad \text{Equation 16-32}$$

The results are not surprising because this is a property of the method of adjustment.

Example 5
Poisson Loglinear Regression

Poisson regression encompasses statistical methods for the analysis of the relationship between an observed count with a Poisson distribution and a set of explanatory variables. The loglinear model is the best known type of Poisson regression. The expected count for observed count n_i is m_i. Its specification is

$$m_i = N_i e^{\beta' x_i}$$

Equation 16-33

for counts n_i with independent Poisson distributions, where n_i denotes the number of events for the ith sample and N_i denotes the corresponding exposure.

The following example illustrates how to use the General Loglinear Analysis procedure to fit Poisson loglinear models. The data are taken from Koch et al. (1986) and show the *age*-by-*region* cross-classification of new melanoma cases among white males during 1969–1971 and estimated populations at risk (see Table 16-4).

Table 16-4
Age-by-region cross-classification

Age group	Melanoma cases, n_{ij}		Estimated population at risk, N_{ij}	
	Northern	**Southern**	**Northern**	**Southern**
less than 35	61	64	2880262	1074246
35–44	76	75	564535	220407
45–54	98	68	592983	198119
55–64	104	63	450740	134084
65–74	63	45	270908	70708
75 +	80	27	161850	34233

The data contain the counts, denoted as n_{ij}, which are the numbers of new melanoma cases reported for the ith age group and jth area where $i = 1, 2, 3, 4, 5, 6$ and $j = 1, 2$. The exposures, denoted as N_{ij}, are corresponding estimated populations at risk. It is of interest to investigate whether the ratios n_{ij}/N_{ij} across areas tend to be homogeneous across age groups or whether the ratios across age groups tend to be homogeneous across areas. Such a structure can be expressed in the loglinear form

$$m_{ij} = N_{ij} e^{\mu + \alpha_i + \beta_j}$$

Equation 16-34

where α_i represents the effect for ith age group and β_j represents jth area effect. The model can be fitted in the General Loglinear Analysis procedure. The data structure is shown in Figure 16-16.

Figure 16-16
Data structure for melanoma data

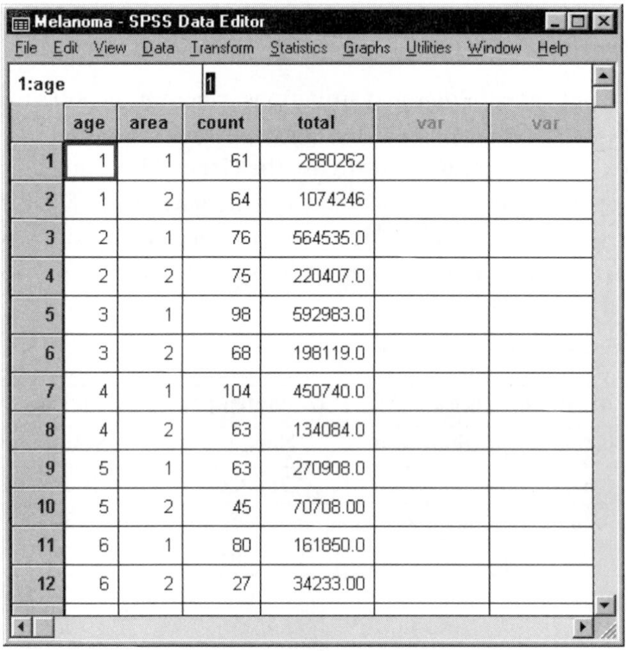

Melanoma - SPSS Data Editor

File Edit View Data Transform Statistics Graphs Utilities Window Help

1:age 1

	age	area	count	total	var	var
1	1	1	61	2880262		
2	1	2	64	1074246		
3	2	1	76	564535.0		
4	2	2	75	220407.0		
5	3	1	98	592983.0		
6	3	2	68	198119.0		
7	4	1	104	450740.0		
8	4	2	63	134084.0		
9	5	1	63	270908.0		
10	5	2	45	70708.00		
11	6	1	80	161850.0		
12	6	2	27	34233.00		

The variables are *age* (age group), *area* (region), *count* (new melanoma cases), and *total* (population at risk). The data are weighted by *count* because the individual cases are already aggregated.

Data
  Weight Cases...
▶ Weight cases by: count

Analyze
  Loglinear
    General...

▶ Factor(s):age area

Cell Structure: total

Model...
  ⊙ Custom
  ▶ Terms in Model (Main effects): age area

Options...
  Display
    ☑ Frequencies
    ☑ Estimates
  Plots: deselect all plots

The goodness-of-fit statistics in Figure 16-17 show that the Poisson loglinear model fits the data fairly well (the significance values are greater than 0.05).

Figure 16-17
Goodness-of-fit statistics

```
Goodness-of-fit Statistics

                       Chi-Square    DF      Sig.
Likelihood Ratio          6.2149      5     .2859
         Pearson          6.1151      5     .2952
```

The output shows that there are nine parameters in the model, including the constant. As shown in Figure 16-18, α_6 and β_2 (parameters 7 and 9) have been identified as redundant and their parameter estimates are set to 0.

Figure 16-18
Correspondence between parameters and terms of the design

```
Parameter   Aliased   Term

        1             Constant
        2             [AGE = 1]
        3             [AGE = 2]
        4             [AGE = 3]
        5             [AGE = 4]
        6             [AGE = 5]
        7        x    [AGE = 6]
        8             [AREA = 1]
        9        x    [AREA = 2]

Note: 'x' indicates an aliased (or a redundant) parameter.
```

The estimates of the remaining six parameters are shown in Figure 16-19. The estimates for parameters 2 through 6 show that different age groups all contribute significant effects to the model and that their effects are not the same. The area effect, parameter 8, is significantly different from 0, as shown by its 95% confidence interval.

Figure 16-19
Parameter estimates

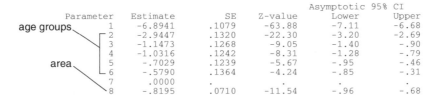

	Parameter	Estimate	SE	Z-value	Asymptotic 95% CI Lower	Upper
age groups	1	-6.8941	.1079	-63.88	-7.11	-6.68
	2	-2.9447	.1320	-22.30	-3.20	-2.69
	3	-1.1473	.1268	-9.05	-1.40	-.90
	4	-1.0316	.1242	-8.31	-1.28	-.79
area	5	-.7029	.1239	-5.67	-.95	-.46
	6	-.5790	.1364	-4.24	-.85	-.31
	7	.0000	.	.	.	.
	8	-.8195	.0710	-11.54	-.96	-.68

To study the difference between different age groups across areas, you can create comparison variables and specify them as contrast variables to obtain the contrast estimate and its confidence interval estimate.

For example, you can compare the second age group with the first age group—that is, $(\alpha_2 - \alpha_1)$—across areas. One way to do this is to create a contrast variable, *G1*. It has the value −1 for the first age group cells, (1,1) and (1,2), and the value 1 for the second age group cells, (2,1) and (2, 2)—the same as the coefficients of α_2 and α_1. The value is 0 for the other cells because they are not included in the comparison currently being considered.

The data with three new contrast variables, *G1*, *G2*, and *G3*, are shown in Figure 16-20. Variable *G2* is for comparing the third age group with the first age group, and *G3* is for comparing the two areas across age groups.

Figure 16-20
Data with contrast variables

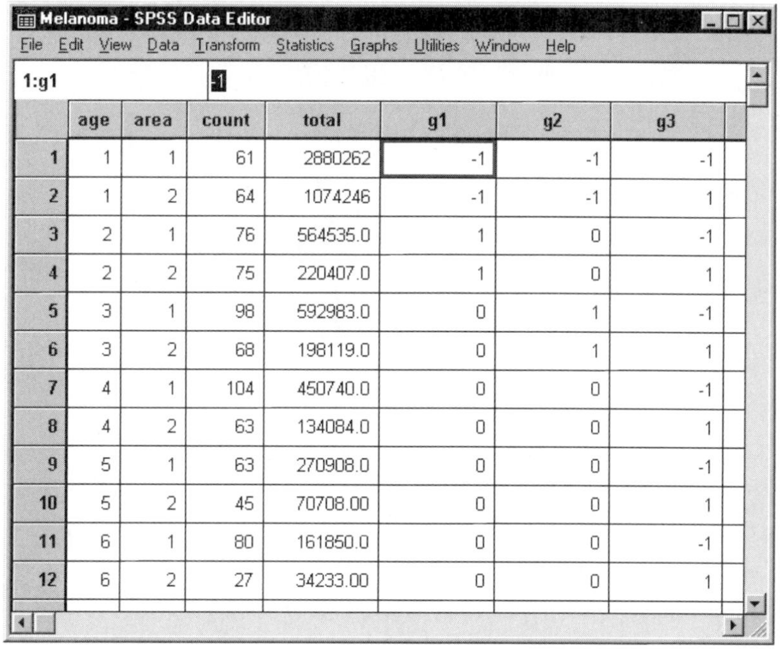

	age	area	count	total	g1	g2	g3
1	1	1	61	2880262	-1	-1	-1
2	1	2	64	1074246	-1	-1	1
3	2	1	76	564535.0	1	0	-1
4	2	2	75	220407.0	1	0	1
5	3	1	98	592983.0	0	1	-1
6	3	2	68	198119.0	0	1	1
7	4	1	104	450740.0	0	0	-1
8	4	2	63	134084.0	0	0	1
9	5	1	63	270908.0	0	0	-1
10	5	2	45	70708.00	0	0	1
11	6	1	80	161850.0	0	0	-1
12	6	2	27	34233.00	0	0	1

To implement the contrast variables, recall the General Loglinear Analysis dialog box and move the three new variables to the Contrast Variable(s) list. The other selections remain the same. The contrast variables *G1*, *G2*, and *G3* are shown in the output in the generalized log-odds ratio (GLOR) coefficients table (see Figure 16-21).

Figure 16-21
Generalized residual and generalized log-odds ratio coefficients

```
Factor      Value                 G1        G2        G3

AGE less than 35
   AREA     northern          -1.000    -1.000    -1.000
   AREA     southern          -1.000    -1.000     1.000

AGE        35-44
   AREA     northern           1.000      .000    -1.000
   AREA     southern           1.000      .000     1.000

AGE        45-54
   AREA     northern            .000     1.000    -1.000
   AREA     southern            .000     1.000     1.000

AGE        55-64
   AREA     northern            .000      .000    -1.000
   AREA     southern            .000      .000     1.000

AGE        65-74
   AREA     northern            .000      .000    -1.000
   AREA     southern            .000      .000     1.000

AGE        75 +
   AREA     northern            .000      .000    -1.000
```

Applying *G1* to Equation 16-34 yields

$$\ln(m_{21}) - \ln(m_{11}) + \ln(m_{22}) - \ln(m_{12})$$
$$= \ln(N_{21}) - \ln(N_{11}) + \ln(N_{22}) - \ln(N_{12}) + 2(\alpha_2 - \alpha_1)$$

Equation 16-35

This equation can be solved for $(\alpha_2 - \alpha_1)$ and evaluated. The estimate for the left side of Equation 16-35 is the GLOR estimate for *G1*, which is calculated by the General Loglinear Analysis procedure. The estimate, shown in the output table in Figure 16-22, is 0.38, with a standard error of 0.24.

Figure 16-22
Generalized log-odds ratio

```
Generalized Log-Odds Ratio
                                           95% Confidence Interval
                                       Log-Odds Ratio      Odds Ratio
Variable   GLOR    SE    Wald   Sig.   Lower   Upper    Lower   Upper
G1          .38    .24   2.48  .1150   -.09     .86      .91    2.35
G2          .56    .24   5.49  .0191    .09    1.02     1.10    2.77
G3        -2.22    .43  27.02  .0000  -3.05   -1.38      .05     .25
```

From the data, you can calculate the first part of the right side of Equation 16-35:

$$\ln(N_{21}) - \ln(N_{11}) + \ln(N_{22}) - \ln(N_{12}) = -3.22$$

Equation 16-36

Next, subtract the result from the GLOR estimate and divide by 2:

$$\frac{0.38 - (-3.22)}{2} = 1.8$$

Equation 16-37

This is the estimate for $(\alpha_2 - \alpha_1)$. The standard error is $0.24/2 = 0.12$. Applying the same operations and using the 95% confidence interval for *G1* $(-0.09, 0.86)$ yields $(1.56, 2.04)$ as the 95% confidence interval for $(\alpha_2 - \alpha_1)$. The figures suggest that the ratio of the rate of new melanoma cases for the second age group (35–44) to the rate for first age group (less than 35) is 6, since

$$e^{1.8} = 6.0$$

Equation 16-38

Two more contrasts, *G2* and *G3*, were created; *G2* compares the third age group with the first age group, and *G3* compares the two areas (see Figure 16-21). Applying both *G2* and *G3* to the natural logarithm of *total* gives -3.27 and -7.11, respectively. Following calculations similar to those for *G1* yields

$$\frac{0.56 - (-3.27)}{2} = 1.915$$

Equation 16-39

as the estimate for $(\alpha_3 - \alpha_1)$. The corresponding 95% confidence interval is $(1.68, 2.15)$.

Similarly, using *G3*, the estimate for $(\beta_2 - \beta_1)$ is

$$\frac{-2.22 - (-7.11)}{6} = 0.815$$

Equation 16-40

It is divided by 6 because we pool the area differences across six age groups. The corresponding 95% confidence interval is $(0.68, 0.96)$, which is the same as that for parameter 8 but has the opposite sign. We can conclude that the rate in the southern area is 2.3 times higher than that of the northern area, since

$$e^{0.815} = 2.3$$

Equation 16-41

Multinomial Logit Models Examples

Multinomial logit models are a special class of loglinear models. In a multinomial logit model, variables are classified as response (or dependent) variables and explanatory (or independent) variables. As their names suggest, the behaviors of the response variables are thought to be explained by the explanatory variables. In these models, response variables are always categorical, while explanatory variables can be either categorical or continuous.

The *logarithm* of the odds of the response variables (instead of the cell count in the loglinear model) is expressed as a linear combination of parameters. Moreover, the counts within each combination of categories of explanatory variables are assumed to have a multinomial distribution. The Logit Loglinear Analysis procedure automatically specifies a multinomial distribution.

There are many kinds of logit models, especially for response variables with more than two categories. Two popular logit models are illustrated later in this chapter—baseline category logit (see "Polytomous Response Variable" on p. 219) and continuation ratio logit (see "Continuation Ratio Logit Model" on p. 233). Two other popular models are cumulative logit and adjacent category logit.

For baseline category logit and adjacent category logit models, there is an equivalent loglinear model for each. In fact, SPSS fits a logit model by fitting its equivalent loglinear model, if it exists. Also, the Logit Loglinear Analysis procedure can handle several response variables that might have more than two categories. The examples in the following sections illustrate how to specify logit models using the Logit Loglinear Analysis procedure and how to interpret the output.

Example 1: One response variable with two categories. Data from a Florida report on accidents relating types of injuries and whether the injured persons were wearing seat belts are analyzed using a Logit Loglinear model. Parameter estimates and the analysis-of-dispersion table are discussed.

Example 2: Two response variables with two categories each. The data are from a study that measured the effects of two respiratory ailments on coal miners in various age groups. The example includes an interaction between covariates.

Example 3: Polytomous response variable. This study investigates how alligators' primary food type varies with their size and the four lakes in which they live. The five categories of food make the response variable polytomous (more than two categories).

Example 4: Model diagnosis, coal miner data revisited. The data from Example 2 are used to generate another model and techniques of model diagnosis are discussed. The second model is shown to be statistically different from the first.

Example 5: Continuation ratio logit model. This model can be used when the response variable is ordinal (has ordered categories). The study investigates how various doses of a chemical affect developing fetuses in mice. Odds of deleterious effects are calculated based on the dosage.

Example 1
One Response Variable with Two Categories

This example shows how to analyze the accident data using the Logit Loglinear Analysis procedure instead of the General Loglinear Analysis procedure ("Complete Table" on p. 168 in Chapter 16). Consider the 1988 Florida automobile accident data again (see Table 17-1).

Table 17-1
1988 Florida automobile accident data

Wearing a seat belt?	Injury type	
	Fatal	Nonfatal
No	1601	162527
Yes	510	412368

The response variable is *injury* (injury type) and the explanatory variable is *qbelt* (whether a seat belt is worn). Each variable has two categories. The data structure is shown in Figure 17-1. The data are weighted by *count*.

Figure 17-1
Data structure for accident data

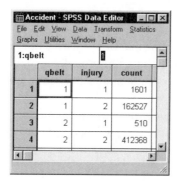

Consider how the odds of having a fatal injury vary with the value of *qbelt*. The observed odds are

$$\frac{n_{11}}{n_{12}} = \frac{1601}{162527} = 0.009851 \qquad \text{Equation 17-1}$$

without seat belts and

$$\frac{n_{21}}{n_{22}} = \frac{510}{412368} = 0.001237 \qquad \text{Equation 17-2}$$

with seat belts. The odds ratio is

$$\frac{n_{11}n_{22}}{n_{12}n_{21}} = 7.964905 \qquad \text{Equation 17-3}$$

These figures suggest that the odds are related to whether or not seat belts are worn. If m_{11} is the expected number of fatal injuries without seat belts, m_{12} is the expected number of nonfatal injuries without seat belts, and so on, the logit model is

$$\ln\left(\frac{m_{i1}}{m_{i2}}\right) = \lambda + \delta_i \qquad i = 1, 2 \qquad \text{Equation 17-4}$$

where λ is the baseline term and δ_i is the term due to *qbelt*. As discussed below, this logit model is equivalent to the loglinear model

$$\ln(m_{ij}) = \alpha_i + \beta_j + \gamma_{ij} \qquad i = 1, 2 \text{ and } j = 1, 2 \qquad \text{Equation 17-5}$$

where α_i is the main-effects term of *qbelt*, β_j is the main-effects term of *injury*, and γ_{ij} is the interaction term between *qbelt* and *injury*. This loglinear model is slightly different from others because the overall intercept term μ is not included in Equation 17-5. The following paragraphs explain why.

Recalling that the logarithm of a ratio is the logarithm of the numerator minus the logarithm of the denominator and using Equation 17-5, we have

$$\ln\left(\frac{m_{i1}}{m_{i2}}\right) = \ln(m_{i1}) - \ln(m_{i2})$$

$$= (\alpha_i + \beta_1 + \gamma_{i1}) - (\alpha_i + \beta_2 + \gamma_{i2}) \qquad i = 1, 2$$

Equation 17-6

Since the α_i terms cancel, Equation 17-6 can be simplified as

$$\ln\left(\frac{m_{i1}}{m_{i2}}\right) = \ln(m_{i1}) - \ln(m_{i2}) = (\beta_1 - \beta_2) + (\gamma_{i1} - \gamma_{i2}) \qquad i = 1, 2$$

Equation 17-7

Comparing Equation 17-4 and Equation 17-7 yields

$$\lambda = \beta_1 - \beta_2 \qquad \text{and} \qquad \delta_i = \gamma_{i1} - \gamma_{i2} \qquad \text{Equation 17-8}$$

Thus, the logit model in Equation 17-4 is equivalent to the loglinear model in Equation 17-5. Furthermore, terms that do not relate to the category of *injury* (that is, the index *j* terms) cancel in Equation 17-6, so it is unnecessary to include the overall intercept term μ in Equation 17-5.

Although it could be further argued that the terms α_i are also unnecessary or that they can have any values (because including them in Equation 17-5 does not affect Equation 17-4), we do need these α_i terms to equate the sum of fitted values to the sum of observed counts for each combination of levels of explanatory variables. Therefore, the Logit Loglinear procedure labels them as constants in the parameter correspondence table and displays their estimates without standard errors in the parameter estimates table.

For the accident data, to weight the data by *count*, from the menus choose:

Data
  Weight Cases...
  ▶ Weight cases by: count

To fit the logit model in Equation 17-4, choose:

Analyze
  Loglinear
    Logit...

  ▶ Dependent: injury
  ▶ Factor(s): qbelt

Options...
  Display
      ☑ Frequencies
      ☑ Estimates
  Plots: deselect all plots
  Criteria
      Delta: 0

The default saturated model is used.

Since the Logit Loglinear Analysis procedure fits the equivalent loglinear model in Equation 17-5, it displays estimates for parameters β_1, β_2, γ_{i1}, and γ_{i2}. Figure 17-2 shows the parameter correspondence table.

Figure 17-2
Parameter correspondence table

```
Correspondence Between Parameters and Terms of the Design

Parameter    Aliased   Term

        1              Constant for [QBELT = 1]
        2              Constant for [QBELT = 2]
        3              [INJURY = 1]
        4        x     [INJURY = 2]
        5              [INJURY = 1]*[QBELT = 1]
        6        x     [INJURY = 1]*[QBELT = 2]
        7        x     [INJURY = 2]*[QBELT = 1]
        8        x     [INJURY = 2]*[QBELT = 2]

Note: 'x' indicates an aliased (or a redundant) parameter.
      These parameters are set to zero.
```

The α_1 and α_2 terms are shown in the table as parameter 1 and parameter 2, respectively, although they are not considered as real parameters in a logit model. Parameters 4, 6, 7, and 8 (β_2, γ_{12}, γ_{21}, and γ_{22}) are identified as aliased and their values are set to 0. Figure 17-3 shows the parameter estimates table.

Figure 17-3
Parameter estimates table

```
Parameter Estimates

  Constant    Estimate

       1      11.9986
       2      12.9297
```

Note: Constants are not parameters under multinomial assumption.
      Therefore, standard errors are not calculated.

Parameter	Estimate	SE	Z-value	Asymptotic 95% CI Lower	Upper
3	-6.6953	.0443	-151.11	-6.78	-6.61
4	.0000	.	.	.	.
5	2.0750	.0509	40.74	1.98	2.17
6	.0000	.	.	.	.
7	.0000	.	.	.	.
8	.0000	.	.	.	.

The parameter estimates are

$$\beta_1 = -6.6953 \qquad \text{Equation 17-9}$$

and

$$\gamma_{11} = 2.0750 \qquad \text{Equation 17-10}$$

Substituting these values into Equation 17-8 yields

$$\lambda = (-6.6953) - 0 = -6.6953$$
$$\delta_1 = 2.0750 - 0 = 2.0750 \qquad \text{Equation 17-11}$$
$$\delta_2 = 0$$

From Equation 17-4,

$$\ln\left[\frac{m_{i1}}{m_{i2}}\right] = -6.6953 + 2.0750\,I \qquad i = 1, 2 \qquad \text{Equation 17-12}$$

where $I = 1$ if $i = 1$ and $I = 0$ if $i = 2$. Hence, the log-odds of having a fatal injury without a seat beat are 2.0750 times that with a seat belt. It is equivalent to saying that the odds of having an injury without a seat belt are

$$e^{2.0750} = 7.9649 \hspace{4cm} \text{Equation 17-13}$$

times higher than the odds with a seat belt.

In addition to parameter estimates, the Logit Loglinear Analysis procedure calculates other statistics useful for investigating the association between response variables and explanatory variables. Two methods for measuring association—entropy and concentration—are used in the logit loglinear model. The Logit Loglinear Analysis procedure produces an analysis-of-dispersion table containing measure-of-association statistics for both entropy and concentration. The analysis-of-dispersion table is analogous to the analysis-of-variance table in regression. The measure of association plays a role similar to R^2 in regression. Following the methods discussed in Haberman (1982), you can use these statistics, shown in Figure 17-4, to compare how the current model differs from the independence model. If the test statistics are not significant, the current model is not substantially different from the independence model.

Figure 17-4
Analysis-of-dispersion table

```
Analysis of Dispersion

Source of Dispersion      Entropy  Concentration       DF

Due to Model           1020.5789        17.0477         1
Due to Residual       12930.7232      4189.5059    577004
Total                 13951.3022      4206.5536    577005

Measures of Association

     Entropy =.0732
Concentration = .0041
```

Consider entropy first. Denoting the entropy due to the model as $S_H(M)$, the chi-square statistic

$$\psi_H = 2\ S_H(M) \hspace{4cm} \text{Equation 17-14}$$

has an asymptotic chi-square distribution. The number of degrees of freedom is given in the column labeled *DF*. In this example,

$$\psi_H = 2 \times 1020.5789 = 2041.1578 \hspace{2cm} \text{Equation 17-15}$$

which has an asymptotic chi-square distribution with 1 degree of freedom. To calculate the *p* value, choose Compute from the Transform menu and create a variable *p*:

$$p = 1 - \text{CDF.CHISQ}(2044.1578, 1) \hspace{2cm} \text{Equation 17-16}$$

The *p* value is practically 0.

The concentration due to the model is denoted as $S_C(M)$ and the concentration due to the residual is denoted as $S_C(R)$. Then the *F* statistic

$$F_C = \frac{S_C(M)/DF(M)}{S_C(R)/DF(R)} \hspace{3cm} \text{Equation 17-17}$$

has an *F* distribution with degrees of freedom *DF(M)* and *DF(R)*. The terms *DF(M)* and *DF(R)* are the degrees of freedom due to the model and due to the residual, respectively.

Using concentration as the measurement,

$$F_C = \frac{17.0477/1}{4189.5059/577003} = 2347.9079 \hspace{2cm} \text{Equation 17-18}$$

with (1, 577003) degrees of freedom. Using the CDF.F function in the Compute Variable dialog box (accessed from the Transform menu), the *p* value is again essentially 0: $p = 1 - \text{CDF.F}(2347.8829)$. Thus, there is strong evidence that *qbelt* and *injury* are not independent.

Note that ψ_H is the same as the likelihood-ratio statistic with the same number of degrees of freedom when an independence model is fitted to these data. Also,

$$\psi_C = \frac{(DF(T) + 1)S_C(M)}{S_C(T)} = 2338.4048 \qquad \text{Equation 17-19}$$

is the same as the Pearson statistic for the independence model, where $DF(T)$ represents the total of degrees of freedom. This is expected, as mentioned in Haberman (1982), because the response variable has two categories.

The association coefficients are $R_H = 0.0732$ and $R_C = 0.0041$. As mentioned in Goodman and Kruskal (1954), it is best not to interpret R_H and R_C in the same manner as we would interpret an R^2 of the same magnitude in a usual regression analysis. The observed R_H and R_C do indicate a fairly strong relation.

Since the data are in a two-way table and the model is saturated, we can calculate R_H and R_C using the Crosstabs procedure. R_H is the uncertainty coefficient with *injury* as the response. R_C is the square of Kendall's tau-*b*.

Example 2
Two Response Variables with Two Categories Each

In some studies, it is common to treat two categorical variables as response variables. We could fit a separate logit model to each response variable using the same set of explanatory variables, or we could study how the associations between response variables are affected by the explanatory variables. Consider an example illustrating the second case.

Figure 17-5 shows data from Ashford and Sowden (1970), where coal miners are classified by breathlessness, wheeze, and age. The data are from a study that measured the effects of two respiratory ailments on 18,282 coal miners in the United Kingdom. The coal miners were smokers without radiological evidence of pneumoconiosis, between 20 and 64 years of age at the time of examination. The aim of this analysis is to study how the association between breathlessness and wheeze changes across levels of age. The variables are *age*, *qbreath*, *qwheeze*, and *count*. The variable *age* is coded into nine groups. The data structure is shown in Figure 17-5.

Figure 17-5
Data structure for coal miner data

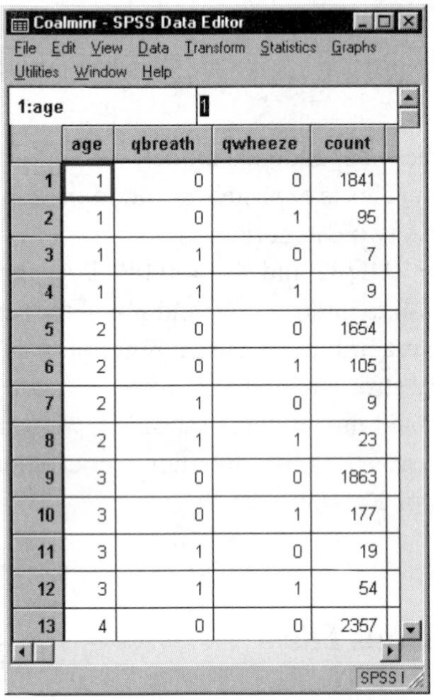

	age	qbreath	qwheeze	count
1	1	0	0	1841
2	1	0	1	95
3	1	1	0	7
4	1	1	1	9
5	2	0	0	1654
6	2	0	1	105
7	2	1	0	9
8	2	1	1	23
9	3	0	0	1863
10	3	0	1	177
11	3	1	0	19
12	3	1	1	54
13	4	0	0	2357

The data are weighted by *count*.

Agresti (1990) fitted the model

$$\ln\left(\frac{m_{11k}m_{22k}}{m_{12k}m_{21k}}\right) = \lambda + k\delta \qquad \text{Equation 17-20}$$

where m_{ijk} is the count for the *i*th category of breathlessness, the *j*th category of wheeze, and the *k*th level of age. Equation 17-20 implies that the association of breathlessness and wheeze, as measured by the log-odds ratio, varies linearly across age. The equivalent loglinear model is

$$\ln(m_{ijk}) = \alpha_k + \beta_i + \omega_j + (\alpha\beta)_{ik} + (\alpha\omega)_{jk} + (\beta\omega)_{ij} + kI\delta \qquad \text{Equation 17-21}$$

where $I = 1$ if $i = j = 1$, and $I = 0$ if *i* or *j* is not 1. The main-effects terms corresponding to *age*, *qbreath*, and *qwheeze* are α_k, β_i, and ω_j. The interaction-effects terms are then denoted by $(\alpha\beta)_{ik}$, $(\alpha\omega)_{jk}$, and $(\beta\omega)_{ij}$. Furthermore, it can be derived from Equation 17-20 and Equation 17-21 that

$$\lambda = (\beta\omega)_{11} - (\beta\omega)_{12} - (\beta\omega)_{21} + (\beta\omega)_{22} \qquad \text{Equation 17-22}$$

To begin the analysis, create a variable *delta*. From the menus choose:

Transform
  Compute...

Target Variable: delta (type the name for the new variable)

Numeric Expression: age*(qbreath=1)*(qwheeze=1)

This sets *delta* equal to the value of the age group when $i = j = 1$; otherwise, *delta* is equal to 0. This is, in fact, an example of an interaction between covariates.

To fit the model in Equation 17-21, from the menus choose:

Analyze
  Loglinear
    Logit...

▶ Dependent: qbreath qwheeze
▶ Factor(s): age
▶ Cell Covariate(s): delta

Model...
  ⊙ Custom
  ▶ Terms in Model (Main effects): age delta

Options...
  Display
    ☑ Frequencies
    ☑ Estimates
  Plot: deselect all plots

Paste

Running the Logit Loglinear Analysis procedure in the dialog box generates all possible interactions between the dependent variable list in the Logit Loglinear Analysis dialog box and the terms in the Logit Loglinear Analysis Model dialog box. To get only the relevant interactions, click Paste and then modify the syntax by removing the extra interactions. The pasted syntax is shown in Figure 17-6. Remove the interactions that are shaded (*delta* remains in the design) and click the Run Current tool.

Figure 17-6
Pasted syntax for coal miner data

```
GENLOG QBREATH QWHEEZE BY AGE WITH DELTA
  /MODEL MULTINOMIAL
  /PRINT = FREQ ESTIM
  /PLOT = NONE
  /CRITERIA =CIN(95) ITERATION(20) CONVERGE(.001) DELTA(.5)
  /DESIGN = QBREATH, QWHEEZE, QBREATH BY QWHEEZE,
            QBREATH BY AGE, QWHEEZE BY AGE,
            QBREATH BY QWHEEZE BY AGE, QBREATH BY DELTA,
            QWHEEZE BY DELTA, QBREATH BY QWHEEZE BY
            DELTA.
```

This model fits the data well, as seen from the goodness-of-fit statistics shown in Figure 17-7. The significance is well above 0.05.

Figure 17-7
Goodness-of-fit statistics

```
Goodness-of-fit Statistics
```

	Chi-Square	DF	Sig.
Likelihood Ratio	6.8017	7	.4498
Pearson	6.8083	7	.4491

Figure 17-8 shows the parameter correspondence table and Figure 17-9 shows the parameter estimates table.

Figure 17-8

Correspondence between parameters and terms of the design

```
Parameter   Aliased   Term
        1             Constant for [AGE = 1]
        2             Constant for [AGE = 2]
        3             Constant for [AGE = 3]
        4             Constant for [AGE = 4]
        5             Constant for [AGE = 5]
        6             Constant for [AGE = 6]
        7             Constant for [AGE = 7]
        8             Constant for [AGE = 8]
        9             Constant for [AGE = 9]
       10             [QBREATH = 0]
       11      x      [QBREATH = 1]
       12             [QWHEEZE = 0]
       13      x      [QWHEEZE = 1]
       14             [QBREATH = 0]*[AGE = 1]
       15             [QBREATH = 0]*[AGE = 2]
       16             [QBREATH = 0]*[AGE = 3]
       17             [QBREATH = 0]*[AGE = 4]
       18             [QBREATH = 0]*[AGE = 5]
       19             [QBREATH = 0]*[AGE = 6]
       20             [QBREATH = 0]*[AGE = 7]
       21             [QBREATH = 0]*[AGE = 8]
       22      x      [QBREATH = 0]*[AGE = 9]
       23      x      [QBREATH = 1]*[AGE = 1]
       24      x      [QBREATH = 1]*[AGE = 2]
       25      x      [QBREATH = 1]*[AGE = 3]
       26      x      [QBREATH = 1]*[AGE = 4]
       27      x      [QBREATH = 1]*[AGE = 5]
       28      x      [QBREATH = 1]*[AGE = 6]
       29      x      [QBREATH = 1]*[AGE = 7]
       30      x      [QBREATH = 1]*[AGE = 8]
       31      x      [QBREATH = 1]*[AGE = 9]
       32             [QWHEEZE = 0]*[AGE = 1]
       33             [QWHEEZE = 0]*[AGE = 2]
       34             [QWHEEZE = 0]*[AGE = 3]
       35             [QWHEEZE = 0]*[AGE = 4]
       36             [QWHEEZE = 0]*[AGE = 5]
       37             [QWHEEZE = 0]*[AGE = 6]
       38             [QWHEEZE = 0]*[AGE = 7]
       39             [QWHEEZE = 0]*[AGE = 8]
       40      x      [QWHEEZE = 0]*[AGE = 9]
       41      x      [QWHEEZE = 1]*[AGE = 1]
       42      x      [QWHEEZE = 1]*[AGE = 2]
       43      x      [QWHEEZE = 1]*[AGE = 3]
       44      x      [QWHEEZE = 1]*[AGE = 4]
       45      x      [QWHEEZE = 1]*[AGE = 5]
       46      x      [QWHEEZE = 1]*[AGE = 6]
       47      x      [QWHEEZE = 1]*[AGE = 7]
       48      x      [QWHEEZE = 1]*[AGE = 8]
       49      x      [QWHEEZE = 1]*[AGE = 9]
       50             [QBREATH = 0]*[QWHEEZE = 0]
       51      x      [QBREATH = 0]*[QWHEEZE = 1]
       52      x      [QBREATH = 1]*[QWHEEZE = 0]
       53      x      [QBREATH = 1]*[QWHEEZE = 1]
       54             DELTA
Note: 'x' indicates an aliased (or a redundant) parameter.
      These parameters are set to zero.
```

Figure 17-9

Parameter estimates

```
Parameter Estimates
  Constant    Estimate
        1      2.4542
        2      3.3158
        3      4.3525
        4      5.3215
        5      5.7848
        6      6.3997
        7      6.8891
        8      7.0824
        9      7.0770
```

Note: Constants are not parameters under multinomial assumption.
      Therefore, standard errors are not calculated.

Parameter	Estimate	SE	Z-value	Asymptotic 95% CI Lower	Upper
10	-2.1462	.2427	-8.84	-2.62	-1.67
11	.0000	.	.	.	.
12	-2.3541	.2375	-9.91	-2.82	-1.89
13	.0000	.	.	.	.
14	4.2330	.3017	14.03	3.64	4.82
15	3.5013	.2347	14.92	3.04	3.96
16	2.9783	.1822	16.35	2.62	3.34
17	2.3722	.1424	16.66	2.09	2.65
18	1.9698	.1275	15.45	1.72	2.22
19	1.5092	.1094	13.79	1.29	1.72
20	.8009	.0989	8.10	.61	.99
21	.4213	.0959	4.39	.23	.61
22	.0000	.	.	.	.
23	.0000	.	.	.	.
24	.0000	.	.	.	.
25	.0000	.	.	.	.
26	.0000	.	.	.	.
27	.0000	.	.	.	.
28	.0000	.	.	.	.
29	.0000	.	.	.	.
30	.0000	.	.	.	.
31	.0000	.	.	.	.
32	1.6556	.1337	12.38	1.39	1.92
33	1.4169	.1287	11.01	1.16	1.67
34	1.0224	.1132	9.03	.80	1.24
35	.8957	.1046	8.56	.69	1.10
36	.5529	.1025	5.39	.35	.75
37	.3639	.0978	3.72	.17	.56
38	.3144	.0958	3.28	.13	.50
39	.2077	.0947	2.19	.02	.39
40	.0000	.	.	.	.
41	.0000	.	.	.	.
42	.0000	.	.	.	.
43	.0000	.	.	.	.
44	.0000	.	.	.	.
45	.0000	.	.	.	.
46	.0000	.	.	.	.
47	.0000	.	.	.	.
48	.0000	.	.	.	.
49	.0000	.	.	.	.
50	3.6762	.1999	18.39	3.28	4.07
51	.0000	.	.	.	.
52	.0000	.	.	.	.
53	.0000	.	.	.	.
54	-.1306	.0295	-4.43	-.19	-.07

In Figure 17-8, $(\beta\omega)_{11}$, $(\beta\omega)_{12}$, $(\beta\omega)_{21}$, and $(\beta\omega)_{22}$ are the 50th, 51st, 52nd, and 53rd parameters, respectively. Then, using Figure 17-9, λ is estimated as $3.6762 - 0 - 0 + 0 = 3.6762$, with a standard error of 0.1999.

Since δ is the 54th parameter, its estimate is -0.1306, with a standard error of 0.0295. The z value is

$$-\frac{0.1306}{0.0295} = -4.4298 \hspace{3cm} \text{Equation 17-23}$$

This implies that δ is significantly far from 0, considering the large sample size. Finally, the estimated log-odds ratio at level k of age is

$$\ln\left(\frac{m_{11k}m_{22k}}{m_{12k}m_{21k}}\right) = +3.6762 - 0.1306\ k \hspace{2cm} \text{Equation 17-24}$$

It is evident from Equation 17-24 that the odds ratio between breathlessness and wheeze decreases at a rate of

$$e^{-0.1306} = 0.88 \hspace{4cm} \text{Equation 17-25}$$

for every level of increase in age.

Example 3
Polytomous Response Variable

A **polytomous response variable** has more than two categories. Data from Delany and Moore (1987) illustrate how to fit a logit model to a polytomous response variable. The data include 219 alligators captured in four Florida lakes in September 1985. The investigators studied how the alligators' primary food type varied with their size and the lakes in which they lived. The response variable *food* categorizes the primary food type. It has five categories—fish, invertebrate, reptile, bird, and other. The explanatory variables are *size* and *lake*. The variable *size* indicates the length of the alligators, in one of two categories. The variable *lake* identifies the area where the alligators were captured.

The data structure is shown in Figure 17-10. The lakes are designated by numbers: Lake Hancock (1), Lake Oklawaha (2), Lake Trafford (3), and Lake George (4). The data are weighted by *count*.

Figure 17-10
Data structure for alligator data

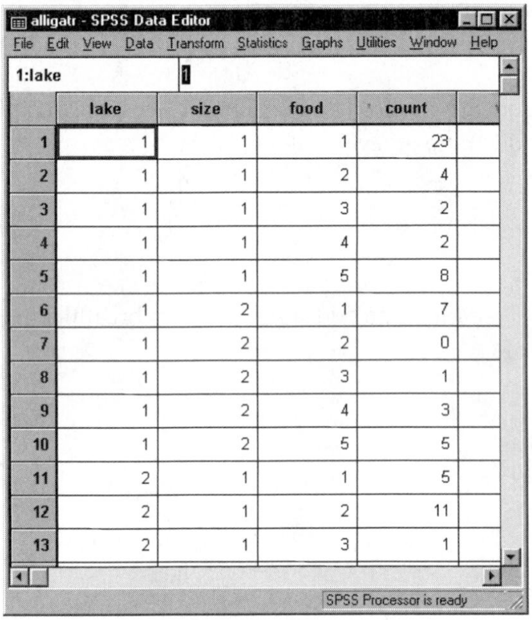

	lake	size	food	count
1	1	1	1	23
2	1	1	2	4
3	1	1	3	2
4	1	1	4	2
5	1	1	5	8
6	1	2	1	7
7	1	2	2	0
8	1	2	3	1
9	1	2	4	3
10	1	2	5	5
11	2	1	1	5
12	2	1	2	11
13	2	1	3	1

Agresti (1990) analyzes these data and fits the logit model

$$\ln\left(\frac{m_{ijk}}{m_{1jk}}\right) = \lambda_i + \omega_{ij} + \upsilon_{ik}, \qquad i = 2, 3, 4, 5 \qquad \text{Equation 17-26}$$

where i is the index for *food*, j is for *size*, and k is for *lake*. This logit model is used to study the preference for fish (*food* 1) versus any other food type. The equivalent loglinear model is

$$\ln(m_{ijk}) = (SL)_{jk} + F_i + (FS)_{ij} + (FL)_{ik} \qquad \text{Equation 17-27}$$

where $(SL)_{jk}$ is the normalizing constant for the *j*th category of *size* and *k*th category of *lake*. F_i is the main-effects term for *food*, $(FS)_{ij}$ and $(FL)_{ik}$ are the terms corresponding to *food* by *size* and *food* by *lake*. From Equation 17-26 and Equation 17-27,

$$\lambda_i = F_i - F_1$$
$$\omega_{ij} = (FS)_{ij} - (FS)_{1j} \qquad \text{Equation 17-28}$$
$$\upsilon_{ik} = (FL)_{ik} - (FL)_{1k}$$

For this logit model, from the menus choose:

Data
 Weight Cases...
▶ Weight cases by: count

Analyze
 Loglinear
  Logit...

▶ Dependent: food
▶ Factor(s): size lake

Model...
 ⊙ Custom
 ▶ Terms in Model (Main effects): lake size

Options...
 Display
  ☑ Frequencies
  ☑ Estimates
 Plot: deselect all plots

This model fits the data well, as shown in the goodness-of-fit statistics in Figure 17-11. The significance is well above 0.05.

Figure 17-11
Goodness-of-fit statistics

	Chi-Square	DF	Sig.
Likelihood Ratio	17.0798	12	.1466
Pearson	15.0435	12	.2391

The measures of association shown in Figure 17-12 are $R_H = 0.1064$ for entropy and $R_C = 0.0921$ for concentration, which suggests that *food* is associated with *lake* and *size*.

Figure 17-12
Analysis of dispersion and measures of association

```
Analysis of Dispersion

Source of Dispersion       Entropy  Concentration       DF

Due to Model               32.1413        14.2409        16
Due to Residual           270.0401       140.3253       856
Total                     302.1815       154.5662       872

Measures of Association

       Entropy =   .1064
 Concentration =   .0921
```

Next, look at the parameter estimates. Figure 17-13 shows the parameter correspondence table, and Figure 17-14 shows the parameter estimates.

Figure 17-13
Correspondence between parameters and terms of the design

```
Parameter   Aliased  Term

        1            Constant for [LAKE = 1]*[SIZE = 1]
        2            Constant for [LAKE = 1]*[SIZE = 2]
        3            Constant for [LAKE = 2]*[SIZE = 1]
        4            Constant for [LAKE = 2]*[SIZE = 2]
        5            Constant for [LAKE = 3]*[SIZE = 1]
        6            Constant for [LAKE = 3]*[SIZE = 2]
        7            Constant for [LAKE = 4]*[SIZE = 1]
        8            Constant for [LAKE = 4]*[SIZE = 2]
        9            [FOOD = 1]
       10            [FOOD = 2]
       11            [FOOD = 3]
       12            [FOOD = 4]
       13       x    [FOOD = 5]
       14            [FOOD = 1]*[SIZE = 1]
       15       x    [FOOD = 1]*[SIZE = 2]
       16            [FOOD = 2]*[SIZE = 1]
       17       x    [FOOD = 2]*[SIZE = 2]
       18            [FOOD = 3]*[SIZE = 1]
       19       x    [FOOD = 3]*[SIZE = 2]
       20            [FOOD = 4]*[SIZE = 1]
       21       x    [FOOD = 4]*[SIZE = 2]
       22       x    [FOOD = 5]*[SIZE = 1]
       23       x    [FOOD = 5]*[SIZE = 2]
       24            [FOOD = 1]*[LAKE = 1]
       25            [FOOD = 1]*[LAKE = 2]
       26            [FOOD = 1]*[LAKE = 3]
       27       x    [FOOD = 1]*[LAKE = 4]
       28            [FOOD = 2]*[LAKE = 1]
       29            [FOOD = 2]*[LAKE = 2]
       30            [FOOD = 2]*[LAKE = 3]
       31       x    [FOOD = 2]*[LAKE = 4]
       32            [FOOD = 3]*[LAKE = 1]
       33            [FOOD = 3]*[LAKE = 2]
       34            [FOOD = 3]*[LAKE = 3]
       35       x    [FOOD = 3]*[LAKE = 4]
       36            [FOOD = 4]*[LAKE = 1]
       37            [FOOD = 4]*[LAKE = 2]
       38            [FOOD = 4]*[LAKE = 3]
       39       x    [FOOD = 4]*[LAKE = 4]
       40       x    [FOOD = 5]*[LAKE = 1]
       41       x    [FOOD = 5]*[LAKE = 2]
       42       x    [FOOD = 5]*[LAKE = 3]
       43       x    [FOOD = 5]*[LAKE = 4]
```

Note: 'x' indicates an aliased (or a redundant) parameter.
These parameters are set to zero.

Figure 17-14
Parameter estimates for alligator data

```
Constant    Estimate

    1       2.2921
    2       1.1327
    3        .0746
    4        .6537
    5       1.4305
    6       1.7612
    7       1.3470
    8        .7674
```

Note: Constants are not parameters under the multinomial assumption.
Therefore, standard errors are not calculated.

Parameter	Estimate	SE	Z-value	Asymptotic 95% CI Lower	Upper
9	1.9043	.5258	3.62	.87	2.93
10	.3553	.5958	.60	-.81	1.52
11	-1.4103	1.1357	-1.24	-3.64	.82
12	-.1888	.7903	-.24	-1.74	1.36
13	.0000	.	.	.	.
14	-.0316	.4483	-.74	-1.21	.55
15	.0000	.	.	.	.
16	1.1267	.5049	2.23	.14	2.12
17	.0000	.	.	.	.
18	-.6828	.6514	-1.05	-1.96	.59
19	.0000	.	.	.	.
20	-.9622	.7127	-1.35	-2.36	.43
21	.0000	.	.	.	.
22	.0000	.	.	.	.
23	.0000	.	.	.	.
24	-.8262	.5575	-1.48	-1.92	.27
25	-.0057	.7766	-7.279E-03	-1.53	1.52
26	-1.5164	.6214	-2.44	-2.73	-.30
27	.0000	.	.	.	.
28	-2.4846	.7432	-3.34	-3.94	-1.03
29	.9316	.7968	1.17	-.63	2.49
30	-.3944	.6263	-.63	-1.62	.83
31	.0000	.	.	.	.
32	.4166	1.2605	.33	-2.05	2.89
33	2.4532	1.2938	1.90	-.08	4.99
34	1.4189	1.1892	1.19	-.91	3.75
35	.0000	.	.	.	.
36	-.1311	.8920	-.15	-1.88	1.62
37	-.6589	1.3686	-.48	-3.34	2.02
38	-.4286	.9383	-.46	-2.27	1.41
39	.0000	.	.	.	.
40	.0000	.	.	.	.
41	.0000	.	.	.	.
42	.0000	.	.	.	.
43	.0000	.	.	.	.

Consider how the size of an alligator affects the odds of its selecting primarily reptiles instead of fish. For $i = 3$, the parameter $\omega_{31} = (FS)_{31} - (FS)_{11}$. Since $(FS)_{31}$ and $(FS)_{11}$ are the 18th and the 14th parameters,

$$\omega_{31} = -0.6828 - (-0.3316) = -0.3512 \qquad \text{Equation 17-29}$$

Similarly,

$$\omega_{32} = (FS)_{32} - (FS)_{12} = 0 \qquad\qquad \text{Equation 17-30}$$

Thus, for a given lake, the estimated odds of preferring primarily reptiles to fish is

$$e^{-0.3512} = 0.70 \qquad\qquad \text{Equation 17-31}$$

times lower for the smaller alligators than for the larger ones.

Next, consider how these odds differ between lakes. One way to do this is to compute the parameter estimates υ_{31}, υ_{32}, υ_{33}, and υ_{34}. By referring to Figure 17-13 and Figure 17-14, we have

$$
\begin{aligned}
\upsilon_{31} &= (FL)_{31} - (FL)_{11} = 0.4166 - (-0.8262) = 1.2428 \\
\upsilon_{32} &= (FL)_{32} - (FL)_{12} = 2.4532 - (-0.0057) = 2.4589 \\
\upsilon_{33} &= (FL)_{33} - (FL)_{13} = 1.4189 - (-1.5164) = 2.9353 \\
\upsilon_{34} &= (FL)_{34} - (FL)_{14} = 0 - 0 = 0
\end{aligned}
\qquad \text{Equation 17-32}
$$

Therefore, the lake effects indicate that the estimated odds of selecting primarily reptiles instead of fish are relatively highest in lake 3, next in lake 2, next in lake 1, and relatively lowest in lake 4. To complete the analysis, the food effect is

$$\lambda_3 = F_3 - F_1 = -1.4103 - 1.9043 = -3.3146 \qquad\qquad \text{Equation 17-33}$$

and the estimated odds are

$$\frac{m_{311}}{m_{111}} = e^{\lambda_1 + \omega_{31} + \upsilon_{31}} = e^{-2.4230} = 0.0887$$

$$\frac{m_{312}}{m_{112}} = e^{\lambda_1 + \omega_{31} + \upsilon_{32}} = e^{-1.2069} = 0.2991$$

$$\frac{m_{313}}{m_{113}} = e^{\lambda_1 + \omega_{31} + \upsilon_{33}} = e^{-0.7305} = 0.4817 \qquad \text{Equation 17-34}$$

$$\frac{m_{314}}{m_{114}} = e^{\lambda_1 + \omega_{31} + \upsilon_{34}} = e^{-3.6658} = 0.0256$$

and

$$\frac{m_{321}}{m_{121}} = e^{\lambda_1 + \omega_{32} + \upsilon_{31}} = e^{-2.0718} = 0.1260$$

$$\frac{m_{322}}{m_{122}} = e^{\lambda_1 + \omega_{32} + \upsilon_{32}} = e^{-0.8557} = 0.4250$$

Equation 17-35

$$\frac{m_{323}}{m_{123}} = e^{\lambda_1 + \omega_{32} + \upsilon_{33}} = e^{-0.3793} = 0.6843$$

$$\frac{m_{324}}{m_{124}} = e^{\lambda_1 + \omega_{32} + \upsilon_{34}} = e^{-3.3146} = 0.0363$$

If you want standard errors or confidence intervals for these odds, you can use a contrast variable to calculate the generalized log-odds ratio (GLOR). You would construct a comparison variable (similar to the variables *G1*, *G2*, and *G3* in "Poisson Loglinear Regression" on p. 196 in Chapter 16) and specify it in the Contrast Variable(s) list in the Logit Loglinear Analysis dialog box.

Example 4
Model Diagnosis: Coal Miner Data Revisited

Consider the coal miner data again, which is discussed in "Two Response Variables with Two Categories Each" on p. 213. The model used is somewhat unusual, although it fits the data well. As in Agresti (1990), this model was developed through model diagnosis on another model. The other model is a logit model that assumes a constant odds ratio across age. The following discussion illustrates how to apply the techniques for model diagnosis to the coal miner data.

For this discussion, the previously fitted model will be called model 1 and another model, to be described below, will be called model 2. Model 2 is given by

$$\ln\left(\frac{m_{11k}m_{22k}}{m_{12k}m_{21k}}\right) = \lambda$$

Equation 17-36

where m_{ijk} is the count for the *i*th category of breathlessness, the *j*th category of wheeze, and the *k*th level of age. The equivalent loglinear model is the one with no three-way interaction. Recall that the variables are *qbreath*, *qwheeze*, and *age*. The setup for running the procedure is similar to "Two Response Variables with Two Categories Each" on p. 213. This time, do not use a covariate.

From the menus choose:

Data
  Weight Cases...
▶ Weight cases by: count

Analyze
  Loglinear
    Logit...

▶ Dependent: qbreath qwheeze
▶ Factor(s): age

Model...
    ⊙ Custom
    ▶ Terms in Model (Main effects): age

Save...
    ☑ Adjusted residuals

Options...
    Display
        ☑ Residuals
    Plot
        ☑ Deviance residuals
        ☑ Normal probability for deviance

Paste

After editing, the final syntax should be:

```
GENLOG QBREATH QWHEEZE BY AGE
 /MODEL=MULTINOMIAL
 /PRINT=RESID ADJRESID DEV
 /PLOT=RESID(DEV) NORMPROB(DEV)
 /DESIGN=QBREATH, QWHEEZE, QBREATH*QWHEEZE, QBREATH*AGE,
  QWHEEZE*AGE
 /SAVE ADJRESID DEV.
```

Figure 17-15 shows the goodness-of-fit information for model 2.

Figure 17-15
Goodness-of-fit statistics

	Chi-Square	DF	Sig.
Likelihood Ratio	26.6904	8	.0008
Pearson	26.6348	8	.0008

Since the sample size $N = 18282$ is large, the two goodness-of-fit statistics follow the chi-square distribution. Since the p values (*Sig.*) are both 0.008, which is considerably smaller than 0.05, this model is unlikely to be the right one.

Next, look at the residuals. When Residuals is selected, the Logit Loglinear Analysis procedure displays three residuals, as shown in Figure 17-16. Notice that the raw residuals and the adjusted residuals all add up to 0 within each level of *age*. This behavior is expected as a property of the multinomial logit model.

Figure 17-16
Residuals for model 2

Factor	Value	Resid.	Adj. Resid.	Dev. Resid.
AGE	20 to 24			
QBREATH No Breathlessness				
QWHEEZE	No Wheeze	1.45	.75	.03
QWHEEZE	Have Wheeze	-1.45	-.75	-.15
QBREATH Have Breathlessness				
QWHEEZE	No Wheeze	-1.45	-.75	-.52
QWHEEZE	Have Wheeze	1.45	.75	.51
AGE	25 to 29			
QBREATH No Breathlessness				
QWHEEZE	No Wheeze	5.91	2.20	.15
QWHEEZE	Have Wheeze	-5.91	-2.20	-.57
QBREATH Have Breathlessness				
QWHEEZE	No Wheeze	-5.91	-2.20	-1.65
QWHEEZE	Have Wheeze	5.91	2.20	1.36
AGE	30 to 34			
QBREATH No Breathlessness				
QWHEEZE	No Wheeze	8.05	2.10	.19
QWHEEZE	Have Wheeze	-8.05	-2.10	-.60
QBREATH Have Breathlessness				
QWHEEZE	No Wheeze	-8.05	-2.10	-1.64
QWHEEZE	Have Wheeze	8.05	2.10	1.16
AGE	35 to 39			
QBREATH No Breathlessness				
QWHEEZE	No Wheeze	9.60	1.77	.20
QWHEEZE	Have Wheeze	-9.60	-1.77	-.59
QBREATH Have Breathlessness				
QWHEEZE	No Wheeze	-9.60	-1.77	-1.30
QWHEEZE	Have Wheeze	9.60	1.77	.90
AGE	40 to 44			
QBREATH No Breathlessness				
QWHEEZE	No Wheeze	6.49	1.13	.15
QWHEEZE	Have Wheeze	-6.49	-1.13	-.39
QBREATH Have Breathlessness				
QWHEEZE	No Wheeze	-6.49	-1.13	-.85
QWHEEZE	Have Wheeze	6.49	1.13	.51
AGE	45 to 49			
QBREATH No Breathlessness				
QWHEEZE	No Wheeze	-2.79	-.42	-.07
QWHEEZE	Have Wheeze	2.79	.42	.16
QBREATH Have Breathlessness				
QWHEEZE	No Wheeze	2.79	.42	.30
QWHEEZE	Have Wheeze	-2.79	-.42	-.17
AGE	50 to 54			
QBREATH No Breathlessness				
QWHEEZE	No Wheeze	5.86	.81	.16
QWHEEZE	Have Wheeze	-5.86	-.81	-.37
QBREATH Have Breathlessness				
QWHEEZE	No Wheeze	-5.86	-.81	-.53
QWHEEZE	Have Wheeze	5.86	.81	.29
AGE	55 to 59			
QBREATH No Breathlessness				
QWHEEZE	No Wheeze	-25.71	-3.65	-.82
QWHEEZE	Have Wheeze	25.71	3.65	1.78
QBREATH Have Breathlessness				
QWHEEZE	No Wheeze	25.71	3.65	2.22
QWHEEZE	Have Wheeze	-25.71	-3.65	-1.25
AGE	60 to 64			
QBREATH No Breathlessness				
QWHEEZE	No Wheeze	-8.86	-1.44	-.38
QWHEEZE	Have Wheeze	8.86	1.44	.79
QBREATH Have Breathlessness				
QWHEEZE	No Wheeze	8.86	1.44	.89
QWHEEZE	Have Wheeze	-8.86	-1.44	-.46

Agresti (1990) observed that the adjusted residuals show a decreasing trend as age increases. Since the adjusted residuals have the same magnitudes within each age group, it would be confusing to look at adjusted residual diagnostic plots provided by the Logit Loglinear Analysis procedure. Instead, consider the diagnostic plots for the deviance residuals. Recall that Deviance residuals and Normal probability for deviance were selected. The plots are shown in Figure 17-17 and Figure 17-18.

Figure 17-17
Matrix plot of observed count versus expected count versus deviance residuals

Loglinear Model

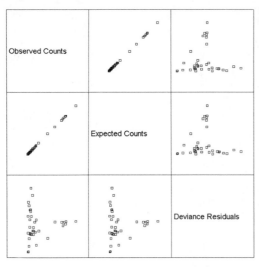

Figure 17-18
Normal Q-Q plot of deviance residuals

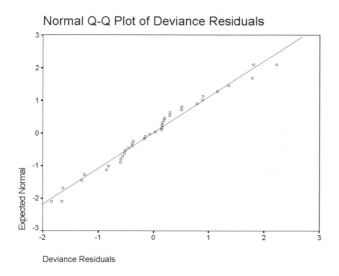

Normal Q-Q Plot of Deviance Residuals

In Figure 17-17, the deviance residuals exhibit a decreasing trend as either the observed or expected count increases. The normal Q-Q plot in Figure 17-18 further suggests that the distribution is not normal.

To verify Agresti's observation, the adjusted residuals are saved into variable *Adj_1* and a scatterplot is created with the Graphs menu. *Adj_1* is plotted versus *age* for cases where *qbreath* is 1 and *qwheeze* is 1. These are the cells for *Have Breathlessness–Have Wheeze*. The scatterplot is shown in Figure 17-19.

Figure 17-19
Scatterplot of adjusted residuals versus age group

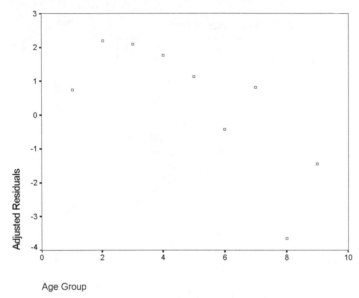

The trend is apparent in Figure 17-19. This suggests that a covariate related to the age group number may be included in the model. Such a variable, *delta*, was created and selected as a covariate in "Two Response Variables with Two Categories Each" on p. 213. Since model 2 is nested within model 1, to test whether the two models are statistically different, you can compare their likelihood-ratio chi-square statistics. Recall that the likelihood-ratio statistic of model 1 is 6.8017 (see Figure 17-7) with 7 degrees of freedom. The difference from the model 2 statistic (see Figure 17-15) is $26.6904 - 6.8017 = 19.8887$ with $8 - 7 = 1$ degrees of freedom.

This corresponds to a p value of 0.0000082. You can calculate the p value by choosing Compute from the Transform menu and creating a new variable $p = 1 - \text{CDF.CHISQ}(19.8887, 1)$. The small p value is strong evidence that model 2 is different from model 1. This is expected because model 1 fits the data well but model 2 does not.

Example 5
Continuation Ratio Logit Model

A categorical variable is called an ordinal variable when there is an unambiguous ordering of its categories. When a response variable is an ordinal variable, we can collect extra information about its association with the explanatory variables. Also, there is a larger class of models for ordinal variables. One of these models is the continuation ratio logit model. Suppose an ordinal variable has categories labeled from 1 to I. Then the jth continuation ratio logit model is defined as

$$L_j = \ln\left(\frac{\pi_j}{\pi_{j+1} + \ldots + \pi_I}\right), \qquad j = 1, \ldots, I - 1 \qquad \text{Equation 17-37}$$

where π_j is the probability that an observation is from the jth category (Agresti, 1990). When I equals 2, this logit model is the same as the standard logit model.

Advantages

There are some advantages in working with continuation ratio logit models. Suppose that $\{n_i\}$ are the observed counts from a multinomial distribution with sample size N and cell probabilities $\{\pi_i\}$. We can decompose the multinomial probability density function as the product of $I - 1$ dependent binomial probability density functions. The jth binomial distribution has probability $\pi_j / (\pi_{j+1} + \ldots + \pi_I)$ and sample size $n_j + \ldots + n_I$. This implies that the continuation ratio logit model can be fitted by using the algorithms or software designed for a standard logit model.

Procedure

The procedure is quite straightforward when you choose Loglinear and then Logit from the Analyze menu. Suppose that the response variable is *resp* and the design is *resp* plus a covariate.

First, choose Recode from the Transform menu to create a dichotomous variable, *resp1*. The first category of *resp1* is the same as that of *resp*. The second category of *resp1* includes the second through the last categories of *resp* combined. Then fit a logit model with the following variables:

■ Response variable *resp1*

■ Design variables *resp1* and the covariate (Logit Loglinear Analysis Model dialog box)

Save the predicted values, creating a variable, *pred1*. Then create a second dichotomous variable, *resp2*. The first category of *resp2* is the second category of *resp*. The second category of *resp2* includes the third through the last categories of *resp* combined. Next, choose Compute Variable from the Transform menu and set the values of *pred1* to 0 for the first category of *resp*. Then fit a logit model with the following variables:

■ Response variable *resp2*

■ Cell structure variable *pred1*

■ Design variables *resp2* and the covariate (Logit Loglinear Analysis Model dialog box)

Save the predicted values, creating variable *pred2*. Repeat these steps until the last category of *resp* is reached.

The overall likelihood-ratio chi-square statistic can be obtained by adding individual chi-square statistics. Furthermore, the observed proportions $n_j/(n_j + \ldots + n_I)$ are each asymptotically independent. Thus, you can assess the fits of the $I - 1$ logit models independently. More details can be found in Fienberg (1980) and Agresti (1990). Although the method sounds complicated, it is in fact practical to use. The following example illustrates how to fit a continuation ratio logit model using SPSS and this method.

Toxicity Study

The data are taken from a developmental toxicity study by Price et al. (1987). The sample consists of 1435 pregnant mice. The purpose of the study was to investigate how various doses of the chemical ethylene glycol dimethyl ether (diEGdiME) affect developing fetuses. The researchers administered diEGdiME in distilled water to pregnant mice for 10 days early in the pregnancy. The mice were divided into five groups according to the concentration of diEGdiME, measured in mg/kg per day. The first group was a control group. The uterine contents of the mice were collected two days later for examination. The results show the status of the fetus. There are three possible outcomes listed in reverse order of desirability—dead, malformed, and normal. These outcomes are recorded in the variable *status* as 1, 2, and 3. The data are shown in Figure 17-20.

Figure 17-20
Data for toxicity study

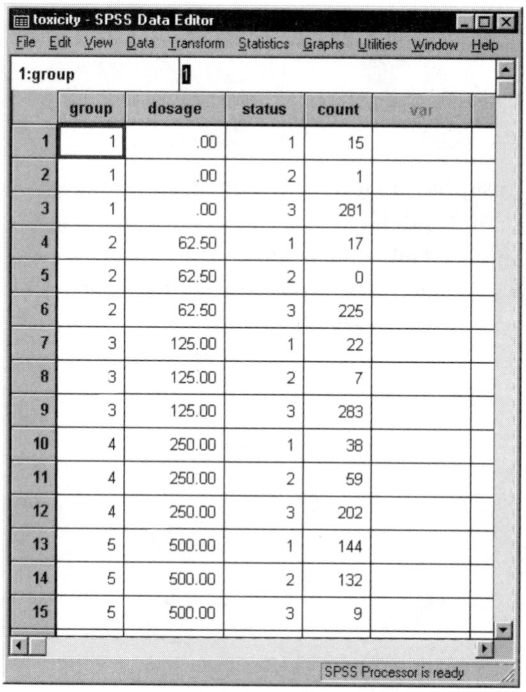

	group	dosage	status	count	var
1	1	.00	1	15	
2	1	.00	2	1	
3	1	.00	3	281	
4	2	62.50	1	17	
5	2	62.50	2	0	
6	2	62.50	3	225	
7	3	125.00	1	22	
8	3	125.00	2	7	
9	3	125.00	3	283	
10	4	250.00	1	38	
11	4	250.00	2	59	
12	4	250.00	3	202	
13	5	500.00	1	144	
14	5	500.00	2	132	
15	5	500.00	3	9	

The variables are *group*, *dosage*, *status*, and *count*. The data are weighted by *count* (using the Data menu).

Since I is equal to 3, there are $I - 1 = 2$ individual logit models. The first logit model compares the number of dead fetuses to that of live fetuses (that is, malformed and normal). The second logit model compares the number of malformed fetuses to that of normal fetuses (provided they are alive). Agresti (1990) suggests the design

$$L_j = \alpha_j + \beta_j x_i \qquad j = 1, 2 \qquad \text{Equation 17-38}$$

where j is the index for *status* and x_i is the *dosage* at the ith group.

To fit the first logit model, the first dichotomous variable, *qalive*, is created.

To create *qalive*, from the menus choose:

Transform
  Recode...

status-->qalive

  Old and New Values...
    1 -->1
    2 thru 3 --> 2

The first group contains all cases having a *status* value of 1, and the second contains all cases having *status* values of 2 and 3.

You do not need to combine the cell counts, since the Logit Loglinear Analysis procedure will aggregate the data internally. Now you can fit a standard logit model with *qalive* as the response (dependent) variable and *group* as a factor.

From the menus choose:

Data
  Weight Cases...
▶ Weight cases by: count

Analyze
  Loglinear
    Logit...

▶ Dependent: qalive
▶ Factor(s): group
▶ Cell Covariate(s): dosage

Model...
  ⊙ Custom
  ▶ Terms in Model (Main effects): dosage

Save...
  ☑ Predicted values

The predicted values will be saved into variable *pre_1* for use in the next logit model.

In the second logit model, the second category of *status* is compared to the third and last category of *status*, making *status* the response variable. The first category of *status* is suppressed by declaring it missing. In the Data Editor, double-click on *status* and specify:

Missing Values...
  Discrete missing values: 1

Next, recall the Logit Loglinear dialog box and choose:

▶ Dependent: status
▶ Factor(s): group
▶ Cell Covariate(s): dosage
▶ Cell Structure: pre_1

Model...
  ⊙ Custom
  ▶ Terms in Model (Main effects): dosage

Save...
  ☐ Predicted values (deselect)

This second custom model uses *status* and the interaction *dosage* by *status* (if you paste the syntax, you can see these variables on the DESIGN subcommand). Since the second logit model is the last logit model in this example, it is not necessary to save the predicted values unless otherwise needed. The goodness-of-fit statistics from the two logit models are shown in Figure 17-21 and Figure 17-22. Both models fit fairly well at the 0.05 level because the significance values are greater than 0.05.

Figure 17-21
Goodness-of-fit statistics for first logit model

	Chi-Square	DF	Sig.
Likelihood Ratio	5.7775	3	.1230
Pearson	5.8257	3	.1204

Figure 17-22
Goodness-of-fit statistics for second logit model

	Chi-Square	DF	Sig.
Likelihood Ratio	6.0609	3	.1087
Pearson	3.9331	3	.2688

The *overall* likelihood-ratio chi-square statistic is the sum of two likelihood-ratio chi-square statistics:

$$5.7775 + 6.0609 = 11.8384 \qquad \text{Equation 17-39}$$

and there are $3 + 3 = 6$ degrees of freedom. To calculate the corresponding p value, from the Transform menu choose Compute and enter

$$p = 1 - \text{CDF.CHISQ}(11.8384, 6) \qquad \text{Equation 17-40}$$

The p value is 0.0657, which is marginally acceptable. The parameter estimates are shown in Figure 17-23 and Figure 17-24.

Figure 17-23
Parameter estimates for first logit model

```
Parameter Estimates
  Constant    Estimate
       1       5.6556
       2       5.4326
       3       5.6602
       4       5.5249
       5       4.9857
Note: Constants are not parameters under multinomial assumption.
      Therefore, standard errors are not calculated.
                                           Asymptotic 95% CI
  Parameter   Estimate      SE    Z-value    Lower      Upper
       6      -3.2479    .1576    -20.60     -3.56      -2.94
       7        .0000       .         .         .          .
       8        .0064    .0004     14.70   5.537E-03  7.241E-03
       9        .0000       .         .         .          .
```

In the first logit model, parameter 8 indicates that

$$\beta_1 = 0.0064 \qquad \text{Equation 17-41}$$

with a standard error of 0.0004 and a z value of 14.70.

Figure 17-24
Parameter estimates for second logit model

```
Parameter Estimates
  Constant    Estimate
       1       -.0170
       2       -.0264
       3       -.0192
       4       -.1892
       5      -3.0716
Note: Constants are not parameters under multinomial assumption.
      Therefore, standard errors are not calculated.
                                           Asymptotic 95% CI
  Parameter   Estimate      SE    Z-value    Lower      Upper
       6        .0000       .         .         .          .
       7      -5.7019    .3322    -17.16     -6.35      -5.05
       8        .0000       .         .         .          .
       9        .0000       .         .         .          .
      10        .0174    .0012     14.16       .01        .02
      11        .0000       .         .         .          .
```

In the second logit model, parameter 10 indicates that

$$\beta_2 = 0.0174 \qquad \text{Equation 17-42}$$

with a standard error of 0.0012 and a z value of 14.16.

Thus, the likelihood of the less desirable fetus status (dead in the first logit model and malformed in second logit model) increases as the concentration of diEGdiME increases. From Equation 17-41, the estimated odds that a fetus is dead increase multiplicatively by a factor of

$$e^{0.0064 \times 100} = 1.9 \qquad\qquad \text{Equation 17-43}$$

for every 100 mg/kg per day increase in the concentration of diEGdiME.

Ordinal Regression

The Ordinal Regression procedure allows you to build models, generate predictions, and evaluate the importance of various predictor variables in cases where the dependent (target) variable is ordinal in nature.

Ordinal Variables

In data analysis, you need to understand the variables you will be analyzing in order to get the most benefit from your data and to be sure that your conclusions are justified. One of the most important features of a variable is its **measurement level**. Many variables represent numerical measurements of some feature, such as an account balance or age. With such variables, you can assume that any particular case (record) can take any value in the range of the variable. In addition, you can also assume that differences are consistent throughout the range of measurements. In other words, for account balances, you can assume that the difference between $2,000 and $3,000 is equivalent to the difference between $14,000 and $15,000. Such variables are referred to as **scale** variables. The usual linear regression methods are designed to model this kind of variable.

There are some important variables that do not fit this profile, however. Consider a credit account status variable, where there are five possible values: paid on time, 30 days past due, 60 days past due, 90 days past due, and uncollectable. It is clear that there is an order to the categories; paid on time is better than 30 days past due, which in turn is better than 60 days past due, and so on. However, it is not clear that differences are consistent. For example, the difference between 90 days past due and uncollectable is of a different magnitude than the difference between 30 days past due and 60 days past due, even though you are comparing adjacent categories in both cases. Such variables are called **ordinal variables**. Other examples of ordinal variables include certain psychological measurements and rank scores. In some cases, apparently continuous variables are best considered as ordinal due to threshold effects. A common example of this is a variable measuring years of education. While time is obviously continuous in the abstract, the fact that there are educational "milestones" effectively changes the relationship between time and the underlying concept of educational achievement. Because students finish their secondary education and receive their diplomas after 12 years of school, the difference between 11 and 12 years is "bigger" than the difference between 10 and 11 years.

When you are trying to predict ordinal responses, the usual linear regression models don't work very well. Those methods can work only by assuming that the outcome (dependent) variable is measured on an interval scale. Because this is not true for ordinal outcome variables, the simplifying assumptions on which linear regression relies are not satisfied, and thus the regression model may not accurately reflect the relationships in the data. In particular, linear regression is sensitive to the way you define categories of the target variable. With an ordinal variable, the important thing is the ordering of categories. So, if you collapse two adjacent categories into one larger category, you are making only a small change, and models built using the old and new categorizations should be very similar. Unfortunately, because linear regression is sensitive to the categorization used, a model built before merging categories could be quite different from one built after.

Regression with Ordinal Outcome Variables

Because of these limitations, special methods are necessary to handle ordinal outcome (dependent) variables. One way to model ordinal variables is to use a scoring scheme, where each category of the ordinal outcome variable is assigned a score on a continuous scale to account for the unequal distances between categories. For example, suppose the credit scoring categories outlined are mapped to a continuous scale of risk. On this risk scale, the categories might have the following values:

Category	Probability of membership	Score
Current	.80	0
30 Days	.07	1
60 Days	.07	3
90 Days	.05	7
Uncollectable	.01	20

Figure 18-1

Mapping categories to continuous scores

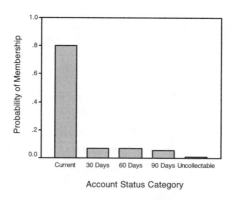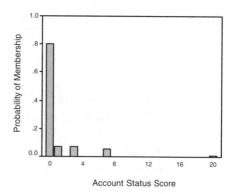

The mapping is shown graphically in Figure 18-1. Once scores have been assigned to cases based on their category, a traditional linear regression model can be applied.

The drawback to this method is that you have to know what score values to assign to the ordinal categories before you start. If you get the score values wrong, your model will be incorrect and your predictions will be inaccurate. Unfortunately, in many cases the appropriate score values cannot be determined *a priori*.

An alternative approach uses a generalization of linear regression called a **generalized linear model** to predict *cumulative probabilities* for the categories. With this method, you get a separate equation for each category of the ordinal dependent variable. Each equation gives a predicted probability of being in the corresponding category or any lower category. For example, look at the distribution shown in

Figure 18-2. With no predictors in the model, predictions are based only on the overall probabilities of being in each category.

Figure 18-2
Cumulative probabilities for ordered categories

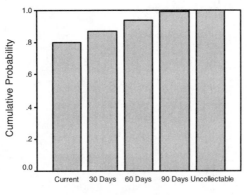

In this case, the predicted cumulative probability for the first category is 0.80. The prediction for the second category is .80 + .07 = .87. The prediction for the third is .80 + .07 + .07 = .94, and so on. The prediction for the last category is always 1.0, since all cases must be in either the last category or a lower category. Because of this, the prediction equation for the last category is not needed.

The Form of the Model

Generalized linear models are a very powerful class of models, which can be used to answer a wide range of statistical questions. The basic form of a generalized linear model is:

$$link(\gamma_j) = \theta_j - [\beta_1 x_1 + \beta_2 x_2 + \ldots + \beta_k x_k]$$

where γ_j is the cumulative probability for the jth category, θ_j is the threshold for the jth category, $\beta_1 \ldots \beta_k$ are the regression coefficients, $x_1 \ldots x_k$ are the predictor variables, and k is the number of predictors. There are several important things to notice here.

■ The model is based on the notion that there is some latent continuous outcome variable (such as the risk scale outlined above), and that the manifest ordinal outcome variable arises from discretizing the underlying continuum into j ordered groups. The cutoff values on this continuous distribution that define the categories are estimated by the thresholds θ_j. In some cases, there is good theoretical justification for assuming such an underlying distribution. However, even in cases in which there is no theoretical concept that links to the latent variable, the model can still perform quite well and give valid results. Note also that in the ordinal regression model, the thresholds are estimated as part of the model and need not be specified *a priori*.

- The thresholds or constants in the model θ_j (corresponding to the intercept in linear regression models) depend only on which category's probability is being predicted. Values of the predictor (independent) variables do not affect this part of the model.

- The prediction part of the model, $[\beta_1 x_1 + \beta_2 x_2 + \ldots + \beta_k x_k]$, depends only on the predictors and is independent of the outcome category. These first two properties imply that the results will be a set of parallel lines or planes—one for each category of the outcome variable.

- Rather than predicting the actual cumulative probabilities, the model predicts a function of those values. This function is called the **link function**, and you choose the form of the link function when you build the model. This allows you to choose a link function based on the problem under consideration to optimize your results. Several link functions (described in "Constructing a Model" on p. 247) are available in the Ordinal Regression procedure.

As you can see, these are very powerful and general models. Of course, there is also a bit more to keep track of here than in a typical linear regression model. There are three major components in an ordinal regression model:

- **Location component.** The portion of the equation shown above, which includes the coefficients and predictor variables, $[\beta_1 x_1 + \beta_2 x_2 + \ldots + \beta_k x_k]$, is called the **location component** of the model. The location is the "meat" of the model. It uses the predictor variables to calculate predicted probabilities of membership in the categories for each case.

- **Scale component.** The **scale component** is an optional modification to the basic model to account for differences in variability for different values of the predictor variables. For example, if men have more variability than women in their account status values, using a scale component to account for this may improve your model. The model with a scale component follows the form

$$link(\gamma_j) = \frac{\theta_j - [\beta_1 x_1 + \beta_2 x_2 + \ldots + \beta_k x_k]}{\exp(\tau_1 z_1 + \tau_2 z_2 + \ldots + \tau_m z_m)}$$

where $\tau_1 \ldots \tau_m$ are coefficients for the scale component and $z_1 \ldots z_m$ are m predictor variables for the scale component (chosen from the same set of variables as the x's).

Here you would include gender, and perhaps some other predictors, in the scale component to adjust for the differences in variability.

- **Link function.** The link function is a transformation of the cumulative probabilities that allows estimation of the model. Five link functions are available in the ordinal regression procedure, summarized in the following table:

Function	Form	Typical application
Logit	$\log\left(\dfrac{\gamma}{1-\gamma}\right)$	evenly distributed categories
Complementary log-log	$\log(-\log(1-\gamma))$	higher categories more probable
Negative log-log	$-\log(-\log(\gamma))$	lower categories more probable
Probit	$\Phi^{-1}(\gamma)$	analyses with explicit normally distributed latent variable
Cauchit (inverse Cauchy)	$\tan(\pi(\gamma-0.5))$	outcome with many extreme values

Example
Credit scoring model

The rest of this chapter will use the analysis of consumer credit data to illustrate how to build and evaluate ordinal regression models. The outcome (dependent) variable is *account status*, with five ordinal levels: no debt history, no current debt, debt payments current, debt payments past due, and critical account. Potential predictors consist of various financial and personal characteristics of applicants, including age, number of credits at the bank, housing type, checking account status, and so on. The data are taken from the "German credit" data set in the University of California, Irvine Repository of Machine Learning Databases (Blake, Keogh, and Merz, 1998).

Constructing a Model

Constructing your initial ordinal regression model entails several decisions. First, of course, you need to identify the ordinal outcome variable. Then, you need to decide which predictors to use for the location component of the model. Next, you need to decide whether to use a scale component and, if you do, what predictors to use for it. Finally, you need to decide which link function best fits your research question and the structure of the data.

Identifying the Outcome Variable

In most cases, you will already have a specific target variable in mind by the time you begin building an ordinal regression model. After all, the reason you use an ordinal regression model is that you know you want to predict an ordinal outcome. In this example, the ordinal outcome is account status, with five categories: no debt history, no current debt, payments current, payments delayed, and critical account.

Choosing Predictors for the Location Model

The process of choosing predictors for the location component of the model is similar to the process of selecting predictors in a linear regression model. You should take both theoretical and empirical considerations into account in selecting predictors. Ideally, your model would include all of the important predictors and none of the others. In practice, you often don't know exactly which predictors will prove to be important until you build the model. In that case, it's usually better to start off by including all of the predictors that you think might be important. If you discover that some of those predictors seem not to be helpful in the model, you can remove them and reestimate the model.

In this case, previous experience and some preliminary exploratory analysis have identified five likely predictors: age, duration of loan, number of credits at the bank, other installment debts, and housing type. We will include these predictors in the initial analysis and then evaluate the importance of each predictor. Number of credits, other installment debts, and housing type are categorical predictors, entered as **factors** in the model. Age and duration of loan are continuous predictors, entered as **covariates** in the model.

Scale Component

The next decision has two stages. The first decision is whether to include a scale component in the model at all. In many cases, the scale component will not be necessary, and the location-only model will provide a good summary of the data. In the interests of keeping things simple, it's usually best to start with a location-only model, and add a scale component only if there is evidence that the location-only model is inadequate for your data. (More information about assessing the need for a scale component is given below.) Following this philosophy, we will begin with a location-only model, and after estimating the model, we will check on whether a scale component is warranted.

Choosing a Link Function

To choose a link function, it is helpful to examine the distribution of values for the outcome variable. Figure 18-3 shows the distribution for the account status categories.

Figure 18-3
Distribution of values for account status

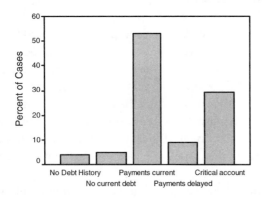

It is clear from this chart that the bulk of cases are in the higher categories, especially categories 3 (payments current) and 5 (critical account). The higher categories are also where most of the "action" is, since the most important distinctions from a business perspective are between categories 3, 4, and 5. For this reason, we will begin with the complementary log-log link function, since that function focuses on the higher outcome categories. The high number of cases in the extreme category 5 (critical account) indicates that the Cauchit distribution might be a reasonable alternative if the complementary log-log link function yields unsatisfactory results.

We are now ready to run the ordinal regression procedure. From the menus choose:

Analyze
  Regression
    Ordinal...

Dependent: Account Status
Factors: Number of Existing Credits, Other Installment Debts, Housing Type
Covariates: Age in years, Duration in Months

Options
  Link: Complementary Log-Log

Output
  Display
    ☑ Test of Parallel Lines
  Saved Variables
    ☑ Predicted Category
    ☑ Predicted Category Probability
    ☑ Actual Category Probability

Evaluating the Model

The first thing you see in the output is the warning shown in Figure 18-4. The reason this warning comes up is that the model includes continuous covariates. Certain fit statistics for the model depend on aggregating the data based on unique predictor and outcome value patterns. For instance, all cases where the applicants have current payments on debt, one other credit at the bank, own their home, have no other installment debts, are 49 years old and are seeking a 12-month loan are combined to form a cell. However, because duration of loan and age are both continuous, most cases have unique values for those variables. This results in a very large table with many empty cells, which makes it difficult to interpret some of the fit statistics. You have to be careful in evaluating this model, particularly when looking at chi-square-based fit statistics.

Figure 18-4
Warning about empty cells

There are 3078 (78.3%) cells (i.e.,
dependent variable levels by factor
levels combinations) with zero
frequencies.

For relatively simple models with a few factors, you can display information about individual cells by selecting *Cell Information* on the Options dialog box. However, this is not recommended for models with many factors (or factors with many levels), or models with continuous covariates, since such models typically result in very large tables. Such large tables are often of limited value in evaluating the model, and they can take a long time to process.

Predictive Value of the Model

Before you start looking at the individual predictors in the model, you need to find out if the model gives adequate predictions. To answer this question, we can examine the Model-Fitting Information table (shown in Figure 18-5). Here we see the -2 log-likelihood values for the intercept only (baseline) model and the final model (with the predictors). While the -2 log-likelihood statistics themselves are suspect due to the large number of empty cells in the model, the difference of log-likelihoods can usually still be interpreted as chi-square distributed statistics (McCullagh and Nelder, 1989). The chi-square reported in the table is just that: the difference between -2 times the log-likelihood for the intercept-only model and that for the final model, $2373.160 - 2019.823 = 353.336$ (within rounding error).

Figure 18-5
Model-fitting information

Model	-2 Log Likelihood	Chi-Square	df	Sig.
Intercept Only	2249.888			
Final	1896.552	353.336	9	.000

Link function: Complementary Log-log.

The significant chi-square statistic indicates that the model gives a significant improvement over the baseline intercept-only model. This basically tells you that the model gives better predictions than if you just guessed based on the marginal probabilities for the outcome categories. That's a good sign, but what you really want to know is *how much* better the model is.

Chi-Square-Based Fit Statistics

The next table in the output is the Goodness-of-Fit table (shown in Figure 18-6). This table contains Pearson's chi-square statistic for the model and another chi-square statistic based on the deviance. These statistics are intended to test whether the observed data are inconsistent with the fitted model. If they are not—that is, if the significance values are large—then you would conclude that the data and the model predictions are similar and that you have a good model.

Figure 18-6
Goodness-of-fit table

	Chi-Square	df	Sig.
Pearson	4688.724	3131	.000
Deviance	1796.915	3131	1.000

These statistics can be very useful for models with a small number of categorical predictors. Unfortunately, these statistics are both sensitive to empty cells. When estimating models with continuous covariates, there are often many empty cells, as in this example. Therefore, you shouldn't rely on either of these test statistics with such models. Because of the empty cells, you can't be sure that these statistics will really follow the chi-square distribution, and the significance values won't be accurate.

Pseudo-R^2 Measures

The next tool to turn to in assessing the overall goodness of fit of the model is the pseudo-R^2 measures. These measures attempt to serve the same function as the coefficient of determination in linear regression models—namely, to summarize the proportion of variance in the dependent variable associated with the predictor (independent) variables. For ordinal regression models, these measures are based on likelihood ratios rather than raw residuals. The results for the initial model are shown in Figure 18-7. Three different methods are used to estimate the coefficient of determination. Cox and Snell's R^2 (Cox and Snell, 1989) is a well-known generalization of the usual R^2 designed to apply when maximum likelihood estimation is used, as with ordinal regression. However, with categorical outcomes, it has a theoretical maximum value of less than 1.0. For this reason, Nagelkerke (1991) proposed a modification that allows the index to take values in the full zero-to-one range. McFadden's R^2 (McFadden, 1974) is another version, based on the log-likelihood kernels for the intercept-only model and the full estimated model.

Figure 18-7
Pseudo-R^2 measures

Cox and Snell	.298
Nagelkerke	.328
McFadden	.149

Here, the pseudo-R^2 values are respectable but leave something to be desired. It will probably be worth the effort to revise the model to try to make better predictions.

The next step in evaluating the model is to examine the predictions generated by the model. Recall that the model is based on predicting cumulative probabilities. However, what you're probably most interested in is how often the model can produce correct predicted categories based on the values of the predictor variables. To see how well the model does, you can construct a **classification table**—also called a **confusion matrix**—by cross-tabulating the predicted categories with the actual categories. The corresponding table for this example is shown in Figure 18-8.

Figure 18-8
Classification table for the initial model

			PREDCAT	
			3.00	5.00
ACCOUNT STATUS	1.00	Count	14	26
		% within ACCOUNT STATUS	35.0%	65.0%
	2.00	Count	41	8
		% within ACCOUNT STATUS	83.7%	16.3%
	3.00	Count	480	50
		% within ACCOUNT STATUS	90.6%	9.4%
	4.00	Count	31	57
		% within ACCOUNT STATUS	35.2%	64.8%
	5.00	Count	73	220
		% within ACCOUNT STATUS	24.9%	75.1%

The model seems to be doing a respectable job of predicting outcome categories, at least for the most frequent categories—category 3 (debt payments current) and category 5 (critical account). The model correctly classifies 90.6% of the category 3 cases and 75.1% of the category 5 cases. In addition, cases in categories 2 are more likely to be classified as category 3 than category 5, a desirable result for predicting ordinal responses.

On the other hand, category 1 (no credit history) cases are somewhat poorly predicted, with the majority of cases being assigned to category 5 (critical account), a category that should theoretically be most dissimilar to category 1. This may indicate a problem in the way the ordinal outcome scale is defined. In the interest of brevity, we will not pursue this issue further here, but in an actual data analysis situation, you would probably want to investigate this and try to discover whether the ordinal scale itself could be improved by reordering, merging, or excluding certain categories.

Identifying Problems

Evaluating the Choice of Link Function

Often, there will not be a clear theoretical choice of link function based on the data. In cases where the initial model performs poorly, it is usually worth trying alternative link functions to see if a better model can be constructed with a different link function. Although some of the link functions perform quite similarly in many instances (particularly the logit, complementary log-log and negative log-log functions), there are situations where choice of link function can make or break your model.

In this example, there are at least two link functions (complementary log-log and Cauchit) that may be appropriate. Although the model does fairly well with the complementary log-log link, it might be possible to improve the model fit by using the Cauchit link function.

Test of Parallel Lines

For location-only models, the test of parallel lines can help you assess whether the assumption that the parameters are the same for all categories is reasonable. This test compares the estimated model with one set of coefficients for all categories (shown on p. 244) to a model with a separate set of coefficients for each category:

$$link(\gamma_j) = \theta_j - [\beta_{1j}x_1 + \beta_{2j}x_2 + \dots + \beta_{kj}x_k]$$

The results for this example are shown in Figure 18-9. You can see that the general model (with separate parameters for each category) gives a significant improvement in the model fit. This can be due to several things, including use of an incorrect link function or using the wrong model.

Figure 18-9
Test of parallel lines

Model	-2 Log Likelihood	Chi-Square	df	Sig.
Null Hypothesis	1896.552			
General	1588.614	307.938	27	.000

Predictors in the Model

Now consider the individual predictors in the model. The parameter estimates are shown in Figure 18-10. For this example, as is often the case, the threshold parameters are not particularly important from a theoretical standpoint. The parameters of most interest are the location parameters, which relate the predictor variables to the cumulative outcome category probabilities.

Figure 18-10
Parameter estimates

| | | Estimate | Std. Error | Wald | df | Sig. | 95% Confidence Interval | |
							Lower Bound	Upper Bound
Threshold	[CHIST = 1.00]	-3.549	.667	28.323	1	.000	-4.856	-2.242
	[CHIST = 2.00]	-2.720	.656	17.167	1	.000	-4.006	-1.433
	[CHIST = 3.00]	-.137	.649	.044	1	.833	-1.408	1.135
	[CHIST = 4.00]	.199	.649	.094	1	.759	-1.072	1.471
Location	AGE	.015	.004	15.128	1	.000	.007	.023
	DURATION	-.002	.003	.379	1	.538	-.009	.005
	[NUMCRED=1.00]	-1.134	.594	3.645	1	.056	-2.298	.030
	[NUMCRED=2.00]	.367	.598	.376	1	.540	-.805	1.538
	[NUMCRED=3.00]	.981	.711	1.902	1	.168	-.413	2.374
	[NUMCRED=4.00]	0	.	.	0	.	.	.
	[OTHNSTAL=1.00]	-.397	.118	11.389	1	.001	-.627	-.166
	[OTHNSTAL=2.00]	-.469	.193	5.913	1	.015	-.848	-.091
	[OTHNSTAL=3.00]	0	.	.	0	.	.	.
	[HOUSNG=1.00]	-.082	.165	.249	1	.617	-.406	.241
	[HOUSNG=2.00]	.132	.139	.897	1	.344	-.141	.404
	[HOUSNG=3.00]	0	.	.	0	.	.	.

You can use the parameter estimates and associated statistical tests to make some judgments about predictors that are candidates for omission from future models. For example, in this case, *duration* seems not to be of much value in the model. Once you have established the proper link function, you can reevaluate the contribution of this covariate and possibly remove it, creating a more parsimonious model. It also seems that housing type (*housng*) is of dubious value to the model, so it will pay to reevaluate that variable after revising the model as well.

Revising the Model

You can now estimate a new model with a Cauchit link function to see whether the change increases the predictive utility of the model. (It is recommended to keep the same set of predictor variables in the model until you have finished evaluating link functions. If you change the link function and the set of predictors at the same time, you won't know which of them caused any change in model fit.) To estimate the revised model, from the menus choose you won't know which of them caused any change in model fit.) To estimate the revised model, from the menus choose:

Analyze
  Regression
    Ordinal...

Dependent: Account Status
Factors: Number of Existing Credits, Other Installment Debts, Housing Type
Covariates: Age in years, Duration in Months

Options
  Link: Cauchit

Output
Display
      ☑ Test of Parallel Lines
    Saved Variables
        ☑ Predicted Category
        ☑ Predicted Category Probability
        ☑ Actual Category Probability

Figure 18-11
Model-fitting information

Model	-2 Log Likelihood	Chi-Square	df	Sig.
Intercept Only	2249.888			
Final	1790.028	459.860	9	.000

Link function: Cauchit.

The model-fitting statistics, shown in Figure 18-11, indicate that this model once again is better than simple guessing. Notice, however, that the chi-square statistic comparing the full model to the intercept-only model is quite a bit larger with the Cauchit link ($\chi^2 = 459.860$) than it was with the complementary log-log link ($\chi^2 = 353.336$). This is encouraging. Next, consider the pseudo-R^2 measures, shown in Figure 18-12.

Figure 18-12
Pseudo-R^2 measures

Cox and Snell	.369
Nagelkerke	.407
McFadden	.194

Once again, you can see that changing the link function has improved the model's ability to account for patterns in the outcome variable.

The classification table is shown in Figure 18-13. This model seems to be slightly better at predicting the lower categories (1, 2, and 3) and slightly worse at predicting the higher categories than the previous model. Since the most important goal of credit scoring is to correctly identify accounts that are likely to become critical (category 5), you would probably choose to retain the original model, even though the fit statistics favor the revised model.

Figure 18-13
Classification table

			PREDCAT	
			3.00	5.00
ACCOUNT STATUS	1.00	Count	15	25
		% within ACCOUNT STATUS	37.5%	62.5%
	2.00	Count	43	6
		% within ACCOUNT STATUS	87.8%	12.2%
	3.00	Count	482	48
		% within ACCOUNT STATUS	90.9%	9.1%
	4.00	Count	36	52
		% within ACCOUNT STATUS	40.9%	59.1%
	5.00	Count	80	213
		% within ACCOUNT STATUS	27.3%	72.7%

Interpreting the Model

With a model that gives an adequate fit to the data, you can make some interpretations based on the parameter estimates, as shown in Figure 18-10.

According to the statistical tests, *age* seems to be an important predictor, whereas *duration* adds little to the model. Also, while there is no single category of number of credits (*numcred*) that is significant on its own, there are two that are marginally significant. Usually, it is worth keeping such a variable in the model, since the small effects of each category accumulate and provide useful information to the model. Other installment debt (*othnstal*) also seems to be an important predictor on empirical grounds. On the other hand, housing type (*housng*) doesn't seem to contribute to the model in a meaningful way and could probably be dropped without substantially worsening the model.

While direct interpretation of the coefficients in this model is difficult due to the nature of the link function, the signs of the coefficients can give important insights into the effects of the predictors in the model. The signs essentially indicate the direction of the effect. Positive coefficients (such as that for *age*) indicate positive relationships between predictors and outcome. In this example, as age increases, so does the probability of being in one of the higher categories of account status. Negative coefficients (such as that for the first category of *numcred*) indicate inverse relationships. In this model, for example, those with one credit at the bank are likely to be in the lower outcome categories.

Using the Model to Make Predictions

Predicted Probabilities

Because the model attempts to predict cumulative probabilities rather than category membership, two steps are required to get predicted categories. First, for each case, the probabilities must be estimated for each category. Second, those probabilities must be used to select the most likely outcome category for each case.

The probabilities themselves are estimated by using the predictor values for a case in the model equations and taking the inverse of the link function. The result is the cumulative probability for each group, conditional on the pattern of predictor values for the case. The probabilities for individual categories can then be derived by taking the differences of the cumulative probabilities for the groups in order. In other words, the probability for the first category is the first cumulative probability; the probability for the second category is the second cumulative probability minus the first; the probability for the third category is the third cumulative probability minus the second; and so on.

From Probabilities to Predicted Category Values

For each case, the predicted outcome category is simply the category with the highest probability, given the pattern of predictor values for that case. For example, suppose you have an applicant who wants a 48-month loan (*duration*), is 22 years old (*age*), has one credit with the bank (*numcred*), has no other installment debt (*othnstal*), and owns her home (*housng*). Inserting these values into the prediction equations, this applicant has predicted values of -2.78, -1.95, 0.63, and 0.97. (Remember that there is one equation for each category *except the last*.) Taking the inverse of the complementary log-log link function gives the cumulative probabilities of $.06$, 0.13, 0.85, and 0.93 (and, of course, 1.0 for the last category). Taking differences gives the following individual category probabilities: category 1: $.06$, category 2: $.13 - .06 = .07$, category 3: $.85 - .13 = .72$, category 4: $.93 - .85 = .08$, and category 5: $1.0 - .93 = .07$. Clearly, category 3 (debt payments current) is the most likely category for this case according to the model, with a predicted probability of 0.72. Thus, you would predict that this applicant would keep her payments current and the account would not become critical.

Life Tables Examples

Contributed by Milton Steinberg, Marymount College.

An insurance company wants to calculate the expected number of years of life remaining for 65-year-old males with angina pectoris. A researcher wants to assess tumor-free time after rats have been injected with a putative carcinogen. The owner of a shopping mall wishes to calculate the probability that a business leasing space in the mall will continue to rent for three years. In each of these instances, the investigator is interested in **survival time**, the time to occurrence of an event, such as death, tumor growth, or rental termination.

The calculations in these situations are complicated by the fact that not all subjects or entities will experience the terminal event during the time of observation. Some of the angina pectoris patients will not die during five years of study. Some of the rats will not develop tumors during 200 days of study. Some of the businesses will not leave during the eight years that the mall has existed.

This chapter discusses techniques for assessing situations in which some of the subjects do not experience the terminal event that is the event of interest. In **life tables** and other methods of **survival analysis**, data from those subjects who do not experience the terminal event can also contribute to the calculation for the probabilities at any interval under study. The terms *survival analysis* and *life tables* refer to the fact that these techniques are often used to assess life expectancies

When to Use Life Tables

If observations can be classified into meaningful equal time intervals such as seconds, days, months, or years, the life table can be used to calculate the probability of a terminal event during any interval under study. If observations cannot be aggregated into equal time intervals, as is the case in many clinical and experimental studies, use the Kaplan-Meier technique, described in Chapter 20. To investigate the relation between survival time and a predictor variable, such as age or tumor type, use the Cox Regression procedures, described in Chapter 21.

Constructing a Life Table

The owner of a small mall with 30 shops wants to determine the probability that a business will continue its lease for three years. During the eight years that the mall has existed, a total of 100 businesses have rented space. Of these 100 businesses, 71 have terminated their leases and moved to other locations. At present, 29 of the 30 shops are occupied.

Figure 19-1 shows the first 15 records of the data as they might be presented for computer processing. There are 100 records total.

Figure 19-1
Computer-ready survival data (first 15 records)

Interval	Status
0	1
0	1
1	1
1	1
1	1
1	1
1	1
1	1
2	1
2	0
2	1
2	1
2	0
2	1
2	1

There are only two columns in this table. In the first column, time intervals are coded by their start times in years. For convenience, the cases have been sorted by interval. The first interval, coded 0, is the interval from the very beginning of a lease up to, but not including, one year. The second interval is from one year up to, but not including, two years, and so on. Each interval indicates the number of years that a business has been under lease, not the year in which the business began to lease. A business with an interval coded 2 could have begun leasing in the sixth year of the mall's eight-year lifetime.

Censored Observations

The second column in Figure 19-1, *Status*, indicates whether the terminal event, lease termination, has occurred. The first nine businesses have terminated their leases (1). The tenth business has not terminated (0). The tenth business is one of the 29 that are still leasing space at the mall even though it has been in business for only two years (two years up to, but not including, three years). This observation on the tenth business is called a **censored** observation because its outcome is hidden from view. The terminal event has not yet occurred.

Calculating Probabilities

In order to determine the probability that a business continues to lease for one year, two years, or more, it is convenient to reorganize Figure 19-1 into intervals of years, as shown in Figure 19-2. The reorganized columns plus additional computed columns constitute a more traditional life table. Notice that the *Status* column from Figure 19-1 has been reorganized into two columns, *Number Withdrawn During Interval*, showing the number of censored observations, and *Number of Terminal Events*.

Figure 19-2
Reorganization of Figure 19-1 with additional, computed columns

Interval Start Time	Number Entering this Interval	Number Withdrawn During Interval	Number of Terminal Events	Number Exposed to Risk	Proportion Terminating	Proportion Surviving	Cumulative Proportion Surviving at End
0	100	0	2	100	.0200	.9800	.9800
1	98	0	6	98	.0612	.9388	.9200
2	92	3	8	90.5	.0884	.9116	.8387
3	81	3	11	79.5	.1384	.8616	.7226
4	67	6	9	64	.1406	.8594	.6210
5	52	8	19	48	.3958	.6042	.3752
6	25	6	9	22	.4091	.5909	.2217
7	10	3	7	8.5	.8235	.1765	.0391
Total		29	71				

This table presents the following information:

- *Interval Start Time* is the start of each interval in years.

- *Number Entering this Interval* is the number of cases surviving at the beginning of the interval. All 100 businesses started leasing at 0 years.

- *Number Withdrawn During Interval* is the number of censored cases. Here, it is the number of businesses that leased less than one year ago and have continued to lease. There were no such cases for the first (0) interval, as can be seen in Figure 19-1.

- *Number of Terminal Events* is the number of cases that experienced the terminal event. Two businesses terminated their leases after less than one year, as shown in Figure 19-1.

- *Number Exposed to Risk* is the number of cases entering the interval minus half the number withdrawn during the interval. It is used to account for the contribution of censored data and will be more fully described below. This column is used as the denominator to calculate the proportion terminating and the proportion surviving.

- *Proportion Terminating* is the proportion of cases that experienced the terminal event during the interval. This is an estimate of the probability that a case will experience termination during an interval. Two businesses out of 100 left the mall during the first year. The probability of a terminal event in the first year (interval 0) is $2/100 = 0.02$.

- *Proportion Surviving* is the proportion of cases that have survived to the end of the interval. Since two businesses terminated their leases, 98 out of 100 were still leasing: $98/100 = 0.98$. This is 1 minus the proportion terminating.

- *Cumulative Proportion Surviving at End* is an estimate of the probability of surviving to the end of any specified interval. The probability for the 0 interval is 0.98. This is also the cumulative probability for the first interval.

For the interval starting at one year, the number entering the interval is 98, since 2 out of 100 were terminated in the previous interval. None of these 98 were censored (withdrawn) during the interval. Six experienced the terminal event. The proportion terminating is thus $6/98 = 0.0612$. The proportion surviving is $1 - 0.0612 = 0.9388$. The probability that a business will survive to the end of the second interval is the probability of survival in the first interval times the probability of survival in the second interval. The cumulative proportion of survival is thus $0.9800 \times 0.9388 = 0.9200$.

Effects of Censoring

The special advantage of survival analysis procedures such as life tables is the ability to use information from censored cases. Ninety-two businesses entered the third interval in the business example. Eight of these became terminal; but, in addition, three businesses are censored. They leased three years ago and are still leasing. Their outcome is unknown, but it is known that they have leased for at least three years. In order to make use of the censored cases, we assume that each of these three businesses were observed for half of the interval. Each is counted as a half-case. Instead of 92 cases, we have $92 - (3 \times 0.5) = 90.5$. This is the number that appears in the *Number Exposed to Risk* column. The number exposed to risk shows the number of cases entering the interval adjusted for censored cases. The proportion terminating becomes the number of terminal events divided by the number exposed to risk ($8/90.5 = 0.0884$) rather than the number of terminal events divided by the number entering the interval ($8/92 = 0.0870$). Our knowledge that the censored cases survived the interval may thus be put to use to increase the estimated probability.

The probability of a business leasing for three years is estimated to be 0.8387 (the cumulative proportion surviving the interval beginning at 2).

Before constructing a life table, you should consider carefully the cases that are to be censored. Use of life tables assumes that the reason for censoring is not related to the cause of termination. In the business example, it must be assumed that those who continued to lease into interval 7 did not do so because they were given more favorable terms than those who terminated their leases. If a cancer patient in remission dies in a workplace accident before experiencing a recurrence of the disease, the case may be considered censored and thus excluded from analysis. The researcher should look carefully at the reasons that the cases under consideration are no longer in the study and decide which cases to censor or drop. For more information on censoring, see Cox and Oakes (1984).

Censored cases, for whom the terminal event has not yet occurred but who have been followed for the duration of the study, are fundamentally different from cases that have been **lost to follow-up**. Cases lost to follow-up are those with whom the investigator has lost contact during the course of the study. They may have experienced the terminal event without the investigator's knowledge during a time period within the purview of the study. Cancer patients lost to follow-up may or may not experience death from cancer during the lifetime of the study; the investigator will not know. Furthermore, those lost to follow-up may be systematically different from those not lost to follow-up. Careful consideration should be given to assigning censored status to these cases or excluding them from the study.

SPSS Life Tables Output

Figure 19-3 shows the result of submitting the data organized as in Figure 19-1 to the SPSS Life Tables procedure.

To produce this table, from the menus choose:

Analyze
  Survival
    Life Tables...

▸ Time: interval
    Display Time Intervals 0 through 8 by 1

▸ Status: status

Define Event...
    Single value: 1

Figure 19-3
Life table

```
Life Table
   Survival Variable  INTERVAL  Interval Start Time
           Number  Number  Number  Number                        Cumul
   Intrvl  Entrng  Wdrawn  Exposd    of    Propn   Propn   Propn   Proba-
   Start    this   During    to    Termnl  Termi-   Sur-    Surv   bility  Hazard
   Time    Intrvl  Intrvl   Risk   Events  nating  viving  at End  Densty   Rate
   ------  ------  ------  ------  ------  ------  ------  ------  ------  ------
      .0   100.0      .0   100.0     2.0   .0200   .9800   .9800   .0200   .0202
     1.0    98.0      .0    98.0     6.0   .0612   .9388   .9200   .0600   .0632
     2.0    92.0     3.0    90.5     8.0   .0884   .9116   .8387   .0813   .0925
     3.0    81.0     3.0    79.5    11.0   .1384   .8616   .7226   .1160   .1486
     4.0    67.0     6.0    64.0     9.0   .1406   .8594   .6210   .1016   .1513
     5.0    52.0     8.0    48.0    19.0   .3958   .6042   .3752   .2458   .4935
     6.0    25.0     6.0    22.0     9.0   .4091   .5909   .2217   .1535   .5143
     7.0    10.0     3.0     8.5     7.0   .8235   .1765   .0391   .1826  1.4000
```

The median survival time for these data is   5.49

```
            SE of   SE of
   Intrvl   Cumul   Proba-  SE of
   Start     Sur-   bility  Hazard
   Time     viving  Densty   Rate
   -------  ------  ------  ------
      .0    .0140   .0140   .0143
     1.0    .0271   .0237   .0258
     2.0    .0369   .0276   .0327
     3.0    .0455   .0329   .0447
     4.0    .0501   .0320   .0503
     5.0    .0533   .0481   .1097
     6.0    .0504   .0450   .1657
     7.0    .0303   .0506   .3779
```

This table presents the following information:

■ *Interval Start Time* is the start of each interval. It extends up to, but not including, the start time of the next interval.

■ *Number Entering this Interval* is the number of cases surviving at the beginning of the interval.

■ *Number Withdrawn During Interval* is the number of censored cases. They have not experienced the terminal event.

■ *Number Exposed to Risk* is the number of cases entering the interval minus half the number withdrawn during the interval. It is used to account for the contribution of censored data.

■ *Number of Terminal Events* is the number of cases that experienced the terminal event. Two businesses terminated their leases after less than one year, as shown in Figure 19-1.

■ *Proportion Terminating* is the proportion of cases that experienced the terminal event during the interval. This is an estimate of the probability that a case will experience termination during an interval. Two businesses out of 100 left the mall during the first year. The probability of a terminal event in the first year (interval 0) is $2/100 = 0.02$.

■ *Proportion Surviving* is the proportion of cases that have survived to the end of the interval. Since two businesses terminated their leases, 98 out of 100 were still leasing: $98/100 = 0.98$. This is 1 minus the proportion terminating.

■ *Cumulative Proportion Surviving at End* is an estimate of the probability of surviving to the end of any specified interval. The probability for the 0 interval is 0.98. This is also the cumulative probability for the first interval.

■ *Probability Density* is an estimate of the probability of failure during a particular time interval.

■ *Hazard Rate* is the proportion of those who have survived up to a particular interval who are expected to fail in that interval. It is a rate and may have a value greater than 1.

■ *Standard Error of the Cumulative Proportion Surviving* is an estimate of the variability of the cumulative proportion surviving.

■ *Standard Error of the Probability Density* is an estimate of the variability of the probability density.

■ *Standard Error of the Hazard Rate* is an estimate of the variability of the hazard rate.

The **median survival time** is the time at which half of the cases experience the terminal event. This is the time when the cumulative proportion surviving is 0.50. Referring to the *Cumulative Proportion Surviving at End* in Figure 19-3, it can be seen that the proportion is 0.6210 at the end of interval 4 (the beginning of the fifth year) and 0.3752 at the end of interval 5 (the beginning of the sixth year); so the median, 0.5, is reached between years 5 and 6. Linear interpolation yields a more accurate estimate. The cumulative proportion surviving reaches 0.50 at 5.49 years. The median is included between the two parts of the table shown in Figure 19-3. It may be roughly estimated from plots of the cumulative proportion surviving against time.

Survival and Hazard Functions

The *Cumulative Proportion Surviving* in Figure 19-3 is an estimate of the **survival function** or **survivorship function** $S(t)$. It is defined as the proportion of cases surviving longer than a specified time t. For example, 37.52% of the cases survive longer than the start of interval 5 (the beginning of the sixth year).

The **hazard function** is a rate—a conditional probability of failure divided by a time interval. The symbol $h(t)$ is used to represent the hazard function. It indicates the expectation that a case will terminate at any particular time period. A high hazard function indicates a high probability of mortality. It can be derived from the survival function $S(t)$ and can take on any value from 0 to infinity.

Survival Function Plots

Figure 19-4 shows a plot of survival (the cumulative proportion surviving at the end of the interval) against the interval start times.

To produce this plot, recall the dialog box and choose:

Options...

☑ Survival

Figure 19-4
Survival plotted against interval start times

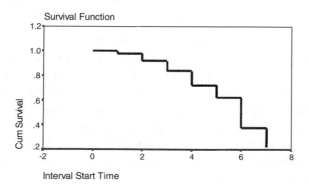

Comparing Groups

Frequently, survival analysis is performed to determine whether one treatment or condition results in longer survival times than another. In the current example, a third column was added to the data called *edu*. It is coded 0 if the renter has no college degree and 1 if the renter has a college degree. The two resulting survival functions are compared using Gehan's generalized Wilcoxon test. Figure 19-5 shows the result of this test for the current example.

To produce this table, recall the dialog box and choose:

▶ Factor: edu

Define Range...
   Minimum 0 Maximum 1

Options...

   Compare Levels of First Factor
   ⊙ Overall

Figure 19-5

Gehan's generalized Wilcoxon test for education level

```
Comparison of survival experience using the Wilcoxon (Gehan) statistic
   Survival Variable    INTERVAL   Interval Start Time
          grouped by    EDU         Education
   Overall comparison    statistic       9.361  D.F.    1   Prob.   .0022
   Group  label                Total N   Uncen    Cen  Pct Cen  Mean Score
      0   No College               57      43      14    24.56    13.8596
      1   College                  43      28      15    34.88   -18.3721
```

Gehan's generalized Wilcoxon test compares each survival time in each group with every survival time in the other group. A case receives a score of 1 if its survival time exceeds that of a case in the other group, a score of −1 if its survival time is less than that of a case in the other group, and a score of 0 if the survival times of the two cases are equal. The *Mean Score* in Figure 19-5 is derived from these scores. The positive value for the *No College* group indicates that this group has longer survival times than the *College* group. This difference is significant, as shown by the probability 0.0022.

The procedure also produced separate survival tables for each condition. From these, it can be seen that the median survival time was greater for the no college group (5.88) than for the college group (4.38).

If a plot is requested, a separate curve is drawn for each level of education. The curve for the no college group, which has the longer survival times, descends more gradually than the curve for the college group. The median for each group can be estimated from these curves.

Figure 19-6

Comparison of survival curves for two levels of education

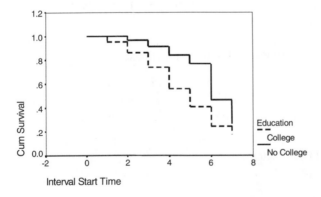

Kaplan-Meier
Survival Analysis Examples

Contributed by Milton Steinberg, Marymount College.

Survival analysis is concerned with the time to occurrence of a critical **event** of interest, such as death, tumor growth, or discharge from employment. The event need not be adverse. It can be an event with a happy outcome, such as time to remission of symptoms or time until finding employment. The time until the event is the **survival time**. Cases can enter a study at various times. Survival time is measured from the time that the case enters the study, not from the beginning of the study itself.

Censored Observations

Survival analysis techniques are unique in that they use information from cases that have not experienced the terminal event during the time of observation. In a study on remission of symptoms, some cases will not show remission during the time of the study. Some job seekers will not find employment during the time of observation. The terminal remission status or employment status of these cases is hidden from view; hence, the term **censored** is applied to them.

When to Use Kaplan-Meier Estimators

In Chapter 19, life tables are constructed for situations in which event times are specified only to an interval. More precise estimates are available when you know exact times by using the **Kaplan-Meier** method. The probability of a terminal event is calculated at every occurrence of the event. This makes Kaplan-Meier techniques useful for studies with few cases where the survival intervals are variable.

Use **life tables** if survival times have been categorized into time intervals such as days, months, or years. Life table techniques determine the probability of the terminal event for each interval by dividing the number of cases experiencing the terminal event during the interval by the number of cases entering the interval alive (after the denominator is adjusted for censored observations).

An Example Using Chemotherapy to Treat Leukemia

Miller (1981) described a data set from a paper by Ebury et al. (1977) in which patients suffering from acute myelogenous leukemia (AML) were brought to remission with chemotherapy. They were then divided into two groups. The experimental group continued to receive maintenance doses of chemotherapy. The control group did not. Did the maintenance doses of chemotherapy increase the number of weeks of remission time?

The data were stored in a file with three columns. Figure 20-1 shows the first five entries.

Figure 20-1
First five cases of AML data file

Chemo	Time	Status
1	9.00	1
1	13.00	1
1	13.00	0
1	18.00	1
1	23.00	1

In the column *Chemo*, a case is coded 1 if subjects received maintenance doses of chemotherapy and 0 if they did not. *Time* is the survival time in weeks. *Status* is coded 1 if the case relapsed and 0 if the case had not relapsed by the end of the study (censored).

Computing Cumulative Survival

We will begin by computing cumulative survival for the experimental subjects who received maintenance doses of chemotherapy. These are the cases for which the *Chemo* column is coded 1. Figure 20-2 contains the *Time* and *Status* columns for all of these cases, just as they appear in Figure 20-1. The other columns in Figure 20-2 are computed from the *Time* and *Status* columns.

Figure 20-2
Time (in weeks) to relapse for AML patients in remission

Time	Status	Prior Number in Remission	Number Remaining	Proportion in Remission	Cumulative Survival
9	1	11	10	10/11	10/11=0.9091
13	1	10	9	9/10	0.9091x(9/10)=0.8182
13	0	9	8		
18	1	8	7	7/8	0.8182x(7/8)=0.7159
23	1	7	6	6/7	0.7159x(6/7)=0.6136
28	0	6	5		
31	1	5	4	4/5	0.6136x(4/5)=0.4909
34	1	4	3	3/4	0.4909x(3/4)=0.3682
45	0	3	2		
48	1	2	1	1/2	0.37x(1/2)=0.1841
161	0	1			

The *Time* column indicates the survival time in weeks to relapse. Any convenient unit of time can be used here. The *Status* column indicates whether the subject has experienced the terminal event or whether the observation is censored. The Kaplan-Meier procedure will accept numbers or string identifiers as definers of status.

The first event occurred nine weeks after the maintenance doses began. One patient relapsed. *Prior Number in Remission* is the number of cases alive prior to the event time. It is 11 prior to the first event time because 11 subjects began the study in remission. Since one subject has relapsed, the *Number Remaining* in remission after the first event is 10. The probability of surviving nine weeks is *Proportion in Remission*, which is *Number Remaining* divided by *Prior Number in Remission*. The next event occurred at 13 weeks. *Prior Number in Remission* is decreased to 10 because of the previous relapse. *Number Remaining* is decreased to 9 because of the current relapse.

The probability of remaining in remission for 13 weeks given that the subject was in remission at 9 weeks is the product of the two probabilities as shown in the *Cumulative Survival* column.

Using Censored Observations

Not all subjects experience relapse at the end of the observation period. The third subject joined the study 13 weeks before its end and was still in remission when the study ended. One strategy would be to drop such subjects from consideration because their outcome is unknown, but this would result in estimated survival probabilities that are too low. This subject provides information about surviving in remission for 13 weeks. Although the probability is not estimated for the third subject, that subject contributes to the total number of subjects, and the number of subjects is decremented for the next event. Decrementing the number of subjects decreases the denominator of *Proportion in Remission* and increases the estimated survival probability.

SPSS Kaplan-Meier Procedure

Figure 20-3 shows part of the output that results from submitting the AML data to the SPSS Kaplan-Meier procedure. The procedure produces a separate survival table for the experimental group that received maintenance doses of chemotherapy and the control group that did not. The separate tables were produced because *chemo* was declared as a factor. If no factor had been declared, the procedure would have produced one survival table for all subjects as though they were from the same group. Only the survival table for the experimental group is shown in Figure 20-3; it is similar to the calculated table in Figure 20-2. To produce the output, from the menus choose:

Analyze
 Survival
  Kaplan-Meier...

▶ Time: time

▶ Status: status

Define Event...
  Single value: 1

▶ Factor: chemo

Figure 20-3

Kaplan-Meier table

```
Survival Analysis for TIME      Time (weeks)

Factor CHEMO = Yes
```

Time	Status	Cumulative Survival	Standard Error	Cumulative Events	Number Remaining
9.00	Relapsed	.9091	.0867	1	10
13.00	Relapsed	.8182	.1163	2	9
13.00	Censored			2	8
18.00	Relapsed	.7159	.1397	3	7
23.00	Relapsed	.6136	.1526	4	6
28.00	Censored			4	5
31.00	Relapsed	.4909	.1642	5	4
34.00	Relapsed	.3682	.1627	6	3
45.00	Censored			6	2
48.00	Relapsed	.1841	.1535	7	1
161.00	Censored			7	0

```
Number of Cases:  11      Censored:   4     ( 36.36%)   Events: 7
```

	Survival Time	Standard Error	95% Confidence Interval	
Mean:	52.65	19.83	(13.78,	91.51)
(Limited to	161.00)			
Median:	31.00	7.36	(16.58,	45.42)

This table presents the following information:

- *Time* is the time of occurrence of the terminal event of interest or the time at which the subject was withdrawn while still in remission (withdrawn alive or censored).

- *Status* indicates whether the subject has experienced the terminal event or has been censored. It contains values or labels, depending on how you have the options set for output labels.

- *Cumulative Survival* is an estimate of the probability of surviving longer than the time listed in the *Time* column. It is not computed for censored events.

- *Standard Error* is the standard error of the *Cumulative Survival* estimate.

- *Cumulative Events* is a count of terminal events that have occurred up to and including the current time. It is not incremented for censored events.

- *Number Remaining* is the number of patients still in remission after the specified time. It is decremented for censored events.

- *Mean Survival Time* is not the arithmetic mean. It is equal to the area under the survival curve for the uncensored cases (Lee, 1992). The survival curve is shown in Figure 20-4.

- *Median Survival Time* is the first event at which cumulative survival reaches 0.5 (50%) or less. It can be estimated more exactly by interpolation within the table.

The mean survival time has been designated as *Limited to 161*. If the cases with the longest survival times are censored, the mean that is calculated using the uncensored cases may be an underestimate. The case with the longest survival time is figured into the calculation, and the mean is reported to be **limited** to the survival time of that censored case (Lee, 1992).

The standard error of the cumulative proportion surviving is calculated as

$$\text{se}(t_k) = S(t_k)\sqrt{\sum_{i=1}^{k}\frac{d_i}{n_i(n_i-d_i)}}$$

where k is the specific event time, $S(t_k)$ is cumulative survival, d_i is the number of events at time t_i, and n_i is the number of cases still in remission (not experiencing the event or censored) prior to time t_i.

Comparing Cumulative Survival Functions: Means and Medians

Did the experimental group that received maintenance doses of chemotherapy have longer survival times in remission than the control group? The output that produced the mean and median for the experimental group, as shown in Figure 20-3, also produced a mean and median for the control group. The mean and median for the experimental group are 52.56 and 31.00, respectively. The mean and median for the control group are 22.71 and 23.00. The larger mean and median for the chemotherapy maintenance group suggests longer survival times for the experimental group.

Comparing Cumulative Survival Functions: Survival Curves

The difference in the two survival functions can be inspected graphically. Figure 20-4 shows a plot with two cumulative survival curves, one for each group in the AML data. Two separate curves were obtained because *chemo* was declared as a factor. If no factor had been declared, one survival function would have been produced, representing all of the cases as though they were from a single group. To obtain this plot from the menu system, use the Dialog Recall button to recall the Kaplan-Meier dialog box and choose:

Options...
    Plots: Survival

Figure 20-4
Cumulative survival function

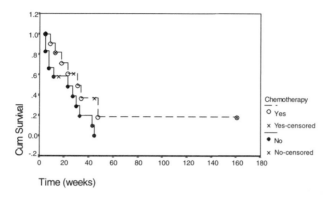

Time (weeks)

The chart in Figure 20-4 was modified in the Chart Editor for presentation in black and white. The default plus signs were changed to X's, and marker display was turned on. The X markers indicate censored cases. The circles represent terminal events (relapse). The curves are step functions because the survival function changes only at terminal events. The survival functions descend because the probability of survival decreases as the pool of survivors decreases (the number of relapses increases). The survival function for the experimental group that received maintenance doses of chemotherapy (*chemo* = 1) descends more gradually than the survival function for the control group. This is consistent with the greater mean and median (longer survival time) for this group.

Comparing Cumulative Survival Functions: Tests of Statistical Significance

In many cases, a researcher wants to be able to make an inference about the population from which the samples are drawn. The Kaplan-Meier procedure provides three statistical tests: the **log rank** (or Mantel-Cox) test, the **Breslow** (or generalized Wilcoxon) test, and the **Tarone-Ware** test. Each of these tests compares the number of terminal events actually observed (D_i) to the number of expected terminal events (E_i), which is calculated from the number at risk and the number of deaths at each event time in the study. The sum of the resulting differences is then calculated:

$$U = \sum_{i=1}^{k} w_i(D_i - E_i)$$

The only difference among the tests is the *w,* or weight, factor. The *w* factor is 1 for the log rank test; hence, all events are weighted equally. The *w* factor is the number at risk at each time point for the Breslow test; hence, early events are weighted more heavily than later events because the number in the risk pool decreases as events occur over time. The *w* factor is the square root of the number at risk for the Tarone-Ware test, so that it weights early cases somewhat less heavily.

The log rank test is considered more powerful than the Breslow test under the special condition that the mortality rate in each group being compared is proportional to that of the others (they differ by a constant multiple). If this is *not* the case, the Breslow test may be more powerful, but the Breslow test has very low power when the percentage of censored cases is large.

Producing Statistical Tests

Figure 20-5 shows the results of three statistical tests performed on the AML data with *chemo* as the factor. The procedure produces complete survival tables for each level of chemo and standard errors and confidence limits for the mean and median of each level of *chemo*. Only the summary comparisons for the two levels of *chemo* and the results of the statistical tests have been reproduced in Figure 20-5. To produce this output, recall the Kaplan-Meier dialog box and select:

Compare Factor...

    Test Statistics:
    ☑ Log rank ☑ Breslow ☑ Tarone-Ware

Figure 20-5
Summary statistics and statistical tests for two levels of chemotherapy

```
Survival Analysis for TIME    Time (weeks)
                         Total      Number      Number       Percent
                                    Events     Censored      Censored
    CHEMO       No        12          11           1           8.33
    CHEMO       Yes       11           7           4          36.36
  Overall                 23          18           5          21.74
    Test Statistics for Equality of Survival Distributions for CHEMO
                  Statistic      df      Significance
    Log Rank         3.40         1         .0653
    Breslow          2.72         1         .0989
    Tarone-Ware      2.98         1         .0842
```

Since the significance levels for each of the three tests are larger than 0.05, the treatments were not significantly different. We cannot conclude that maintenance doses of chemotherapy would increase survival times in the population.

Stratification: The Interaction of Two Variables

More than one factor may be present, which, in combination with other factors, might affect survival time. In a cancer study, a stratification technique might be used to separate different stages of disease or different histologic groups. Or a researcher might expect that both the presence or absence of positive axillary lymph nodes and the pathologic tumor size would affect survival times. In other words, does tumor size determine survival time, whether or not a patient has lymph node involvement? A study of breast cancer patients at the University of Chicago (Heimann, unpublished) contains data on overall survival times, tumor size, and lymph nodes. A subset of the data was used for this example.

To answer the question, a Kaplan-Meier analysis was performed on overall survival time (*time*) with pathologic tumor size categories (*pathscat*) as the factor and the presence of lymph nodes (*ln_yesno*) as the strata. To produce the output, from the menus choose:

Analyze
  Survival
    Kaplan-Meier...

▶ Time: time
▶ Status: status

Define Event...
  Single value: 1

▶ Factor: pathscat
▶ Strata: ln_yesno

Compare Factor...

  Test Statistics:
  ☑ Log rank
  ⊙ For each stratum

Options...

  ☐ Survival table(s) (deselect)
  Plots:
  ☑ Survival

Figure 20-6 and Figure 20-7 show the descriptive statistics for each level of *pathscat* when *ln_yesno* is *No* or *Yes*. The output has been condensed to facilitate relevant comparisons.

Figure 20-6
Mean survival times for pathologic tumor sizes for patients with no positive lymph nodes

```
Survival Analysis for TIME     Time (months)
Strata LN_YESNO = No
Factor PATHSCAT = <= 2 cm
             Survival Time   Standard Error   95% Confidence Interval
Mean:         127.56              1.40         (  124.82,    130.30 )
(Limited to   133.80 )
Median:          .                 .           (    .   ,       .   )

Strata LN_YESNO = No
Factor PATHSCAT = 2-5 cm
             Survival Time   Standard Error   95% Confidence Interval
Mean:         113.19              3.51         (  106.32,    120.07 )
(Limited to   128.57 )
Median:          .                 .           (    .   ,       .   )

Strata LN_YESNO = No
Factor PATHSCAT = > 5 cm
             Survival Time   Standard Error   95% Confidence Interval
Mean:          42.21              8.35         (   25.85,     58.57 )
(Limited to    52.43 )
Median:          .                 .           (    .   ,       .   )
```

When there is no lymph node involvement, the mean survival times for the different tumor sizes get smaller as the tumor size gets larger. The mean survival times are 127.56, 113.19, and 42.21 months when the tumor size goes from small to large.

Figure 20-7
Mean survival times for pathologic tumor sizes in patients with positive lymph nodes

```
Survival Analysis for TIME     Time (months)
Strata LN_YESNO = Yes
Factor PATHSCAT = <= 2 cm
             Survival Time   Standard Error   95% Confidence Interval
Mean:         119.47              2.88         (  113.81,    125.12 )
(Limited to   129.03 )
Median:          .                 .           (    .   ,       .   )

Strata LN_YESNO = Yes
Factor PATHSCAT = 2-5 cm
             Survival Time   Standard Error   95% Confidence Interval
Mean:          89.99              5.87         (   78.48,    101.49 )
(Limited to   117.23 )
Median:          .                 .           (    .   ,       .   )

Strata LN_YESNO = Yes
Factor PATHSCAT = > 5 cm
             Survival Time   Standard Error   95% Confidence Interval
Mean:          62.57             12.33         (   38.41,     86.73 )
(Limited to    80.00 )
Median:        45.13               .           (    .   ,       .   )
```

Similarly, in Figure 20-7, when the patients do have positive lymph nodes, the mean survival time also gets shorter as the tumor size gets larger. The mean is again limited to the last censored case (as in Figure 20-3).

The median survival time cannot be calculated for most groups here because less than 50% of the at risk cases in the group experienced the terminal event. See Chapter 19 for a discussion of the median. Figure 20-8 shows summaries of the number of events, number censored (alive), and percentage censored in each combination of categories.

Figure 20-8
Summaries of lymph node involvement and pathologic tumor size

```
Survival Analysis for TIME        Time (months)
                          Total    Number      Number      Percent
                                   Events      Censored     Censored
LN_YESNO      No          860        39          821        95.47
  PATHSCAT    <= 2 cm     666        21          645        96.85
  PATHSCAT    2-5 cm      190        17          173        91.05
  PATH        > 5 cm        4         1            3        75.00
LN_YESNO      Yes         261        27          234        89.66
  PATHSCAT    <= 2 cm     160        10          150        93.75
  PATHSCAT    2-5 cm       93        16           77        82.80
  PATHSCAT    > 5 cm        8         1            7        87.50

Overall                  1121        66         1055        94.11
```

Figure 20-9 shows that the survival times for different categories of pathologic tumor size were significantly different, both for patients with no positive lymph nodes and for patients having positive lymph nodes. The significance is well under the conventional value of $p = 0.05$.

Figure 20-9
Test statistics

```
Test Statistics for Equality of Survival Distributions for PATHSCAT
 For LN_YESNO = No
                  Statistic     df      Significance
 Log Rank          20.50         2         .0000
Test Statistics for Equality of Survival Distributions for PATHSCAT
 For LN_YESNO = Yes
                  Statistic     df      Significance
 Log Rank          14.02         2         .0009
```

These statistics are for each stratum. Since the conclusion is the same in both strata, *Pooled over strata* could be used. If the conclusions for the separate strata are not the same, then do not pool. These tests indicate only that the pathologic tumor size categories are different from one another, but not which specific categories are different. For comparing all distinct pairs of factor categories, select pairwise statistics.

Separate charts for each level of lymph node involvement with survival functions for each category of tumor size are shown in Figure 20-10. In each chart, the curves representing the larger size categories descend more rapidly than the curve for the smallest category. The longer survival for smaller tumor sizes is apparent. For the largest size category (> 5 cm), there is only a small number of steps in each chart, reflecting the small number of cases in this category.

Figure 20-10

Comparison of the survival functions for pathologic tumor sizes with no lymph node involvement

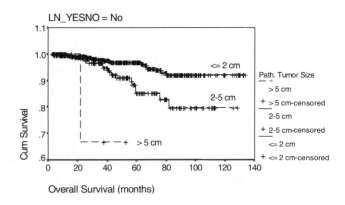

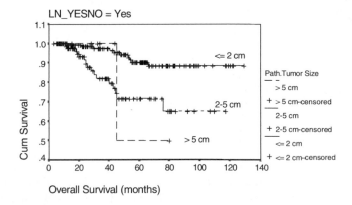

Cox Regression Examples

Contributed by Milton Steinberg, Marymount College.

A series of measurements was taken at the University of Chicago (Heimann, unpublished) on more than 1000 conservatively treated breast cancer cases. Among the measurements were pathologic tumor size, estrogen receptor status, and number of positive axillary lymph nodes. Can any of these factors be used to predict the risk of death from breast cancer? What is the relative risk of death for breast cancer patients who have a positive estrogen receptor status as compared with breast cancer patients who have a negative estrogen receptor status? Do cases with positive estrogen receptor status survive longer than those with negative estrogen receptor status?

As described in the *SPSS Base Applications Guide*, multiple linear regression is a technique used to determine the influence of predictor variables on a dependent variable. However, linear regression has no mechanism for handling censored cases. A nonlinear model is also more reasonable as an approximation for a variable, such as survival time or hazard rate, that cannot take on negative values.

The Cox Regression Model

As explained more fully in Chapter 19, some observations in survival studies are commonly censored. Censored cases do not experience the event of interest in the study, such as death from cancer or recovery from depression, before the end of the study. Cox Regression, like other survival techniques, makes use of the contribution of censored cases.

The Cox **proportional hazards** regression model is popular in part because it requires fewer assumptions than some other survival models. However, it should be used only if the assumption of proportional hazards is met (see "Checking for

Proportional Hazards" on p. 301). If the proportional hazards assumption is violated, an extended version of the Cox model must be used.

The Hazard Function

Cox Regression uses the **hazard function** to estimate the relative risk of failure. The hazard function, *h(t)*, is a rate. It is an estimate of the potential for death per unit time at a particular instant, given that the case has survived until that instant (see Kleinbaum, 1996). A high hazard function indicates a high rate of mortality. For example, the hazard function representing the risk of human mortality is high during the first days of life, becomes low and stable through the middle years, and begins to increase with advancing age. Note that the hazard function is not a probability and can therefore exceed 1. It can take on any value from 0 to infinity.

The **survival function** or **survivorship function**, *S(t)*, was introduced in Chapter 19. It is an estimate of the probability of surviving longer than a specified time. The **cumulative hazard function**, *H(t)*, is related to the survival function and can be derived from the survival function (see Lee, 1992: $H(t) = -\ln S(t)$).

The Cox Regression model used to determine the influence of predictor variables on a dependent variable is most simply expressed in terms of the hazard function. Predictor variables are termed **covariates** in this model. A simple model comparing treatment to control, or condition to no condition, can be written as

$$h(t) = [h_0(t)]e^{(BX)}$$

Equation 21-1

Here *X* is a dichotomous covariate that takes the value 0 for control or no condition and the value 1 for treatment or condition. *B* is a regression coefficient, *e* is the base of the natural logarithm (about 2.718), and $h_0(t)$ is the **baseline hazard function** when *X* is set to 0 (the expected risk without the treatment or condition). The expected risk of death for a particular case with condition *X* is equal to the risk of death without condition *X* multiplied by the quantity *e* raised to the power *(BX)*. In the breast cancer example, the expected risk of death from cancer in a patient who has a positive estrogen receptor status *h(t)* is equal to the expected risk of death for a patient who has a negative estrogen receptor status $h_0(t)$ multiplied by *e* raised to the power *(BX)*. In this example, *X* takes the value of 0 for negative or 1 for positive receptor status, and *B* is the regression coefficient. It is estimated by maximizing a partial likelihood (Cox and Oakes, 1984; Kalbfleisch and Prentice, 1980).

There are other ways to express Equation 21-1 that are helpful in interpreting the output from Cox Regression. If both sides of Equation 21-1 are divided by $h_0(t)$, the result is

$$h(t)/h_0(t) \ = \ e^{(BX)}$$

Equation 21-2

The quantity $h(t)/h_0(t)$ is called the **relative hazard** or the **hazard ratio**. It indicates the increase (or decrease) in risk incurred by applying the treatment or condition.

If the natural log is taken of both sides of Equation 21-2, the result is

$$\ln[h(t)/(h_0(t))] \ = \ BX$$

Equation 21-3

The quantity $\ln[h(t)/(h_0(t))]$ is the log relative hazard, which can be used to compare the relative risk for patients with and without the treatment. If the quantity $\ln[h(t)/(h_0(t))]$ is set equal to Y, then Equation 21-3 becomes $Y = BX$. This closely resembles an ordinary regression equation.

A subset of the cases in the original breast cancer data was used for the examples in this chapter. In order to submit the data to the Cox Regression procedure, the file must contain at least two variables: a survival time indicator (the dependent variable) and a status indicator that records whether the event has occurred for the case or if the case is censored. Usually a third, predictor (independent), variable is also entered. In this example, the dependent variable, *time*, indicates months of survival of breast cancer cases. The status indicator variable, *status*, is coded 0 for censored cases and 1 for cases that have died of breast cancer. The predictor variable, estrogen receptor status (*er*), is coded 0 for negative status and 1 for positive status. To produce the output, from the menus choose:

Analyze
  Survival
    Cox Regression...

▶ Time: time

▶ Status: status

Define Event...
  Single value: 1

▶ Covariates: er

Figure 21-1

Statistics for estrogen receptor status

Variables in the Equation

	B	SE	Wald	df	Sig.	Exp(B)
ER	-.651	.281	5.346	1	.021	.522

The table in Figure 21-1 presents the following information:

- *B* is the estimated coefficient. It is interpreted as the predicted change in log hazard for a unit increase in the predictor.

- *S.E.* is the standard error of the estimated coefficient, *B*.

- *Wald* is the Wald statistic. If $df = 1$, the Wald statistic can be calculated as $(B/S.E.)^2$. It is used to test whether the estimated coefficient *B* is different from 0 in the population. It is distributed as chi-square.

- *df* is degrees of freedom for the Wald statistic. The degrees of freedom for the Wald statistic is 1 except for categorical variables. While the degrees of freedom for each category is 1, the degrees of freedom for the overall test of the categorical variable is the number of categories minus 1.

- *Sig* is the significance level for the Wald statistic.

- *Exp(B)* is $e^{(B)}$ as in Equation 21-2, $h(t)/h_0(t) = e^{(BX)}$. For a dichotomous variable in which there are two levels, 0 and 1, *Exp(B)* is the **relative risk**, which is the ratio of the risk with *X* at 0 compared to the risk with *X* at 1.

Is estrogen receptor status an effective predictor that can be used to predict the risk of death from breast cancer? The negative value of the regression coefficient means that as the value of *er* increases, the risk decreases. Since *er* is coded 0 for negative and 1 for positive, it means that the death rate is expected to be less when estrogen receptor status is positive. This estimated coefficient is significantly different from 0; the Wald statistic is large, and the significance level is small. Estrogen receptor status does appear to be an effective predictor variable in this model where no other variables are considered. Since *Exp(B)* is less than 1, it indicates that there is a decreased relative risk when estrogen receptor status is positive. The hazard from breast cancer with positive estrogen receptor status is about 52% that of the hazard with negative estrogen receptor status, when no other variables are considered. An increased risk would have been indicated by a number greater than 1.

The hazard function for estrogen receptor status can be written as

$$h(t) = [h_0(t)]e^{(-0.6507X)}$$

where X is 0 or 1 (negative or positive receptor status) and $h_0(t)$ is the baseline hazard function.

The difference in risk of breast cancer death between negative and positive estrogen receptor status can be seen graphically. Figure 21-2 shows cumulative hazard functions for positive and negative estrogen status (*er*). To produce the output, recall the dialog box and choose:

Categorical...
  ▶ Categorical Covariates: er (Indicator(first))

Plots...
Hazard
  ▶ Separate Lines for: er(Cat)

Figure 21-2
Cumulative hazard function for positive and negative estrogen receptor status

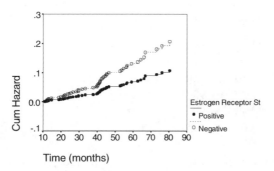

Note: Charts in this chapter have been modified in the Chart Editor for black and white presentation.

In Figure 21-2, the line representing the cumulative hazard function for negative estrogen receptor status is above the line representing positive estrogen receptor status. This shows a higher hazard for cases with negative estrogen receptor status.

Declaring the estrogen receptor status variable categorical has divided it into two patterns because there are two levels of the variable, 0 and 1, and it is categorical. The Cox Regression procedure can also produce plots for more than two patterns.

Generating Cumulative Hazard and Survival Estimates for Individual Cases

The hazard function and the survival function are closely related, and both can be calculated by the Cox Regression procedure. To add cumulative hazard and survival functions to the data, recall the dialog box and choose:

Save...
  Survival:
  ☑ Function
  Diagnostics:
  ☑ Hazard function

Two new variables appear in the Data Editor, *sur_1* and *haz_1*. Figure 21-3 shows values for six uncensored cases, three with negative and three with positive estrogen receptor status.

Figure 21-3
Cumulative hazard and survival estimates for a few selected cases

ID	Estrogen Receptor Status	Time	sur_1	haz_1
1182	Negative	11.03	.99818	.00182
1103	Negative	12.00	.99635	.00366
1153	Negative	13.10	.98891	.01115
1180	Positive	12.20	.99713	.00288
1169	Positive	12.43	.99616	.00385
1155	Positive	13.03	.99518	.00483

The cumulative hazard for case 1153 (with negative estrogen receptor status and surviving for 13.10 months) is 0.01115. The cumulative hazard for the case 1155 (surviving for 13.03 months with positive estrogen receptor status) is 0.00483. The smaller hazard reflects the lesser risk expected for the positive status. Similarly, from the survival column *sur_1*, 99.64% of the cases continue alive after the event at 12.00 months *(er negative)* and 99.71% of the cases continue alive after the event at 12.20 months *(er positive)*. This reflects the higher survival rate expected for positive status as compared with negative status.

Plotting Survival Functions

Just as the overall differences in risk for estrogen receptor positivity and negativity are clarified by a graph of the cumulative hazard function, the answer to the question of whether cases with positive estrogen receptor status survive longer than those with negative estrogen receptor status is clarified by viewing the survival functions.

To plot the survival functions, recall the dialog box and from the menus choose:

Plots...

☑ Survival
Separate Lines for: er(Cat)

The plot is shown in Figure 21-4. The curve for estrogen receptor positivity is higher than the curve for estrogen receptor negativity. It reflects an expectation of longer survival times with estrogen receptor positive status.

Figure 21-4
Survival curves for estrogen receptor status data

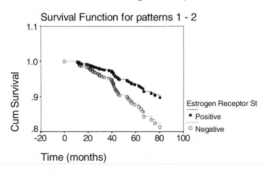

A regression equation can be written for *S(t)* similar to that for *h(t)*:

$$S(t) = [S_0(t)]^p$$

Equation 21-4

where $p = e^{(BX)}$. Instead of $S_0(t)$ being multiplied by $e^{(BX)}$, it is raised to the power $e^{(BX)}$. This creates a more complicated function than that for *h(t)* in Equation 21-1.

Multiple Covariates

As with multiple linear regression, the model for Cox Regression can be expanded to include more than one covariate:

$$h(t) = [h_0(t)]e^{(B_1 X_1 + B_2 X_2 + \ldots + B_p X_p)}$$ Equation 21-5

where $X_1 \ldots X_p$ are the covariates. The covariates can be continuous or categorical. Dichotomous covariates, such as estrogen receptor status, can be treated as categorical or continuous on an interval scale, since the single interval between 0 and 1 must be an "equal" interval. See the appendix for more information on coding schemes and their interpretation. The Cox Regression procedure automatically codes any variables designated as categorical and permits inclusion of interaction terms in the model.

Suppose the variable representing estrogen receptor status (*er*) is joined in the model with two other variables, one representing the number of positive axillary lymph nodes (*lnpos*) and another representing pathologic tumor size (*pathsize*). The variable *er* is dichotomous and can be considered continuous or categorical. *Lnpos* and *pathsize* are continuous variables.

Figure 21-5 shows the Cox Regression output from the model with three variables included. To produce the output, from the menus choose:

Analyze
  Survival
    Cox Regression...

▶ Time: time
▶ Status: status
Define Event...
  Single value: 1

▶ Covariates: er lnpos pathsize

Figure 21-5
Statistics for model with three variables

Variables in the Equation

	B	SE	Wald	df	Sig.	Exp(B)
ER	-.565	.295	3.653	1	.056	.569
LNPOS	.145	.036	16.274	1	.000	1.156
PATHSIZE	.400	.117	11.717	1	.001	1.492

The interpretation is similar to that for Figure 21-1. There are now three estimated coefficients (*B* values), one for each variable. The regression equation can now be written as

$$h(t) = [h_0(t)]e^{((-0.565 \times er) + (0.145 \times lnpos) + (0.400 \times pathsize))}$$

Notice that the estimated coefficient for *er* is not the same as in Figure 21-1. The contribution of each variable to the regression model is considered in the light of the contribution of all the other variables in the model. The value of *B* for *er* was computed as a partial weight after partialing out the influence of the other two variables. This *B* is no longer significant at the 0.05 level. Should *er* be removed from the model?

For multiple level variables, *Exp(B)* estimates the percentage change in risk with each unit change in the covariate. Each unit increase in the number of positive lymph nodes (*lnpos*) is expected to increase the risk of death about 16%, since $Exp(B) = 1.156$. For the dichotomous variable *er,* the percentage change in risk with each unit change in the covariate can be interpreted as the relative risk, since the covariate takes only the values 0 and 1.

Testing the Overall Model

Does the inclusion of any of the three predictors *er, lnpos,* and *pathsize* do a better job of predicting the hazard rate than a baseline model in which each *B* is set to 0 (the covariates are ignored)? This question is answered by testing whether any of the population *B* values are nonzero. In Cox Regression, coefficients are estimated by maximizing the partial likelihood function, *L*. The partial likelihood is determined by finding the risk of failure at each failure point and taking the product of all of these risks. The natural log of *L* is called the log likelihood, *LL*. Minus 2 times the log likelihood (-2 log likelihood) for the model of interest can be compared with -2 log likelihood for the baseline model in which all *B*'s are set to 0 to test whether all population *B*'s are 0.

Figure 21-6
Comparing regression models

Block 0: Beginning Block

**Omnibus Tests
of
Model Coefficients**

| -2 Log
Likelihood |
| --- |
| 596.064 |

Block1: Method = Enter

**Omnibus Tests of[1,2]
Model Coefficients**

| -2 Log
Likelihood | Change From
Previous step | | | Change From
Previous Block | | | Overall (score) | | |
| --- | --- | --- | --- | --- | --- | --- | --- | --- | --- |
| | Chi-
square | df | Sig. | Chi-
square | df | Sig. | Chi-
square | df | Sig. |
| 560.175 | 35.888 | 3 | .000 | 35.888 | 3 | .000 | 56.953 | 3 | .000 |

[1]. Beginning Block Number 0, initial Log Likelihood function: -2 Log likelihood: -596.064

[2]. Beginning Block Number 1. Method: Enter

The output in Figure 21-6 presents the following information:

- *Block Number 0* refers to the baseline model with all *B*'s set to 0.

- *Block Number 1* refers to the model with the predictor variables included.

- *Change from Previous Block* is the difference between -2 log likelihood for block 0 and block 1. This is the **likelihood-ratio (LR)** test.

- *Change from Previous Step* refers to stepwise regression procedures (see below).

- *Overall (score)* is another test of whether all of the coefficients (*B*) in the model are 0 in the population. It is distributed as chi-square and is an approximation to *LR*. This test is also called the **global chi-square** or **overall chi-square**.

- *df* is the number of variables in the present model minus the number of variables in the previous model.

- *Sig* is based on the chi-square test. Both the score and -2 log likelihood are distributed as chi-square for large samples.

In the current model, the change in -2 log likelihood from the previous block, in which all B's were set to 0, is $590.06 - 560.18 = 35.88$. Since $p < 0.0001$, the inference is that at least one population B is nonzero. The score agrees with the likelihood ratio.

Finding a Good Model

Does the model using *er*, *lnpos*, and *pathsize* include the best predictors of survival? The estimated coefficient B for *er* is no longer significantly different from 0 when *lnpos* and *pathsize* are added to the model. Should *er* be removed from the model? The basic strategy for answering such questions involves adding various combinations of variables to the model and then testing each model to determine which has the best predictive power. But be aware that determination of a best model is not a purely mechanical procedure. The model that best fits the present data was specifically constructed to do so for the sample being used. It may not be the same as the one that best fits other samples from the same population. Practical and theoretical considerations also play a part in choosing a model. Some variables or interactions that seem to be part of the optimal model may be difficult to interpret or hard or expensive to measure.

Methods for Selecting Models

The coefficient for *er* changed when *lnpos* and *pathsize* were added to the model. It no longer made a significant contribution to the prediction of risk. But, the contribution of any one variable is determined in the context of the contribution of all other variables in the model. If other variables were included in the model, *er* might be found to make a significant contribution. Several methods are available for adding and deleting variables from the model. The method used so far has been **forced entry**. All of the variables have been forced into the model in one step. Two stepwise methods are available, **forward selection** and **backward selection,** in which variables are entered and deleted according to specified criteria.

In forward selection, the model begins as the baseline model without any variables in it. Variables are considered one at a time. They are added to the model if they meet the selection criterion based on the p value for the score statistic. The default value for inclusion is 0.05. As each new variable is added, the variables already present are evaluated for removal. One of three criteria for removal can be selected: the likelihood-ratio statistic based on the maximum partial likelihood estimates, the likelihood-ratio statistic based on conditional parameter estimates, and the Wald statistic. The default for removal from the model is a *p* value of 0.10 for the selected statistic. The maximum partial likelihood estimates criterion may be superior to the others, but it requires recomputation of the model after each variable is deleted in turn. The conditional parameter estimates criterion does not require recomputation of the model and usually gives results similar to those for the maximum partial likelihood estimates criterion. When no more variables meet entry or removal criteria, or when the last model is identical to a prior model, the algorithm stops.

In backward selection, all of the selected variables are entered into the model at the first step. Each variable is then considered for removal. All of the variables that meet removal criteria are removed. Then the excluded variables are reconsidered for inclusion. When no more variables can be entered or removed, the algorithm stops.

Stepwise Regression: Forward Selection Example

For this section, two other variables, age and histologic grade (*histgrad*) have been added to the model. Histologic grade has been treated as a categorical variable with three levels coded as indicator or dummy variables and with the first category as the reference category. A forward selection procedure with removal based on conditional parameter estimates has been selected.

Figure 21-7 shows Cox Regression output using forward selection. To produce the output, from the menus choose:

Analyze
  Survival
    Cox Regression...

▶ Time: time
▶ Status: status

Define Event...
    Single value: 1

▶ Covariates: er lnpos pathsize age histgrad

 Method: Forward:Conditional

Categorical: histgrad (Indicator(first))

(Deselect any Plots or Save variables)

Figure 21-7
Forward selection: Block 0

**Variables not[1,2]
in the Equation**

	Score	df	Sig.
ER	3.643	1	.056
LNPOS	21.847	1	.000
PATHSIZE	24.656	1	.000
AGE	9.305	1	.002
HISTGRAD	5.534	2	.063
HISTGRAD(1)	1.498	1	.221
HISTGRAD(2)	4.586	1	.032

[1]. Residual Chi Square = 43.487 with 6 df Sig. = .000

[2]. Beginning Block Number 0, initial Log Likelihood
function: -2 Log likelihood: -463.880

The forward selection statistics contain the following information:

- *Block Number 0* is the baseline model with all variables excluded.

- *Variables not in the Equation* includes all of the variables in the model because forward selection begins with all of the variables excluded.

- *Residual Chi Square* tests whether all of the coefficients for the variables not in the equation are 0.

- *Score* statistic is used to determine inclusion in the model. For categorical variables, an overall score statistic and score statistics for each of the components are printed. The significance of the overall score statistic determines inclusion.

- *df* for the score statistic is 1 except for categorical variables and interaction terms with two or more components. In that case, the degrees of freedom is the number of components. In a categorical variable, this is one less than the number of levels.

- *Sig* of the score statistic is the criterion for inclusion in the model. The default value for inclusion is 0.05.

The categorical variable, *histgrad*, has an overall score statistic and a statistic for each of its components. The overall score determines whether *histgrad* is included in the model. The degrees of freedom for *histgrad*, overall, is 2. It has three levels that are reduced to two components by the coding scheme.

Because the residual chi-square is significant ($p < 0.0001$), at least one coefficient is implied to be nonzero in the population. The variables *lnpos*, *pathsize*, and *age* all meet the criteria for inclusion at this stage because significance of the chi-squares for their score statistics is less than 0.05. The variable with the lowest *Sig* level will be added at the next step. Figure 21-8 shows the model after the addition of *pathsize*, the variable with the lowest *p* value (*Sig*) for its score statistic.

Figure 21-8
Block 1, step 1

Omnibus Tests [4,5]
of Model Coefficients

Step: 1 [1]

-2 Log Likelihood	Change From Previous step			Change From Previous Block			Overall (score)		
	Chi-square	df	Sig.	Chi-square	df	Sig.	Chi-square	df	Sig.
444.685	19.195	1	.000	19.195	1	.000	24.656	1	.000

1. Variable(s) Entered at Step Number 1: PATHSIZE

4. Beginning Block Number 0, initial Log Likelihood function: -2 Log likelihood: -463.880

5. Beginning Block Number 1. Method: Forward Stepwise (Conditional LR)

Variables in the Equation

Step 1 PATHSIZE

B	SE	Wald	df	Sig.	Exp(B)
.605	.123	24.241	1	.000	1.832

**Variables
not in the Equation**[1]

		Score	df	Sig.
Step 1	ER	1.700	1	.192
	LNPOS	8.072	1	.004
	AGE	4.442	1	.035
	HISTGRAD	3.097	2	.213
	HISTGRAD(1)	.786	1	.375
	HISTGRAD(2)	2.381	1	.123

[1]. Residual Chi Square = 13.109 with 5 df Sig. = .022

Model if Term Removed

Term Removed		Loss Chi-square	df	Sig.
Step 1	PATHSIZE	19.195	1	.000

With *pathsize* entered into the model, -2 log likelihood is calculated and compared with -2 log likelihood for the baseline model. The likelihood-ratio chi-square is significant, as is the chi-square for the score statistic. The variable *pathsize* has a positive coefficient (*B*), so the larger the pathologic tumor size, the greater the hazard. Examination of *Exp(B)* shows that there is approximately an 83% increase in hazard for each unit increase in *pathsize*.

The *Model if Term Removed* column helps test *pathsize* for removal using the *conditional* criterion requested as Method in the dialog box. Since the *p* value for the chi-square is less than the 0.10 exclusion criterion, *pathsize* is retained in the model.

The residual chi-square for the variables not in the equation is significant. The variable *lnpos* now has the smallest *p* value. It will be selected in the next step.

Figure 21-9 shows step 2.

Figure 21-9
Block 1, step 2

Omnibus Tests of Model Coefficients

Step: 2^2

	Change From Previous step			Change From Previous Block			Overall (score)		
-2 Log Likelihood	Chi-square	df	Sig.	Chi-square	df	Sig.	Chi-square	df	Sig.
438.522	6.163	1	.013	25.358	2	.000	38.818	2	.000

2. Variable(s) Entered at Step Number 2: LNPOS

Variables in the Equation

		B	SE	Wald	df	Sig.	Exp(B)
Step 2	LNPOS	.125	.045	7.798	1	.005	1.133
	PATHSIZE	.503	.129	15.140	1	.000	1.654

Variables not in the Equation [1]

		Score	df	Sig.
Step 2	ER	2.144	1	.143
	AGE	4.092	1	.043
	HISTGRAD	2.612	2	.271
	HISTGRAD(1)	.842	1	.359
	HISTGRAD(2)	2.077	1	.150

1. Residual Chi Square = 13.109 with 5 df Sig. = .022

Model if Term Removed

Term Removed		Loss Chi-square	df	Sig.
Step 2	LNPOS	6.216	1	.013
	PATHSIZE	12.916	1	.000

Change from Previous Step shows the difference between -2 log likelihood for the model constructed at step 1 and the model constructed at step 2. *Change from Previous Block* shows the difference between -2 log likelihood for the baseline model constructed in block 0 and for the model constructed in step 2. Both likelihood ratios show a significant improvement in the model. The model is then reevaluated with both *pathsize* and *lnpos*. Both variables make significant contributions.

Of the variables not in the equation, only *age* has a *p* value that falls below the 0.05 cutoff. It will be selected in the next step. Both *pathsize* and *lnpos* are below criteria for removal from the model, and therefore they are retained in the next step.

Figure 21-10 shows step 3 of the forward selection process.

Figure 21-10
Block 1, step 3

Omnibus Tests of Model Coefficients

Step: 3[3]

	Change From Previous step			Change From Previous Block			Overall (score)		
-2 Log Likelihood	Chi-square	df	Sig.	Chi-square	df	Sig.	Chi-square	df	Sig.
434.321	4.200	1	.040	29.558	3	.000	41.232	3	.000

3. Variable(s) Entered at Step Number 3: AGE

Variables in the Equation

		B	SE	Wald	df	Sig.	Exp(B)
Step 3	LNPOS	.127	.047	7.136	1	.008	1.135
	PATHSIZE	.437	.135	10.429	1	.001	1.548
	AGE	-.027	.013	4.040	1	.044	.973

Variables not in the Equation [1,2,3]

		Score	df	Sig.
Step 3	ER	.851	1	.356
	HISTGRAD	1.535	2	.464
	HISTGRAD(1)	.420	1	.517
	HISTGRAD(2)	1.102	1	.294

1. Residual Chi Square = 13.109 with 5 df Sig. = .022

2. Residual Chi Square = 5.964 with 4 df Sig. = .202

3. Residual Chi Square = 1.937 with 3 df Sig. = .585

Model if Term Removed

		Statistic		
Term Removed		Loss Chi-square	df	Sig.
Step 3	LNPOS	5.838	1	.016
	PATHSIZE	9.179	1	.002
	AGE	4.203	1	.040

When the model with *lnpos*, *pathsize*, and *age* is reevaluated, each has a loss chi-square *p* value below the 0.10 cutoff, and all three variables make a significant contribution to predicting hazard or survival. Since *age* has a negative coefficient, increases in age lead to decreases in hazard.

The variables not in the equation, *er* and *histgrad*, have score statistics with *p* values that exceed the 0.05 cutoff criterion. *No more variables can be added or deleted*, and the algorithm stops.

Checking for Proportional Hazards

The proportional hazards model assumes that the hazard function $h(t)$ for the model that includes a particular covariate is proportionally related to the baseline hazard, $h_0(t)$. This expectation is implied in Equation 21-2, where $h(t)$ and $h_0(t)$ are in constant proportion to one another; that is, they are related to one another as a power of e. To see what this means, observe plots of the baseline hazard functions for estrogen receptor positive status and negative status (*er*) in Figure 21-11. To produce the output, from the menus choose:

Analyze
  Survival
    Cox Regression...

▶ Time: time

▶ Status: status

Define Event...
  Single value: 1

▶ Strata: er

Plots...
  Plot Type:
  ☑ Hazard
  ☑ Log minus log

Figure 21-11
Baseline hazard functions for estrogen receptor status data

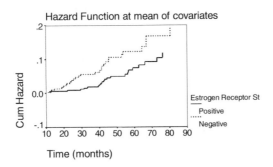

The variable *er* was declared as *strata* rather than as a covariate. This caused baseline hazard functions to be calculated for each level of the variable. Although the coefficients of the hazard functions are different for the baselines of estrogen receptor positivity and negativity, the proportions are approximately the same throughout. Estrogen receptor negative diverges from estrogen receptor positive at a nearly constant rate so that the difference between the two curves remains proportional over time.

Another useful plot for determining whether the assumption of proportional hazards is met is the **log-minus-log** (LML) plot of the survival function. If the hazards are proportional, the curves generated by LML should be parallel. The curves in Figure 21-12 seem sufficiently parallel to confirm that the proportional hazards assumption is met.

Figure 21-12
Log-minus-log plot for two levels of estrogen receptor response

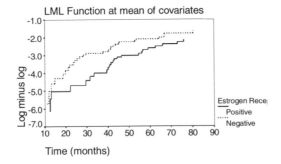

Nonproportional Hazards

Carter, Wampler, and Stablein (1983) reproduced a data set published from Stablein, Carter, and Wampler (1980) that demonstrates a model that violates the assumption of proportional hazards. Mice were injected with leukemia cells and then treated with different doses of the drug ICRF-159. Figure 21-13 compares baseline cumulative hazard functions for two dose strata, 0.0 mg/kg and 112.5 mg/kg.

Figure 21-13
Baseline hazard functions for two doses of ICRF-159

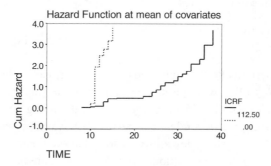

The two curves do not appear to increase proportionally. They diverge radically. The LML plot for the same data in Figure 21-8 confirms this departure from proportionality, since the plotted curves are not parallel.

Figure 21-14
Log-minus-log plot for two doses of ICRF-159

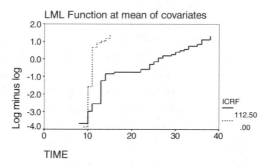

Cox Regression with Time-Dependent Covariates

Since the proportional hazards model implies that the effect of the covariate on the relative hazard is constant over time, it cannot be used to determine the efficacy of ICRF-159; its hazard function was determined to be nonproportional over time. But the covariate can be combined in a product with the survival time variable, or some function of the survival time variable, to create a **time-dependent covariate**. The time-dependent covariate can then be used to fit a nonproportional hazards model in which time is included as a predictor. It can also be used to check on the assumption of proportional hazards. The relative hazard function in such a model is free to vary with time.

$$h(t) = [h_0(t)]e^{(B_1 X_1 + B_2 X_1 * \text{T\_COV\_})}$$
Equation 21-6

In Equation 21-6, B_2 is the coefficient of a compound covariate formed by the product of X_1 with a variable called $T\_COV\_$, which is some function of the survival time variable for the model that includes X_1. SPSS provides a separate dialog box for calculating Cox Regression with time-dependent covariates. Both Cox Regression and its variant, Cox Time-Dependent, use the Newton-Raphson method, a numerical iterative procedure for solving nonlinear equations, in order to estimate parameters. However, the Cox Regression dialog box also permits saving diagnostics and graph generation.

To set up a Cox time-dependent analysis, from the menus choose:

Analyze
  Survival
    Cox w/ Time-Dep Cov...

At the top of the variables list on the left of the dialog box, a new variable, called $T\_$, has been inserted. The inserted variable, $T\_$, was generated by the time-dependent procedure. It assumes the same values as the variable in the database that is designated as the survival *time* indicator. $T\_$ can be transformed in many ways. For example, if $T\_$ is in months, $T\_/12$ would measure years. After you enter the information in the dialog box, the transformed version is stored in a variable called $T\_COV\_$. The strategy is to use $T\_COV\_$ as a covariate in interaction with other variables to generate a regression equation in which variables are free to change as a function of time.

Figure 21-15 shows output for the model that includes *icrf* and the interaction *T_COV_*icrf*. To produce the output, from the menus choose:

Analyze
  Survival
    Cox w/ Time-Dep Cov...

Expression for T_COV_: T_

Model...

▶ Time: time

▶ Status: status

Define Event...
  Single value: 1

▶ Covariates: icrf, T_COV_*icrf

Figure 21-15
Cox Regression with a time-dependent covariate

Variables in the Equation

	B	SE	Wald	df	Sig.	Exp(B)
ICRF	-.025	.004	44.932	1	.000	.975
T_COV_*ICRF	.001	.000	24.675	1	.000	1.001

The Time-Dependent procedure calculates the values of the covariates at each event time for each case still at risk at that time. In this example, *T_COV_* has been assigned the value of *T_*, which is nothing more than the survival times in the time *variable*. The *icrf* coefficient gives the per unit change log hazard for time equal to 0. The coefficient for the product *T_COV_*icrf* is also significant. The significant interaction term indicates that the model that includes *icrf* does indeed violate the proportional hazards assumption and that the creation of the time-dependent variable *T_COV_*icrf* was necessary in order to evaluate *icrf* using Cox Regression.

Segmented Time-Dependent Covariates

The time-dependent covariate, *T_COV_*icrf,* was specifically created as an interaction term to permit the modeling of nonproportional hazards. Another type of time-dependent covariate, the **segmented time-dependent covariate,** is a variable that *intrinsically* varies with time (for example, blood pressure measurements that are taken more than once during a study). Crowley and Hu (1977) provide an example of the analysis of a heart transplant study in which the survival times of transplant patients were compared to those of nontransplant patients. In the version reported here, the covariates placed in the model are *waittime* (waiting time until transplant), *age* (at time of transplant), and *mismatch* (a tissue mismatch score). The transplant patients are not equivalent to the nontransplant patients. Only those who survive long enough to receive a heart can become recipients, so those with longer survival times are more likely to receive a heart. A time-dependent variable is therefore set up as an indicator. It has the value 0 before transplant and assumes the value 1 at the time of transplant (see Cox and Oakes, 1984). The syntax commands for the three time-dependent variables are as follows:

```
TIME PROGRAM.
COMPUTE xplant = (T_ >= waittime).
If missing(waittime) xplant=0.
COMPUTE xplntage = (T_ >= waittime) * age .
If missing(waittime) xplntage=0.
COMPUTE score = (T_ >= waittime) * mismatch .
If missing(waittime) score=0.
COXREG
    survival  /STATUS=followup(1)
  /METHOD=ENTER   xplant xplntage score
  /CRITERIA=PIN(.05) POUT(.10) ITERATE(20) .
```

The variable *waittime* indicates when transplant has occurred. In the first transformation,

COMPUTE xplant = (T_ >= waittime)

the covariate *xplant* assumes a value of 0 if survival time is shorter than the waiting time until transplant, and *xplant* assumes a value of 1 if survival time is equal to or exceeds the waiting time until transplant. The 1 and 0 are results of true or false evaluation of the logical expression in parentheses. In the second transformation,

If missing(waittime) xplant = 0

all missing values of *xplant* are set to 0. All elements of the variable must have some value or the coefficients will not converge. Similarly, the values of the variable *xplntage* will be 0 for all times less than *waittime* (before transplant), and the values of *xplantage* will be the same as the values for *age* for all times greater than or equal to *waittime*. Finally, *score* has the value 0 before transplant and the value of *mismatch* after transplant.

The COXREG portion of the commands produced the table in Figure 21-16. (The CRITERIA subcommand contains default values, which are listed if you paste the syntax from the dialog box.)

Figure 21-16
Cox Regression with time-dependent covariates for heart transplant data

Variables in the Equation

	B	SE	Wald	df	Sig.	Exp(B)
XPLANT	-3.178	1.186	7.179	1	.007	.042
XPLNTAGE	.055	.023	5.965	1	.015	1.057
SCORE	.444	.280	2.512	1	.113	1.559

More Than Two Segments

It is possible to construct segmented covariates with more than two segments. Suppose radiation treatments are administered at the start of each of three months, and tumor size is assessed at the end of each month. A time-dependent covariate might be defined as

$$(T\_ > 1) * size1 + (T\_ >= 1 \& T\_ < 2) * size2 + (T\_ >= 2 \& T\_ < 3) * size3$$

If the survival time is between zero and one month (but not including one month), then *T_COV_* will have the values for *size1*. If survival time is between one and two months (but not including two months), then *T_COV_* will have the values for *size2*, and, similarly, for a survival time between two and three months, the values of *size3*.

Diagnostics

Graphic displays can be used to test whether the assumption of proportional hazards in Cox Regression is met, whether the **log relative hazard** (Equation 21-3) is linear as is assumed in Cox Regression, or whether cases in the data set may have an excessive influence on the outcome of the Cox Regression. The Cox Regression procedure permits you to save the cumulative hazard function (which is also called the **Cox-Snell** residual), **partial residuals**, **DfBeta**, and **X'Beta** to assist in making these determinations.

Cox Regression was performed for the breast cancer example with *age* as the only covariate. To produce the output, from the menus choose:

Analyze
  Survival
    Cox Regression...

▶ Time: time

▶ Status: status

Define Event...

Single value: 1

▶ Covariates: age

Save...

Diagnostics: ☑ Hazard function ☑ Partial residuals ☑ DfBeta(s)

☑ X*Beta

The Save options each add a new variable to the data: *haz_1*, *pr1_1*, *dfb1_1*, and *xbe_1*, respectively. These new variables can be saved with the data file. If there had been more than one covariate, a complete set of new variables would have been added to the data file for each covariate and named uniquely, as in *haz_2*, *pr1_2*, etc.

Using the Partial Residual for Checking Proportional Hazards

Partial residuals (Schoenfeld residuals) do not depend on time; hence, they may be plotted against time to test for violations of the proportional hazards assumption (Hess, 1995). Figure 21-17 shows a simple scatterplot of the partial residuals for *age* against survival time in the breast cancer data.

Figure 21-17

Plot of partial residuals for age against survival time

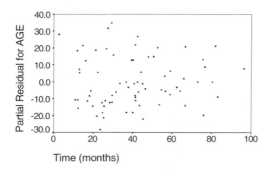

The partial residuals are calculated for uncensored cases only; they can be used for covariates that are not time-dependent. The partial residual for each case is the difference between the observed value of the case and its expected value. The expected value is calculated from all of the cases still at risk when the current case fails. The difference between a case and its expected value should be approximately 0 if proportionality holds. Figure 21-17 shows that the partial residuals are distributed fairly evenly in a band around 0, which is expected if the assumption of proportional hazards is met.

Linearity of the Log Hazard Function

Equation 21-3 defines the log relative hazard. It indicates that the log of the relative hazard is expected to be linearly related to the predictors.

At one time, the Cox-Snell residual (cumulative hazard function) was used to assess linearity. It is now standard practice to use the cumulative hazard function to construct **martingale residuals**. If the status indicator is coded 0 for censored cases and 1 for uncensored cases, martingale residuals are simply the hazard function subtracted from the status indicator. However, the following routine will work in all situations: if the case is censored, use Compute on the Transform menu to set *martgale = -(haz_1)*. If the case is uncensored, then the transformation is *martgale = 1 - haz_1*. Plots of martingale residuals against the covariate (Figure 21-18) or against the linear predictor *X'Beta* (Figure 21-19) should be linear. To find *X'Beta*, multiply each mean-corrected case value by each of its coefficient values (*B*), and add these products together. In this example, there is only one covariate and one coefficient.

Figure 21-18
Plot of martingale residuals against age

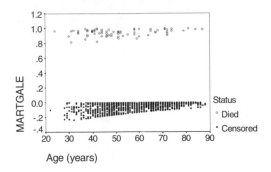

Figure 21-19
Plot of martingale residuals against X'Beta

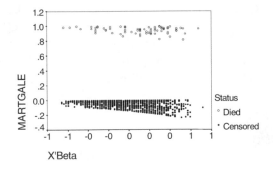

Since the martingale transformation treats censored and uncensored cases differently, it tends to separate them in the plot. In this data, there are many more censored cases than uncensored cases. They have been represented with closed and open circles, respectively, to clearly differentiate them. The censored cases form a fairly straight line around 0, and the uncensored cases form a fairly straight line around 1.

Influential Cases

Influential cases are those that have a disproportionate effect on the result of Cox Regression. The estimates for the regression coefficients are markedly different when such cases are included in the model and when they are removed from the model. DfBetas for each case can be calculated by performing the regression with and without each case in the model and finding the difference between the resulting coefficients for the predictor. This procedure is estimated by an approximation in Cox Regression. Figure 21-20 shows DfBeta for age plotted against the identification number (*id*) for each case.

Figure 21-20
Plot of DfBeta for age by id for each case

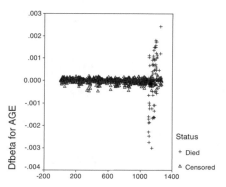

The censored cases are represented by open circles, and the uncensored cases, by plus signs. The uncensored cases seem to have a greater influence than the censored cases. Cases with little influence should form a band around 0. The DfBetas in this example are quite small. No case is outstanding. Extreme cases can be marked with the case number, using the Chart Editor. Case 1113 is the most extreme case in this data set.

Figure 21-21 shows that case 1113 is the oldest uncensored case in the data set. The censored cases in this chart have been hidden in the Chart Editor by making them tiny and white.

Figure 21-21
Plot of survival time against age

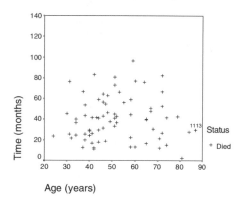

Categorical Variable Coding Schemes

In many SPSS procedures, you can request automatic replacement of a categorical independent variable with a set of contrast variables, which will then be entered or removed from an equation as a block. You can specify how the set of contrast variables is to be coded, usually on the CONTRAST subcommand. This appendix explains and illustrates how different contrast types requested on CONTRAST actually work.

Deviation

Deviation from the grand mean. In matrix terms, these contrasts have the form:

$$
\begin{array}{llllll}
\text{mean} & (\ \ 1/k & 1/k & ... & 1/k & 1/k\ ) \\
\text{df}(1) & (\ 1-1/k & -1/k & ... & -1/k & -1/k\ ) \\
\text{df}(2) & (\ -1/k & 1-1/k & ... & -1/k & -1/k\ ) \\
. & & . \\
. & & . \\
. & & . \\
\text{df}(k-1) & (\ -1/k & -1/k & ... & 1-1/k & -1/k\ )
\end{array}
$$

where k is the number of categories for the independent variable and the last category is omitted by default. For example, the deviation contrasts for an independent variable with three categories are as follows:

$$
\begin{array}{rrr}
(\ 1/3 & 1/3 & 1/3\ ) \\
(\ 2/3 & -1/3 & -1/3\ ) \\
(-1/3 & 2/3 & -1/3\ )
\end{array}
$$

To omit a category other than the last, specify the number of the omitted category in parentheses after the DEVIATION keyword. For example, the following subcommand obtains the deviations for the first and third categories and omits the second:

```
/CONTRAST(FACTOR)=DEVIATION(2)
```

Suppose that *factor* has three categories. The resulting contrast matrix will be

```
(  1/3    1/3    1/3 )
(  2/3   -1/3   -1/3 )
( -1/3   -1/3    2/3 )
```

Simple

Simple contrasts. Compares each level of a factor to the last. The general matrix form is

```
mean     (  1/k    1/k    ...    1/k    1/k )
df(1)    (   1      0     ...     0     -1 )
df(2)    (   0      1     ...     0     -1 )
  .                  .
  .                  .
df(k-1)  (   0      0     ...     1     -1 )
```

where k is the number of categories for the independent variable. For example, the simple contrasts for an independent variable with four categories are as follows:

```
( 1/4    1/4    1/4    1/4 )
(  1      0      0     -1 )
(  0      1      0     -1 )
(  0      0      1     -1 )
```

To use another category instead of the last as a reference category, specify in parentheses after the SIMPLE keyword the sequence number of the reference category, which is not necessarily the value associated with that category. For example, the following CONTRAST subcommand obtains a contrast matrix that omits the second category:

```
/CONTRAST(FACTOR) = SIMPLE(2)
```

Suppose that *factor* has four categories. The resulting contrast matrix will be

$$
\begin{pmatrix}
1/4 & 1/4 & 1/4 & 1/4 \\
1 & -1 & 0 & 0 \\
0 & -1 & 1 & 0 \\
0 & -1 & 0 & 1
\end{pmatrix}
$$

Helmert

Helmert contrasts. Compares categories of an independent variable with the mean of the subsequent categories. The general matrix form is

$$
\begin{array}{lc}
\text{mean} & (& 1/k & 1/k & \dots & 1/k & 1/k) \\
\text{df}(1) & (& 1 & -1/(k-1) & \dots & -1/(k-1) & -1/(k-1)) \\
\text{df}(2) & (& 0 & 1 & \dots & -1/(k-2) & -1/(k-2)) \\
\cdot & & & & & & \\
\cdot & & & \cdot & & & \\
\text{df}(k-2) & (& 0 & 0 & 1 & -1/2 & -1/2) \\
\text{df}(k-1) & (& 0 & 0 & \dots & 1 & -1)
\end{array}
$$

where k is the number of categories of the independent variable. For example, an independent variable with four categories has a Helmert contrast matrix of the following form:

$$
\begin{pmatrix}
1/4 & 1/4 & 1/4 & 1/4 \\
1 & -1/3 & -1/3 & -1/3 \\
0 & 1 & -1/2 & -1/2 \\
0 & 0 & 1 & -1
\end{pmatrix}
$$

Difference

Difference or reverse Helmert contrasts. Compares categories of an independent variable with the mean of the previous categories of the variable. The general matrix form is

```
mean     (        1/k        1/k        1/k     ...    1/k )
df(1)    (        −1          1          0      ...     0 )
df(2)    (       −1/2       −1/2         1      ...     0 )
 .                                 .
 .                                 .
df(k–1)  (     −1/(k–1)  −1/(k–1)  −1/(k–1)     ...     1 )
```

where k is the number of categories for the independent variable. For example, the difference contrasts for an independent variable with four categories are as follows:

```
(  1/4    1/4    1/4   1/4 )
( −1      1      0     0 )
(−1/2   −1/2     1     0 )
(−1/3   −1/3   −1/3    1 )
```

Polynomial

Orthogonal polynomial contrasts. The first degree of freedom contains the linear effect across all categories; the second degree of freedom, the quadratic effect; the third degree of freedom, the cubic; and so on for the higher-order effects.

You can specify the spacing between levels of the treatment measured by the given categorical variable. Equal spacing, which is the default if you omit the metric, can be specified as consecutive integers from 1 to k, where k is the number of categories. If the variable *drug* has three categories, the subcommand

```
/CONTRAST(DRUG)=POLYNOMIAL
```

is the same as

```
/CONTRAST(DRUG)=POLYNOMIAL(1,2,3)
```

Equal spacing is not always necessary, however. For example, suppose that *drug* represents different dosages of a drug given to three groups. If the dosage administered to the second group is twice that to the first group and the dosage administered to the third group is three times that to the first group, the treatment categories are equally spaced, and an appropriate metric for this situation consists of consecutive integers:

```
/CONTRAST(DRUG)=POLYNOMIAL(1,2,3)
```

If, however, the dosage administered to the second group is four times that given the first group, and the dosage given the third group is seven times that to the first, an appropriate metric is

```
/CONTRAST(DRUG)=POLYNOMIAL(1,4,7)
```

In either case, the result of the contrast specification is that the first degree of freedom for *drug* contains the linear effect of the dosage levels and the second degree of freedom contains the quadratic effect.

Polynomial contrasts are especially useful in tests of trends and for investigating the nature of response surfaces. You can also use polynomial contrasts to perform nonlinear curve fitting, such as curvilinear regression.

Repeated

Compares adjacent levels of an independent variable. The general matrix form is

$$
\begin{array}{ll}
\text{mean} & (1/k \quad 1/k \quad 1/k \quad ... \quad 1/k \quad 1/k\,) \\
\text{df}(1) & (\ \ 1 \quad -1 \quad 0 \quad ... \quad 0 \quad 0\,) \\
\text{df}(2) & (\ \ 0 \quad\ \ 1 \quad -1 \quad ... \quad 0 \quad 0\,) \\
\ \ \cdot & \qquad\qquad\ \cdot \\
\ \ \cdot & \qquad\qquad\ \cdot \\
\text{df}(k-1) & (\ \ 0 \quad\ \ 0 \quad 0 \quad ... \quad 1 \quad -1\,)
\end{array}
$$

where k is the number of categories for the independent variable. For example, the repeated contrasts for an independent variable with four categories are as follows:

$$
\begin{array}{rrrr}
(1/4 & 1/4 & 1/4 & 1/4\,) \\
(\ \ 1 & -1 & 0 & 0\,) \\
(\ \ 0 & 1 & -1 & 0\,) \\
(\ \ 0 & 0 & 1 & -1\,)
\end{array}
$$

These contrasts are useful in profile analysis and wherever difference scores are needed.

Special

A user-defined contrast. Allows entry of special contrasts in the form of square matrices with as many rows and columns as there are categories of the given independent variable. For MANOVA and LOGLINEAR, the first row entered is always the mean, or constant, effect and represents the set of weights indicating how to average other independent variables, if any, over the given variable. Generally, this contrast is a vector of ones.

The remaining rows of the matrix contain the special contrasts indicating the desired comparisons between categories of the variable. Usually, orthogonal contrasts are the most useful. Orthogonal contrasts are statistically independent and are nonredundant. Contrasts are orthogonal if:

■ For each row, contrast coefficients sum to 0.

■ The products of corresponding coefficients for all pairs of disjoint rows also sum to 0.

For example, suppose that *treatment* has four levels and that you want to compare the various levels of treatment with each other. An appropriate special contrast is

(	1	1	1	1)	weights for mean calculation
(	3	−1	−1	−1)	compare 1st with 2nd through 4th
(	0	2	−1	−1)	compare 2nd with 3rd and 4th
(	0	0	1	−1)	compare 3rd with 4th

which you specify by means of the following CONTRAST subcommand for MANOVA, LOGISTIC REGRESSION, and COXREG:

```
/CONTRAST(TREATMNT)=SPECIAL( 1  1  1  1
                             3 -1 -1 -1
                             0  2 -1 -1
                             0  0  1 -1 )
```

For LOGLINEAR, you need to specify:

```
/CONTRAST(TREATMNT)=BASIS SPECIAL( 1  1  1  1
                                   3 -1 -1 -1
                                   0  2 -1 -1
                                   0  0  1 -1 )
```

Each row except the means row sums to 0. Products of each pair of disjoint rows sum to 0 as well:

Rows 2 and 3: $(3)(0)+(-1)(2)+(-1)(-1)+(-1)(-1) = 0$

Rows 2 and 4: $(3)(0)+(-1)(0)+(-1)(1)+(-1)(-1) = 0$

Rows 3 and 4: $(0)(0)+(2)(0)+(-1)(1)+(-1)(-1) = 0$

The special contrasts need not be orthogonal. However, they must not be linear combinations of each other. If they are, the procedure reports the linear dependency and ceases processing. Helmert, difference, and polynomial contrasts are all orthogonal contrasts.

Indicator

Indicator variable coding. Also known as dummy coding, this is not available in LOGLINEAR or MANOVA. The number of new variables coded is $k-1$. Cases in the reference category are coded 0 for all $k-1$ variables. A case in the ith category is coded 0 for all indicator variables except the ith, which is coded 1.

Bibliography

Agresti, A. 1990. *Categorical data analysis.* New York: John Wiley and Sons.

Ashford, J. R., and R. D. Sowden. 1970. Multivariate probit analysis. *Biometrics*, 26: 535–546.

Berenson, M. L., and D. M. Levine. 1992. *Basic business statistics, concepts and applications.* Englewood Cliffs, N.J.: Prentice Hall.

Bishop, Y. M. M., and S. E. Fienberg. 1969. Incomplete two-dimensional contingency tables. *Biometrics*, 25: 119–128.

Bishop, Y. M. M., S. E. Fienberg, and P. W. Holland. 1975. *Discrete multivariate analysis: Theory and practice.* Cambridge, Mass.: MIT Press.

Blake, C., E. Keogh, and C.J Merz. 1998. *UCI Repository of machine learning databases* [http://www.ics.uci.edu/~mlearn/MLRepository.html]. Irvine, CA: University of California, Department of Information and Computer Science.

Bowker, A. H., and G. J. Lieberman. 1972. *Engineering statistics.* 2nd ed. Englewood Cliffs, N.J.: Prentice Hall.

Box, G. E. P., and N. R. Draper. 1969. *Evolutionary operation: A statistical method for process improvement.* New York: John Wiley and Sons.

Carter, W. H., Jr., G. L. Wampler, and D. M. Stablein. 1982. *Regression analysis of survival data in cancer chemotherapy.* New York: Marcel Dekker.

Corbeil, R. R., and S. R. Searle. 1976. Restricted maximum likelihood (REML) estimation of variance components in the mixed model. *Technometrics*, 18: 31–38.

Cox, D. R., and D. O. Oakes. 1984. *Analysis of survival data.* London: Chapman and Hall.

Cox, D. R., and E. J. Snell. 1989. *The analysis of binary data, 2nd.* Ed. London: Chapman and Hall.

Crowley, J., and M. Hu. 1977. Covariance analysis of heart transplant survival data. *Journal of the American Statistical Association,* 72: 27–36.

Delany, M. F., and C. T. Moore. 1987. American alligator food habits in Florida. Unpublished manuscript.

Embury, S. H., L. Elias, P. H. Heller, C. E. Hood, P. L. Greenberg, and S.L. Schrier. 1977. Remission maintenance therapy in acute myelogenous leukemia. *Western Journal of Medicine*, 126: 267–272.

Friereich, E. J., et al. 1963. The effect of 6-mercaptopurine on the duration of steroid-induced remission in acute leukemia. *Blood*, 21: 699–716.

Giesbrecht, F. G. 1983. An efficient procedure for computing MINQUE of variance components and generalized least squares estimates of fixed effects. *Communications in Statistics, Part A— Theory and Methods*, 12: 2169–2177.

Goodnight, J. H. 1979. A tutorial on the SWEEP operator. *The American Statistician*, 33: 149–158.

Haberman, S. J. 1973. The analysis of residuals in cross-classified tables. *Biometrics*, 29: 205–220.

_____. 1979. *Analysis of qualitative data*. Vol. 2. New York: Academic Press.

_____. 1982. Analysis of dispersion of multinomial responses. *Journal of the American Statistical Association*, 77: 568–580.

Heimann, R. Unpublished breast cancer data. Department of Radiation Oncology, University of Chicago.

Hemmerle, W. J., and H. O. Hartley. 1973. Computing maximum likelihood estimates for the mixed A.O.V. model using the W transformation. *Technometrics*, 15: 819–831.

Hess, K. R. 1995. Graphical methods for assessing violations of the proportional hazards assumption in Cox regression. *Statistics in Medicine*, 14: 1707–1723.

Hicks, C. R. 1982. *Fundamental concepts in the design of experiments*. 3rd ed. New York: Holt, Rinehart and Winston.

Hocking, R. R. 1985. *The analysis of linear models*. Monterey, Calif.: Brooks/Cole.

Huynh, H., and G. K. Mandeville. 1979. Validity conditions in repeated measures design. *Psychological Bulletin*, 86: 964–973.

Jennrich, R. I., and P. F. Sampson. 1976. Newton-Raphson and related algorithms for maximum likelihood variance component estimation. *Technometrics*, 18: 11–17.

Jennrich, R. I., and M. D. Schluchter. 1986. Unbalanced repeated measures models with structured covariance matrices. *Biometrics*, 42: 805–820.

Johnson, N. L., S. Kotz, and A. W. Kemp. 1992. *Univariate discrete distributions*. New York: John Wiley and Sons.

Johnson, R. A., and D. W. Wichern. 1988. *Applied multivariate statistical analysis*. London: Prentice Hall International, Inc.

Kalbfleisch, J. D., and R. L. Prentice. 1980. *The statistical analysis of failure time data.* New York: John Wiley and Sons.

Kleinbaum, D. G. 1996. *Survival analysis: A self-learning text.* New York: Springer-Verlag.

Koch, G., S. Atkinson, and M. Stokes. 1986. Poisson regression. In: *Encyclopedia of Statistical Sciences*, Vol. 7, S. Kotz and N. Johnson, eds. New York: John Wiley and Sons.

LaMotte, L. R. 1973. On non-negative quadratic unbiased estimation of variance components. *Journal of the American Statistical Association*, 68: 728–730.

Lee, E. T. 1992. Statistical methods for survival data analysis. New York: John Wiley and Sons.

Mauchly, J. W. 1940. Significance test for sphericity of a normal n-variate distribution. *Annuals of Mathematical Statistics*, 11: 204–209.

McCullagh, P., and J. A. Nelder. 1989. *Generalized linear models.* New York: Chapman & Hall.

McCullagh, P., and J. A. Nelder. 1989. *Generalized linear models.* 2nd ed. London: Chapman and Hall.

McFadden, D. 1974. Conditional logit analysis of qualitative choice behavior. In P. Zarembka (Ed.), *Frontiers in Econometrics.* New York: Academic Press.

Miller, R. G. 1981. *Survival analysis.* New York: John Wiley and Sons.

Milliken, G. A., and D. E. Johnson. 1992. *Analysis of messy data.* Vol. 1, *Designed experiments.* New York: Chapman and Hall.

Nagelkerke, N. J. D. 1991. A note on the general definition of the coefficient of determination. *Biometrika, 78(3),* 691-692.

Olsen, C. L. 1976. On choosing a test statistic in multivariate analysis of variance. *Psychological Bulletin*, 83: 579–193.

Patterson, H. D., and R. Thompson. 1971. Recovery of inter-block information when block sizes are unequal. *Biometrika*, 58: 545–554.

Potthoff, R. F., and S. N. Roy. 1964. A generalized multivariate analysis of variance model useful especially for growth curve problems. *Biometrika*, 51: 313–326.

Rao, C. R. 1973. *Linear statistical inference and its applications.* 2nd ed. New York: John Wiley and Sons.

Rao, C. R., and J. Kleffe. 1988. *Estimation of variance components and applications.* Amsterdam: North-Holland.

Searle, S. R. 1987. *Linear models for unbalanced data.* New York: John Wiley and Sons.

Searle, S. R., G. Casella, and C. E. McCulloch. 1992. *Variance components.* New York: John Wiley and Sons.

Searle, S. R., F. M. Speed, and G. A. Milliken. 1980. Population marginal means in the linear model: An alternative to least squares means. *The American Statistician*, 34:4, 216–221.

Snedecor, G. W., and W. G. Cochran, 1980. *Statistical methods.* 7th ed. Ames: Iowa State University Press.

Speed, F. M. (1979). Choice of sums of squares for estimation of components of variance. *Proceedings of Statistical Computing Section*, 55–58. Alexandria, Va.: American Statistical Association.

Stablein D. M., W. C. Carter, Jr., and G. L. Wampler. 1980. Survival analysis of drug combinations using a hazards model with time-dependent covariates. *Biometrics*, 36: 537–546.

Winer, B. J., D. R. Brown, and K. M. Michels. 1991. *Statistical principles in experimental design*. New York: McGraw-Hill.

Index